KU-181-773

To the Trotskyist militants
of General Drivers Union Local 544
and to the comrades of the Socialist
Workers Party who so loyally backed
them in a time of great need

330865

Farrell Dobbs

Contents

List of Illustrations

Acknowledgments

This book, for which I bear sole responsibility as the author, has been written with generous assistance from all who were asked to cooperate in its preparation.

Marvel Scholl, my close and dear companion throughout our adult lives, has drawn freely upon her abundant qualifications to provide help. Having shared the whole Teamster experience with me, she served as a valuable source through which to supplement my own memory of previously unrecorded happenings and to recount those episodes in keeping with the spirit of the times. Sharon Lee Finer performed the hard task of typing final copies of the manuscript, which are so neat and accurate that they should prove a copy setter's delight. She did this, moreover, with prompt attention to each successive chapter as it was turned over to her in draft form, no matter what other things were taxing her time and energy; and her enthusiasm for the project served as a constant inspiration to me.

Ray Rainbolt, who served as recording secretary of Local 544 during the critical 1941 events, made available his file containing minutes of meetings held by the union's job stewards. Jack Maloney related a personal experience which gave an example of unscrupulous methods used by the FBI in trying to cook up false testimony against frame-up victims. Harry DeBoer, a militant Teamster leader throughout the 1934-41 period, scanned each chapter of the manuscript to verify its accuracy.

Valuable files kept by the late Harold Swanson of Local 544's Federal Workers Section were placed at my disposal through the initiative of Pauline (Swanson) DeBoer. Margaret Winter dug into bulky volumes of legal records to provide factual data about the court history of the Smith Act. George Breitman supplied

7

background information about the Ludlow amendment. George Tselos, while doing his own research of official AFL correspondence available in public archives, thoughtfully made copies for me of items he found relating to internal affairs of the International Brotherhood of Teamsters.

Both the Minnesota Historical Society and the public library in Berkeley, California, graciously responded to requests for help in obtaining reference material. A boost was also received from the Berkeley branch of the Socialist Workers Party, which went out of its way to equip me with excellent working facilities.

Some of the facts set forth in this book have come from files I kept both as a trade union and a political organizer. In addition I have drawn upon the Minneapolis Teamster papers *Northwest Organizer* and *Industrial Organizer,* and the AFL organs *Minneapolis Labor Review* and *Minnesota Teamster.* Extensive use has been made of the weeklies *The Militant* and the *Socialist Appeal,* together with the magazine *Fourth International,* all Trotskyist publications. On some pertinent matters, quotations have been taken from capitalist dailies in Minneapolis and Saint Paul, Minnesota.

In describing the 1941 sedition trial, lengthy citations were taken from the official Abstract of Record, United States Circuit Court of Appeals, Eighth Circuit, No. 12,195 Criminal: *United States of America* v. *V. R. Dunne et al.* This source was supplemented by material from two pamphlets: *Socialism on Trial,* by James P. Cannon; and *In Defense of Socialism,* by Albert Goldman.

Throughout the writing of my contribution to Teamster history I have had the benefit of George Novack's editorial skills. Some years ago both he and Ray Dunne began pressing me to undertake the job. But I had a problem in that connection. My experience had centered mainly on trade union work, political organizing, and public speaking related to those functions. I had done little writing. Therefore, I was hesitant about trying to set down on paper an account of Teamster events in which I had participated. Sensing my difficulty, George proffered full cooperation on the literary aspects of the project. Once he got me started through such encouragement, his aid was given continuously in most handsome fashion; and it is with deep appreciation of George Novack's help that I am now able to look upon the task as completed.

Preface

This is the concluding volume of a series on Teamster history. Three previous books covered the following subjects:

Teamster Rebellion described the bloody strikes through which General Drivers Union Local 574, an affiliate of the International Brotherhood of Teamsters, AFL, established itself as a power in the Minneapolis trucking industry.

Teamster Power told how Local 574 fought off an attempt by IBT President Daniel Tobin to expel it from the international union; won reinstatement under a new charter as Local 544; and proceeded thereafter to spearhead an organizing campaign among over-the-road drivers in the upper Mississippi Valley, which opened the way for transformation of the IBT into a massive and potentially dynamic movement on a national scale.

Teamster Politics dealt with questions of independent labor political action, especially as these were reflected within the Farmer-Labor Party in Minnesota; employer counterattacks on Local 544 as the national labor upsurge of the 1930s began to subside; an FBI assault on midwest Teamster locals; and a national strike of Works Progress Administration workers in 1939, followed by a legal frame-up of WPA strike leaders in Minneapolis by the federal government.

The present volume winds up the series with extensive accounts of an antiwar campaign initiated by the Minneapolis Teamsters; a new clash that developed between Local 544 and Tobin over the war issue; and federal charges of sedition against militants of Local 544 and the Socialist Workers Party, on the basis of which eighteen were railroaded to prison.

Trade Union Campaign
Against War

1. Let the People Vote on War

Shortly after the 1936 elections, President Franklin D. Roosevelt began a rightward shift in policy—a step that was to have profound effects upon the Minnesota labor movement. There were two basic aspects to the turn. He backed off from earlier promises to concentrate on social reforms in this country and centered his attention, instead, on "defense of American interests" abroad. This change in emphasis was designed to further a deliberate and disguised imperialist plan, the essence of which may be perceived through a brief look at preceding developments.

When Roosevelt first took office in 1933, the country was caught in the paralyzing grip of a deep economic depression. The resulting hardships caused rebellious moods to grow in intensity among the workers and small farmers. So extensive was the mass discontent, in fact, that the capitalists became worried about the danger that a revolutionary situation might emerge.

To get out of this bind, the boss class acquiesced in a promise by the incoming president to give the "ill-fed, ill-clothed, ill-housed" of the nation a "New Deal." His program, however, consisted primarily of increased government spending to "prime the economic pumps," along with "fair-trade" regulations devised to raise prices and increase profit-taking.

Just enough social concessions were added to revive faith among workers and farmers that their problems could be taken care of through repair of the capitalist system. In that connection, expecially, the aims of the New Deal were supported by the trade union bureaucracy, the social democrats and—beginning in 1935—the Communist Party.

As a consequence of those combined factors, the labor upsurge was confined to struggles at the trade union level; the workers were blocked from taking the road of independent political action and forming their own party; and the capitalist ruling class kept a firm hold on the reins of government.

In one respect, though, the "miracle" of the New Deal remained flawed. It had failed to overcome the economic crisis. Although a limited industrial recovery had temporarily developed in response to "pump-priming" measures and an upturn in the world economy, contradictions inherent in the capitalist system continued to operate in a manner that brought another deep slump, beginning in 1937. That trend made it imperative for ruling-class strategists to seek other ways of propping up their outlived system. So they resorted to a method that could be incorporated into plans for the solution of yet another problem they faced—in the international arena.

Imperialist rivals were encroaching upon territories abroad which this country's ruling class, with its global interests, had staked out for exploitation. Among those competing governmental gangs, two loomed as the most formidable opponents of their Wall Street counterparts. One operated from within Hitlerite Germany; the other had its base in Japan, where a militarist regime held power. Both had their eyes on the superprofits United States banking combines and monopoly corporations were raking in from foreign holdings; Germany and Japan were out to grab a larger piece of the action.

It was in this rivalry between imperialist cutthroats that Roosevelt was dedicating himself to the protection of "American interests." But that wasn't what he talked about during the 1936 elections. Instead, he campaigned on the basis of his phony image, built up during his first term, as a champion of the exploited masses. Then, after being returned to office, he began to apply his real line in foreign policy. Budgetary provisions were made for increased military spending, using the argument that such action would expand industrial hiring and reduce the jobless rolls. At the same time Washington employed every available propaganda device in an effort to justify the handling of foreign affairs in a manner that led toward war.

At that point General Drivers Local 544, in Minneapolis, Minnesota, set out to organize trade union opposition to Roosevelt's preparations for use of the workers as imperialist cannon fodder. Local 544, an affiliate of the International Brotherhood of Teamsters, AFL, was led by Trotskyist militants. They were revolutionary socialists, whose training and experience enabled them to grasp the real meaning of the scheme being cooked up in Washington.

The leaders of Local 544 were also seasoned campaigners, well versed in the organization of mass actions. Thus it was apparent to them that the first task was to alert the union ranks to the dangers arising from the new course taken by the White House and to explain why the workers' vital interests were threatened. Only in that way could the necessary forces be drawn together to launch a broad protest movement.

Fortunately, there was an excellent vehicle at hand to undertake that beginning. The Minneapolis Teamsters had a weekly paper, the *Northwest Organizer*, published initially by the General Drivers Union. In 1936 it had been made the official organ of the Teamsters Joint Council, a body composed of representatives from all IBT locals in the city. Its editor was Miles Dunne, one of Local 544's central leaders. A method had been worked out whereby the entire membership of all Council affiliates received the paper regularly; and it was distributed similarly to the ranks of a few other unions that worked closely with the IBT forces—for example, organizations of furniture and power workers. There were also numerous labor militants throughout the city and state who subscribed to the paper as individuals. All in all, the Teamster organ had a prime body of readers, among whom the initial protest forces could be mobilized.

The educational phase of the campaign was opened through an editorial in the April 22, 1937, issue of the paper. It was pegged to the upcoming celebration of May Day, the international working-class holiday which had come into being in direct relationship to class battles during the latter part of the nineteenth century. Liberal capitalist politicians often attempt to exploit such occasions for purposes contrary to the workers' interests, and this was used as an opening to begin discussion of the war issue and its implications for the labor movement.

"May Day will continue to express the interlocking nature of economics and politics," the editorial said in part. "But although puny politicians may try to turn the occasion into a common election rally, the workers will be turning their attention to much broader and sounder implications, namely independent working-class action. Proper economic subjects such as hours, wages, jobs, relief and organization, will be amplified by consideration of political relations such as civil liberties, war and the other struggles ahead. . . .

"Wars and rumors of war are . . . necessary implements of great capitalist competitors. Not one of them can remain peaceable but each must strive until his power is broken, to gain world-wide supremacy by ruthless terror and destruction. Here, too, petty politics are of no avail. Why? Because government, 'the executive committee of the ruling class,' must not only conduct war for its master, but must prepare the way by subduing all opposition and assuring 'unity at all costs' at home. May Day therefore calls for renewed defense of workers' rights."

Some weeks later, in July 1937, the Japanese military invaded North China. Shortly thereafter two United States soldiers stationed in the war zone were wounded, and the capitalist propagandists seized upon the incident to build up anti-Japanese sentiment here in this country. At that point the Teamster paper set out to counter the jingoistic line, opening with an editorial which asserted:

"The reason the United States has its garrisons in China and its warships in the Far Pacific is to protect American capitalism in the Orient. The American worker has nothing whatever at stake, the American bosses have millions of dollars of investments that must be protected. The American worker has nothing to gain and everything to lose by a war fought to protect American capitalism. . . . In the present crisis in the Far East, the interests of the American workers lie with the interests of the downtrodden people of China.

"For an understanding of the whole problem of Imperialism and its relation to the American trade union movement, the *Northwest Organizer* recommends to its readers a series of articles on this subject beginning in the next issue."

Five articles written by Tex Norris, a revolutionary socialist educator, were then published. His main points, which were illustrated by historical examples, may be summarized as follows:

Imperialists are capitalists with investments in foreign countries. By 1937 United States business interests were making increasingly large investments in every possible quarter of the world. Those who benefited from this development were trying to keep the facts hidden from the workers, who always came out losers in such a situation, and it was the duty of the labor movement to explain what was happening.

Profits made by gouging U.S. labor, Norris continued, were being used in the form of capital to exploit foreign workers at starvation wages, even lower than those paid here. In order to maximize such exploitation, the imperialists, acting just as they did at home, sought to use the governments of the particular foreign countries to break strikes by native workers and, wherever possible, to crush their trade unions. The accomplishment of those aims helped, moreover, to hold down wage rates in this country, thus enabling the imperialists to reap superprofits at the expense of both U.S. and foreign labor.

In an effort to cope with this problem, some within the trade unions were promoting "Buy American" campaigns, hoping thereby to protect jobs and wages in this country. But such notions were misleading, he pointed out. In the long run, no nation could sell more to foreign nations than it bought from them. Efforts to build walls around nations were, therefore, bound to result in restricted production and a reduced standard of living. Instead of pursuing that false course, the answer to the difficulty lay in cooperation between U.S. and foreign workers in a common struggle to win better conditions for all.

There were also other characteristics of capitalism which led to imperialism, Norris explained. Among them was the growth of monopoly. Since that trend was directed toward complete domination of industry, it was only natural that the monopolies should expand outside the nation to control foreign supplies, factories, and markets. In banking, likewise, concentration and monopoly occurred, with a few banking groups competing to extend their control throughout the world.

Imperialism, he added, was a natural development in any advanced capitalist nation. Just as U.S. business operated outside its home base, so did British, French, Italian, Japanese. The competition between those different imperialist interests within a contracted world market was growing keener daily, and that was leading to the most terrible of all the consequences of imperialism—war.

Protection of U.S. business interests in that sharpening conflict, Norris emphasized, had become the main concern of the Roosevelt administration. Its State Department had consuls searching for foreign investment opportunities. Prospective investors were being shown where diplomatic and military protection could be offered. Acquisition of military bases was going on in regions where capitalist investments abroad were concentrated, and Washington was preparing to pull millions of workers into the armed forces for war against its rivals.

If workers in the U.S. were to resist this mad course, he

concluded, they needed to fight against capitalism itself, of which imperialism was a deadly offspring. That, in turn, called for the clasping of workers' hands in other countries in a grip of international labor solidarity.

While presenting the foregoing explanation of imperialism, the *Northwest Organizer* added editorially: "The army is not our army, but belongs to the rulers of America and is for THEIR use—to protect THEIR investments and interests in foreign lands, and in case of domestic crises, to protect the same interests at home against the workers. . . . There is not a capitalist country in the world which has not at one time or another used its army against striking workers at home. As long as capitalism exists, there is not a government—no matter who leads it—that would dare move to abolish its professional army and depend upon a popular militia to keep order."

Attention was also focused upon the concrete situation in Asia, concerning which the Teamster paper said: "In the fast-moving epoch that we live in, the time has passed when organized labor can afford to disregard what is taking place on the other side of the earth. The truth is that today the world is so interlocked and interdependent that a crisis in any country in the world soon makes itself felt in every other country. Such an event is the Sino-Japanese war. . . . The boss press, following out the dictates of its masters, more and more boldly points out the tremendous interests which American employers have in the Far East. Daily, the government becomes more aggressive in defense of these interests. . . . All this talk of 'national defense' . . . is only a mask by means of which the exploiters cover up their predatory appetites and bloody brawls for booty. . . ."

Then, on October 5, 1937, Roosevelt made a major foreign policy address. If "aggression" triumphed elsewhere in the world, he contended, it would be a threat to the United States. On that premise he called for a "quarantine" against "aggressor nations." In presenting that line, however, the slippery demagogue gave no clear definition of what "quarantine" meant. So the *Northwest Organizer* offered an explanation of what the president obviously had in mind.

"The official mobilization of public opinion, the keystone of war preparations in the modern world, is now formally launched," the union organ predicted. "From now own, workers can expect anti-Japanese stories to mount in number and fervor. One can anticipate a vast increase in the armaments budget at the next session of Congress, together with the enactment of various industrial and military mobilization plans. . . . 'Quarantine' is nothing but a new and peculiarly ingenious method of turning sentiment for peace into support of war. In threatening to swallow all of China, Japanese imperialism has at last hit too close to the vitals of American business. . . . These considerations explain Roosevelt's new and aggressive policy in Far Eastern affairs."

Before long further developments began to confirm that analysis. On December 12, 1937, Japanese planes bombed the U.S.S. *Panay*, a gunboat lying at anchor on the Yangtse, and three Standard Oil tankers. A massive wave of anti-Japanese propaganda followed in this country. "Our" flag had been insulted, the capitalist press howled. "We" had to take strong measures to assure the safety of U.S. citizens in China.

"What do they mean by 'we' and 'our'?" the Teamster paper replied. "Who are the [U.S.] citizens in China? Who sent them there? Do they represent the American people? No, they are businessmen who went to China for the purpose of squeezing profits out of the terribly oppressed and exploited Chinese masses. Why should we send one penny or one man to China to 'protect' them? If the investments of the Standard Oil Company are in jeopardy, that's Rockefeller's headache, not ours. . . . We've got war enough right here at home. The war for the oppressed and exploited, against their oppressors and exploiters. . . . Let's fight that war and win it! And let's drown out the war-howlers with the peace cry of the masses. Withdraw all American armed forces from China!"

At that point the *Northwest Organizer* presented a review of labor's experiences in Minnesota during World War I. The aim was to make its readers aware of the devious methods employed to hoodwink the workers, split their ranks, and use them to advance imperialist aims. This educational project was undertaken through a series of articles written by Carlos Hudson, a revolutionary socialist journalist.

Soon after the first world conflict erupted in 1914, he recalled, numerous peace societies sprang up in this country. Those formations dedicated themselves to the mobilization of a large pacifist movement, harboring the belief that such action could prevent U.S. involvement in the imperialist slaughter. Among them was the Minnesota Peace Society, which quickly grew to a membership of about seventy thousand. But size alone did not make it an effective antiwar instrument; that was soon confirmed by the test of events.

In 1916 the Democratic Party ran Woodrow Wilson for reelection as U.S. president, using the campaign slogan: "He kept us out of war." The pacifist movement fell for that line and welcomed the return of Wilson to office. During the same period the imperialist tricksters launched a campaign for a "nonsectarian" armament program to provide an "adequate system of defense." In this case as well, pacifist muddleheadedness was demonstrated when Dr. Cyrus Northrup, president of the Minnesota Peace Society, backed the scheme. "We should prepare against war," Northrup said. "This is not militarism and we do not believe in militarism. But we realize that we are inadequately prepared should we have to defend ourselves. . . ." The thousands yearning for peace, who had placed their trust in that pacifist organization, were thus entrapped into support of preparations for war.

Opposition to U.S. involvement in the European conflict had also developed within the Minnesota labor movement, Hudson continued. In 1915 the left-wing forces succeeded in putting the AFL State Federation of Labor on record against the "senseless clamor of the jingoes" for war. Continuation of the sentiment was manifested during the next two years, especially through mass protests against Wilson's switch in policy after he was reelected.

The labor protests were triggered when, in February 1917, the president who "kept us out of war" severed diplomatic relations with Germany. At the same time, he armed U.S. merchant vessels transporting war supplies to England and France, using the pretext that they were in danger of attack by German submarines; and his actions were accompanied by propaganda urging all "loyal" citizens to "stand by President Wilson."

In Minneapolis, Hudson stressed, such propaganda failed to get the intended results. A huge working-class rally was held to protest against the government's belligerent tactics. But that antiwar stand was not backed by the top union bureaucrats. Early in March, the national officials of the AFL came out in support of Wilson's line, an act that served the ruling class by dividing labor on this vital issue.

Three weeks later, on April 6, 1917, the U.S. Congress voted to declare war on Germany. A vicious assault was then made on the antiwar forces. Workers whom the imperialists had failed to fool were subjected to increasingly harsh forms of repression. As a consequence one trade union after another began to capitulate to Wilson, and labor's opposition to the war was whittled down to little more than the revolutionary wing of the working class.

Publication of the above review by Hudson, which has been outlined in very condensed form, was completed in January 1938. By that time a flare-up had occurred in the incumbent Congress over the handling of foreign policy. It stemmed from an earlier move made by Representative Louis L. Ludlow, a Democrat from Indiana.

In 1935 Ludlow had introduced a resolution in the House calling for an amendment to the U.S. Constitution. The key passage of the Ludlow amendment read: "The authority of Congress to declare war shall not become effective until confirmed by a majority of votes cast thereon in a nation-wide referendum."

For two years the resolution had been bottled up in a House committee where it was expected to expire from prolonged neglect. Then, in December 1937, the situation changed when Roosevelt sought to use the *Panay* incident as a means to whip the country into an anti-Japanese frenzy. His action backfired. It tended to deepen mass fears of war, as shown by a Gallup Poll in which 72 percent favored the Ludlow amendment. Under those circumstances, backers of that measure were able to force it onto the House floor for consideration. A similar resolution was introduced in the Senate by Robert M. La Follette, Jr., of Wisconsin.

During the ensuing debate, Roosevelt sent a letter to Congress flatly opposing any notion of a referendum on war. "Such an amendment as that proposed," he argued, "would cripple any President in his conduct of our foreign relations, and it would encourage other nations to believe that they could violate American rights with impunity."

In January 1938 the Ludlow amendment came to a vote in the House, where it was defeated 209-188, a margin of only 21 votes. Made cockier than ever by the strangulation of democratic rights, Roosevelt called upon Congress to authorize a big jump in the military budget. Under his pressure it was increased to an amount representing the largest peacetime appropriation—up to then—in U.S. history.

Those events took place just as this country's Trotskyist movement was being consolidated in the form of the Socialist Workers Party. At first the SWP merely differentiated itself from the movement backing the referendum demand. It did so by concentrating on criticism of the pacifist agitation connected with the Ludlow measure, which created illusions that simple modification of the Constitution could prevent the imperialists from plunging the U.S. into war. Peace could be maintained, the party stressed, only by labor taking state power away from the capitalist class.

A bit later, in February 1938, some advice was offered on the subject by Leon Trotsky, founding leader of the Fourth International, to which the SWP was then affiliated. He recommended that the party take a more flexible and positive stand on the Ludlow resolution. Roosevelt's opposition to the measure, he observed, represented the conceptions and interests of the imperialists, who wanted a free hand to declare war. Ludlow's initiative, in contrast, reflected apprehensions among the masses about the imperialists' intentions. Even though it was an illusion to think that a referendum could put the brakes on the drive toward war—and the SWP should continue to say so openly—the illusion had progressive antiwar features. Therefore, he said, it was advisable for revolutionists to go through this experience with the masses around the referendum issue, giving critical support to their democratic demand.

After weighing the question for a time, the SWP's national committee decided to accept Trotsky's advice. Thereafter, the party's fight against Roosevelt's foreign policy was conducted around the slogan: "Let the people vote on war."

That shift in tactics coincided with new developments in the Minnesota labor movement. The antiwar campaign, which the Trotskyist leaders of Local 544 had launched early in 1937, had gotten a boost from the dispute over the Ludlow measure. Support of the referendum demand was increasing within the trade unions, especially in Minneapolis. Thus a realistic basis existed to give organized expression to working-class disapproval of Roosevelt's line and, at the same time, to isolate those within labor's ranks who supported his course toward war.

The first major advance in that direction was registered within the Minneapolis Central Labor Union, a body composed of delegates from all AFL locals in the city. A resolution on foreign policy, introduced by the left wing of that body, was adopted toward the end of March. It branded the government's imperialist aims "a mortal danger to organized labor" and denounced Roosevelt's attempts to throttle opponents of his line, "as revealed by the lynch spirit" organized against supporters of the

Ludlow amendment. "Therefore be it resolved," the resolution said:

"1. That the Central Labor Union of Minneapolis, voicing the determination of fifty thousand trade unionists, declares its unalterable opposition to all war preparations and military budgets, and any and all bills in which they are embodied, and stigmatizes the war being prepared as a war of imperialist conquest, and declares its firm opposition to any war launched by the Government;

"2. That we demand that all war funds now proposed for the military budget and naval expansion be transferred immediately to the relief of the unemployed;

"3. That we demand the immediate withdrawal of any and all armed forces of the United States from the Far East, since it is only Big Business and not Labor that has any interests there to protect;

"4. That we assert militant Labor's determination to support . . . the brave Chinese people in their fight for independence against the Japanese invaders and all other foreign exploiters;

"5. That we shall join with all other forces in the labor movement who share our views for the purpose of consolidating the strongest possible movement of resistance to war and to the war-mongers."

Since the AFL central body in Minneapolis represented the strongest section of the Minnesota labor movement, its action gave a boost to left-wing efforts to put the Farmer-Labor Party on record against Roosevelt's foreign policy. That was a complex and difficult task, however, due to the contradictory basis on which the party had developed.

The FLP, which had arisen during World War I, ran candidates against both the Republicans and the Democrats in state elections. By 1930 it had displaced the Democrats as the main opponent of the Republicans in Minnesota. The strength thus shown by the FLP derived from its mass base among the workers and small farmers, who wanted genuinely independent political action. But those supporters of the party who had illusions that their problems could be solved through reforms within the existing social system accepted the idea of making political blocs with liberal capitalist politicians. That opened the way for unprincipled careerists inside the party to steer it onto a class-collaborationist course, one that had come to include ward-heeling political relations with the Roosevelt administration.

In 1935 the latter problem became aggravated when the Communist Party made an abrupt turn from its previous ultraleft policies to a "people's front" line. The essence of the change in course was defined by the *Northwest Organizer* as follows: "*People's Front*, a new name for class collaboration based on the proposal that organizations and parties representing the working class, and sections of the capitalist class, should unite on a common program to defend capitalist democracy. A People's Front government is a coalition of working class and capitalist parties, in defense of capitalism. Through a People's Front agreement the workers' party must give up its program and accept the program of the non-workingclass organizations. In a People's Front coalition, therefore, the workingclass parties always lose and the non-workingclass parties always gain."

As applied in the United States, the new CP line centered on a pair of concepts: unqualified support of the national administration, coupled with efforts to secure reciprocity in the form of a U.S. alliance with the Soviet Union. Proceeding accordingly, the Stalinists subordinated the workers' interests to those of the Kremlin bureaucrats, who had dictated the above policy to them. They opposed the use of class-struggle criteria in politics, arguing that the only effective distinction to be made was between "progressives" and "reactionaries." To serve "progress," they contended, it was necessary to back Roosevelt's domestic and foreign policies.

In Minnesota, once the turn began, the CP rushed its forces into the Farmer-Labor Party. There the Stalinists made a bloc with politicians of the right wing, helping them to consolidate machine control over the party within the framework of a pro-Roosevelt line.

Such was the situation when left-wing trade unionists sought in 1938 to precipitate a realignment of forces within the FLP around the war issue. Two resolutions intended to serve that purpose had been passed in the Minneapolis Central Labor Union. One called upon the FLP to speak out against Roosevelt's foreign policy. The other proposed a plank in the party's election platform demanding that funds earmarked for war be diverted into an expanded federal relief program for jobless workers.

These moves resulted in a temporary cleavage between the pro-war Stalinists and some semipacifist right-wingers in the Farmer-Labor Party. An example was the tendency on the part of some right-wingers to back the Ludlow amendment. That view was the opposite of the line taken by the Communist Party. Through the *Daily Worker*, a Stalinist organ, the CP denounced the Ludlow measure and linked its supporters to the Nazis.

In an effort to deepen this rift, Local 544's executive board made use of a dispute in Congress over the military budget. A telegram on the subject was sent to U.S. Senator Ernest Lundeen, a Farmer-Laborite from Minnesota; and the action was timed to precede an FLP state convention, scheduled for the end of March 1938.

"The first test vote on the naval appropriations bill has revealed the complete collapse of purely pacifist non-workingclass opposition to Roosevelt's war preparations," Local 544's telegram said. "Not in the halls of Congress but in the trade unions and farmers' organizations, in the mines, fields and factories, will the real, unalterable opposition to imperialist war be organized. For our part we pledge to rally the workers and farmers of the Northwest to struggle against the war. In that task, if they will, the Farmer-Labor delegation in the House and Senate can play an important role.

"We urge you to call together the Farmer-Labor congressmen and senators for joint action independently of the Republicans and Democrats. The Farmer-Labor delegation—you, Shipstead, Teigan, Bernard, Kvale, Johnson, Buckler—can utilize the platforms of House and Senate as a tribune from which to call the masses to demonstrate their irreconcilable opposition to the war-makers. Members of your delegation should tour the country to help rally the workers against the naval appropriations bill. We will provide you a platform for that purpose here on twenty-four hours notice. If the naval appropriations bill is permitted to pass without mass opposition, the rest of the administration's war program will follow. We urge you to subordinate all other problems to the most important problem before the American people—the struggle against war."

Parallel with the above action, the *Northwest Organizer* addressed itself editorially to the FLP leadership in Minnesota. If the party was to reflect the deepest feelings of the rank and file, the Teamster paper asserted, it had to dissociate itself from Roosevelt's war plans.

Nothing of the kind was done, however, when the FLP convention took place. It quickly became clear that the Stalinists and semipacifist right-wingers had more or less patched over their differences. First they combined forces to rig the gathering against labor, using that advantage to block the resolutions submitted by the Minneapolis Central Labor Union. Then they forced through a line designed to support Roosevelt in essence and yet avoid an open collision with antiwar workers and farmers.

In the election platform adopted by the convention, for example, not a word was said in support of the Ludlow amendment. A vague declaration against increased armament was thrown in, but nothing was added about the reasons for the military policy emanating from the White House. Cooperation with "all forces genuinely seeking peace" was advocated, the FLP machine obviously intending to include Roosevelt in that category. In short, as the *Northwest Organizer* pointed out, the convention's line on the war issue was "the polar opposite of the militant stand taken by the Minneapolis Central Labor Union."

Ordinarily, the success against the left wing in the Farmer-Labor Party would have emboldened right-wingers in the trade unions to become more aggressive. In this instance, though, other factors intervened to retard such a development. A several-sided anti-union offensive had recently been opened by the Minneapolis ruling class. An outfit called the Silver Shirts was mobilizing fascist-minded thugs, with the aim of conducting terrorist assaults on workers' organizations. Efforts were under way to launch a citywide company union movement. A handful of finks had instituted a boss-inspired court suit designed to pry into Local 544's internal affairs, and that step implied subsequent moves of the same kind against other labor formations.

Because of the sweeping offensive aimed at the entire labor movement, there was little room for conservative trade unionists to collaborate with the employers in opposing the left-wing forces. Instead, the right-wingers were under pressure from the ranks to lend at least verbal support to measures taken in defense of the trade unions. That circumstance strengthened the hand of the revolutionists, who initiated a union defense guard to ward off the Silver Shirt threat and organized a counterattack on the company unionists. In the process, moreover, it became possible to intensify the campaign against Roosevelt's foreign policy.

The antiwar movement got a boost toward the latter end when, late in 1938, a new issue came to the fore nationally. By then Hitlerite Germany was subjecting the Jewish people to mass victimizations of a horrendous nature. For Jews—and other antifascists—who had managed to escape the Nazi terror, it had thus become a matter of life and death to find asylum in another country.

Taking cognizance of their desperate need, Local 544's executive board adopted a resolution on November 16, 1938, which stated: "The working thousands enrolled under the banner of General Drivers Union Local 544 extend their keen sympathy to the victims of the repulsive and abominable fascist terror in Germany. . . . Local 544 demands of President Roosevelt that he open the gates of the United States to the oppressed of Europe."

An editorial on the subject followed in the *Northwest Organizer*. It was intended to deepen the workers' understanding of ruling-class policy in Germany by linking it to the Silver Shirt experience locally. The union paper said: "The fight against Hitler's terror begins at home. There are groups in the United States, in Minnesota, in Minneapolis who are striving to bring Hitler's brand of 'law and order' into being here. The Minneapolis labor movement stands ready to protect and enforce observance of the civil rights of minorities here, and to move against any group that seeks to violate these rights. Labor backs up this position with the Union Defense Guard."

Other class aspects of the issue were also stressed in the Teamster paper: "Roosevelt seeks to turn the public outcry against the Nazi terror into support for putting across his colossal armament plans. . . ." "While hardly a single American big shot has come out with public support for the demand to open the doors of the United States to the victims of Hitler, workers' organizations throughout the country continue to swell the demand to admit the refugees. Never has the moral superiority of the workers over their masters been more clearly shown than in the conflict over this issue."

There was good cause for the above reference to Roosevelt's cynical use of the refugees' plight. On the heels of the 1938 elections, he initiated another hike in military spending, calling simultaneously for drastic cuts in appropriations for the Works Progress Administration. His victim in that "fiscal economy," the WPA, was a federal setup created to provide the unemployed—of whom there were still millions—with stingy relief allowances through "make-work" projects.

Pinpointing the meaning of the administration's double-barreled action, the Teamster paper observed: "Today there are no longer funds to support both the army of the unemployed and the army of the General Staff. One army will get the gravy. The government has already made its choice. . . ."

When large-scale WPA layoffs soon followed, the *Northwest Organizer* reminded the workers: "In 1936 Franklin D. Roosevelt said the following in a speech delivered in Buenos Aires: 'The employment given by armament programs is a false employment. It builds no permanent structure and creates no consumer goods for the maintenance of a lasting prosperity. We know that nations guilty of these follies inevitably face the day either when their weapons of destruction must be used against their neighbors or when an unsound economy, like a house of cards, will fall apart.'"

Then the union organ, emphasizing Roosevelt's about-face since 1936, said of the situation at the beginning of 1939: "No funds for the hungry and homeless unemployed. Plenty of funds to finance the coming imperialist war. . . . No miracle can save the unemployed. They must answer the phony 'no funds' line of Washington by organizing and demanding, all war funds to the unemployed."

By July 1939 the plight of the WPA workers had become so desperate that those still on the federal projects launched a massive national strike in protest against the layoffs and wage cuts imposed by the administration. Roosevelt responded by taking punitive action against the strikers. In doing so, he cracked down hardest in Minneapolis, where the jobless were well organized and led by experienced revolutionists. On the antidemocratic premise that "You can't strike against the government," several leaders of Local 544's unemployed unit, the Federal Workers Section, were railroaded to jail.

Those harsh measures gave added evidence of the rightward shift in administration line. As the Socialist Workers Party noted at its 1939 convention, the New Deal policy of liberal demagogy and social concessions to the masses had ended in collapse. U.S. capitalism was shaping an aggressive foreign policy course in an effort to solve its problems by acquiring a greater share of the world market, and Roosevelt had firmly taken the leadership in making preparations toward that end.

With the country's ruling class thus getting ready to challenge its rivals abroad, there was good reason for labor to grow increasingly concerned about developments in Europe. For an imperialist war was about to begin there, one destined to become global in its scope.

2. Stalin-Hitler Pact

A startling announcement on August 21, 1939, caused press wires to hum throughout the world. Germany and the Soviet Union had signed a "nonaggression" treaty. Under its terms Hitler promised to maintain peaceful relations with Stalin, and in return he was tacitly given a free hand to attack any other country without Soviet objection.

Eleven days later the Nazis invaded Poland. Quickly thereafter England declared war on Germany, as did France; and Italy entered the conflict on Berlin's side. An imperialist holocaust had started that would culminate in a most hideous crime, the atom bombing of Japan by the United States.

Judging by appearances, the Kremlin's pact with Hitler had been negotiated behind the backs of the Stalinists in this country. Right up to August 21, the Communist Party had continued with its pro-Roosevelt, anti-Hitler line. If anything, "people's frontism" was being carried to new, superpatriotic extremes, as shown by a 1939 public meeting in Minneapolis where William Z. Foster, the best-known CP leader, was the featured speaker.

Leaflets advertising the affair were printed in red, white, and blue. The hall decorations gave the impression that a rally of the chauvinistic Daughters of the American Revolution was to be held, and the program opened with the singing of the national anthem.

Acting with similar pro-war zeal during the July 1939 WPA tie-up, the CP introduced motions at strike meetings advocating a third term for Roosevelt. That was followed by the introduction of a resolution at an AFL convention in Minnesota, praising the faker in the White House and condemning "Hitlerism and Nazi Germany." That resolution was hastily withdrawn after the August 21 announcement.

There was still another indication that news of the pact with Hitler came as a thunderbolt to Stalin's lackeys in this country.

The first reaction of the national CP leaders was one of complete silence on the subject. They needed time to get details of the new line from Moscow and to figure out how it could be applied here.

Soon, though, a public switch in policy was initiated. Former support of U.S. participation in a war "against German fascism" to "defend democracy" was replaced by appeals to "keep America out of war"—against Germany. Those previously hailed as "peace lovers," who favored all-out support of England and France, suddenly became "warmongers." To differentiate from them, the Stalinists coined a new slogan: The Yanks are not coming.

Attempting to conceal the real cause of their shift in line, the CP hacks pretended they were making a left turn toward principled opposition to imperialist war. "Peace Committees" were formed within the labor movement, using all possible means to give them a non-Stalinist coloration. But in every case those setups propagated the new line handed down by the Kremlin—that the U.S. should take a neutral stance concerning the war in Europe.

At the same time, the Stalinists reversed themselves on the question of a third term for Roosevelt. Previously he had been touted as the representative of "progressive" capitalists, who deserved labor's support against the "reactionaries." But those credentials had suddenly disappeared, according to a resolution adopted by the CP's political committee.

As reported in the *Daily Worker* of October 15, 1939, the resolution declared: "Pressed by the imperialist bourgeoisie, the Roosevelt government, despite its avowed intention of 'keeping out of war,' more and more takes a course which threatens to involve the U.S.A. in the imperialist war. . . . the slogans of anti-fascism no longer give the main direction of the struggle of the working class and its allies as they formerly did in the period of the struggle for the anti-fascist peace front and people's front. . . . [The difference] between the New Deal and anti–New Deal camps is losing its former significance. Both are parties of the bourgeoisie and seek in various ways to realize and promote the predatory interests of American imperialism. . . ."

Meanwhile, Roosevelt had been quick to use the European developments to implement his foreign policy. A scare was raised about the "vulnerability" of Washington and New York if a foreign army landed on the Atlantic coast. On that pretext, large-scale "war games" were held to practice "defensive maneuvers."

As a further means of creating patriotic hysteria, a "limited state of national emergency" was declared, and in that setting a special session of Congress was called for September 21, 1939.

Convening of the special session was accompanied by a White House announcement that two submarines of "unknown nationality" had been sighted off the coast of North America. The administration also released a "confidential report" that messages had been intercepted from Berlin and Moscow which instructed their "friends" in the U.S. to press for continuation of the existing official embargo on arms shipments to warring nations.

Such was the atmosphere in which a so-called Neutrality Act was rushed through Congress. It lifted the arms embargo and provided a legal formula for the shipment of military supplies to the Anglo-French imperialist combine. That step served, in turn, as a means to build up this country's munitions industry in preparation for the day when the ruling class would be ready to enter the "war against fascism" on its own account.

Among those advocating such aims—with double-talk about "defense of American interests"—was J. P. Morgan, a banker-monopolist. He was answered by the *Northwest Organizer,* which said:

"J. P. Morgan has a gun. He has just returned from a sojourn in Scotland where he was shooting grouse. If he wants to defend his investments, let him take his gun and fight for them. But don't let him try to force us to fight for him. And don't let him try to lie about any fake 'war for democracy.'"

What appeared to be a forthright stand against the Morgan-Roosevelt line came from yet another quarter. The *Minneapolis Times-Tribune,* speaking from a pacifist viewpoint, raised a warning against moves to involve the U.S. in the European conflict. But that approach to the vital issue of war and peace had a history of trickery, as the Teamster organ pointed out in an open letter to the editors of the capitalist daily.

"During the past several weeks," the open letter stated, "your paper, addressing itself to the fathers, to the mothers, and to the youth of the Northwest, has made fervent appeals 'against any movement to involve the United States in the present European war' and against sending 'American boys abroad as soldiers.' . . . The feelings that the masses have about this monstrous bloody brawl between the imperialist slave-holders of different camps are the feelings that you express. And yet, gentlemen, WE DOUBT YOU. . . .

"Let us turn back the pages of history twenty-five years . . . to the quiet summer days of August, 1914. How young and bright and healthy the world seemed then. And like a flash of heat lightning the First World War broke about the heads of startled mankind. . . . In your editorial of August 5th [1914]—you called it 'The Only Refuge is Peace'—you wrote: 'All the news is that the world is rushing to the bloodiest war ever fought among men. Were it justified by issues as solemn as any that have ever provoked war, the price would still be too great. But it is justified in nothing. . . .'

"How like your words today. Indeed, your pages then seemed to foreshadow in an unbelievably accurate way the steps that President Roosevelt is taking now. On August 6th, 1914, your leading front-page story told of the President's [Wilson's] mobilization of the army and navy—of the precautionary measures taken 'to enforce neutrality.'. . . 'This mobilization,' you assured your readers, 'is not intended for war or for defense from impending attack. The sole purpose of the preparations being made is to protect American neutrality.'

"The war progresses. Millions of men, the flower of all nations, march into the valley of death. The day of April [6,] 1917 strikes. . . . From your pacifism of the start of the war, you went all the way over, to become the blatant leader of the war-mongering pack that urged the people on to war—'for democracy and civilization,' you said. . . . And how effective a trick it was! The *Minneapolis Tribune,* the leader of the antiwar sentiment in the Northwest, endorsing the war. Why, if the *Tribune,* who hates war, endorses the war, the war must be a good war, a just war. What assurances can you give us today that you won't repeat your performance of 1917?"

In a follow-up editorial, calling attention to the *Times-Tribune's* failure to answer the open letter, the *Northwest Organizer* added: "Pacifism alone can never stop war. There have always been pacifists and there have always been wars. Pacifism is not enough. The people must have a chance to decide, they must demand of Congress that it give to the people a direct popular referendum vote in the case of any and all wars. . . . And if Congress denies this democratic and fundamental right, the people must find other means to stop the war-makers."

Those sentiments were widely shared, as a declaration by the

1939 convention of the Minnesota State Federation of Labor demonstrated. "We," the delegates asserted, "demand the adoption of a constitutional amendment that would take the warmaking power out of the hands of Congress and refer it to a vote of the people."

A few weeks later hostilities broke out between the Soviet Union and Finland. Tear-jerking pleas for sympathy with "poor little Finland" quickly followed in a further effort by the imperialists to create public sympathy at home for "defense of democracy" abroad.

Such propaganda was denounced as a capitalist trick by the Minneapolis Central Labor Union, which restated its antiwar views through a resolution introduced by Miles Dunne of the Teamsters. The concluding passage stated that the CLU "again declares its unalterable opposition to any war launched by the government; that we again demand that all war funds be transferred immediately to the relief of the unemployed; that we oppose intervention by the United States on either side of the present war in Europe; that we declare our support for a national referendum binding on Congress for any and all wars."

Use of the formulation "binding referendum" stemmed from a recent development in Congress. Senator Robert M. La Follette had tried, in typical liberal fashion, to soften ruling-class opposition to the referendum demand by submitting a watered-down version of the Ludlow amendment. His substitute called for a national "advisory" vote, before Congress would declare war. What this plebiscite meant, of course, was that an expression of the people's will would have no binding effect on Congress, and the CLU opposed any such retreat on the issue.

There was evidence, moreover, of concern on the part of many others about binding control over the pro-war forces in government. Public opinion polls, which had been taken from time to time, continued to show a majority in favor of the referendum demand, and in those circumstances the belligerent capitalists were quick to order rejection of La Follette's pitch. They wanted no snarls whatever in the strings used to manipulate their congressional puppets.

Jingoistic propaganda emanating from Washington soon mounted to higher intensity when, in the spring of 1940, Germany invaded Norway and Denmark. And once again the Minneapolis CLU warned the workers against being taken in by the enemy class. In its unanimous statement on the subject the

AFL central body said: "We declare in favor of international, militant working class solidarity to stop the war."

To help explain what was really going on, the *Northwest Organizer* added in reporting the CLU action: "Day after day, speech after speech, one move after another—in the Pacific, in Europe, at home—the President is hurtling this nation down the road that Wilson strode, to war. . . . The heartfelt anti-fascist sentiments of the American people are being systematically manipulated to get them to support a war of the United States whose real purpose has nothing whatever to do with freeing the peoples of Europe from fascism and military dictatorship. . . . The interests of American capitalism demand that new fields of investment, new markets, new sources of raw materials, be made available for America's Sixty Families. Like Hitler Germany, like every other imperialist nation, the United States must expand, or capitalism will die. That is what the war is all about, and that is all it is about. All the talk about 'democracy' is hogwash."

In its next issue, the Teamster organ took up the question of progressive and reactionary wars. "The revolutionary war fought by the original colonies," it explained, "was a progressive war because it served to liberate this nation from the clutches of the English crown, it served to insure that the budding American manufacturers could develop and furnish America with a higher standard of living for the masses.

"The Civil War on the part of the Northern army was also a progressive war insofar as it represented a victory of the capitalist North over the . . . [slaveholding] South, and insofar as it served to free the Negro slaves. It was progressive because capitalism represented a more progressive social system. . . .

"With the growth of American imperialism, however, the point was reached where it was no longer possible for this nation's government to fight a progressive war. . . . Of all the wars that are being conducted today in the world, only one may be said to be a progressive war, the war of China against Japan insofar as the Chinese are fighting to free themselves from imperialism. Certainly, nothing progressive can come out of the war in Europe so long as the governments now leading the nations involved remain at the head of the people. Not until the war is converted into a war of the people against their governments and against the capitalists who have brought about the mass slaughter will the war be a progressive war, a liberating war, a war that can carry mankind to higher economic and cultural levels."

Not long thereafter Roosevelt took a new step in his preparations to lead the country into the imperialist slaughter. In the summer of 1940 a measure calling for peacetime conscription, the Burke-Wadsworth bill, was introduced in Congress. The *Northwest Organizer* responded to the move by putting forward a military policy for the working class, which had been developed by Leon Trotsky in talks with leaders of the Socialist Workers Party.

"With few exceptions," the union paper emphasized, "the toilers of this nation have indicated their opposition to compulsory military conscription under a war machine dominated by anti-labor interests. . . . It is not the idea of military training itself that is objectionable to labor. No worker would be opposed to understanding the furthest reaches of the military art. It is partly the idea of taking this training under the heel of a notoriously anti-democratic and anti-union military clique that labor objects to. Millions of toilers further sense that the war for which they will be trained to fight will be a war that is definitely not in their interests, a war that is not fought for any higher ideal than that of profiting Big Business. . . .

"Despite the mass opposition to the Burke-Wadsworth bill, it must be clear to all but a handful of pacifist blockheads that some sort of compulsory military training is going to be insisted upon by Big Business. . . . Pacifism is a bankrupt philosophy in our modern world. Any union man who has ever been through a strike can tell you this. There isn't a union that could last one year if it adopted a pacifist attitude towards the finks and thugs and strike-breakers sent against it by the employers. . . .

"A frank recognition of the truth reveals that at present organized labor is neither strongly enough organized nor of the mind to abolish or stop the war machine. But American labor is well enough organized to protect the interests of the workers in the army, just as we protect the workers in their jobs. We oppose corralling the workers into the regular army. . . . If Big Business insists that the masses be taught the military arts, we propose that the trade union movement be given control of the military training of the workers.

"We want to see union men trained in the military arts, not in the bosses' way, not for the defense of American imperialism, but in the union way, for the defense of the workers' homes and lives and jobs against enemies at home and abroad. We want to see the workers trained in the military arts under their own union officials, whom they can control and trust, at government expense."

After the conscription bill had breezed through Congress, as was becoming more and more the case with Roosevelt's moves toward war, the Teamster organ added the following observations on the subject:

"Congress has furnished us these last few weeks with a revolting spectacle—and an excellent political lesson. How ready was the United States Senate to conscript the wealth of the common man, his labor power, and subject him to the military dictatorship of the army, at scab wages and non-union conditions. And how outraged Congress becomes at the mere thought of conscripting the wealth and source of power of the rich: their factories and machines. . . . Hard on the poor and easy on the rich—that's Congress all over when it comes to national defense.

"Washington's actions become all the more indefensible in the light of recent revelations about the hoggishness of Big Business and its refusal to even start production on army goods until it is guaranteed exorbitant super-profits, until the government will give it the factories in which it will coin gold from the sweat of the regimented workers. . . .

"We would like to see the government expropriate every big industry in the nation and place it under trade union control. Then you would see no sit-down strike of capital. Then efficient production could really be organized, with real concern for the rights of the workers and the unemployed."

By that time a major political question had arisen. Roosevelt was campaigning for reelection and many workers wanted to run a labor candidate against him. Sentiment of the kind had been growing among trade unionists nationally ever since the second economic slump of the decade began in 1937. What is more, the feeling had been strengthened by the administration's subordination of the unemployed workers' needs to the capitalist arms program—a callous policy that had just been topped off with a peacetime draft.

Among those sensitive to the changing mass mood was Farmer-Laborite Ernest Lundeen. Speaking as a U.S. senator, he called for a new, nationwide movement of the Farmer-Labor type. Such a party could win in the 1940 elections, he predicted, because the workers and farmers had nothing to hope for from the Republicans and Democrats. Unfortunately, however, Lundeen died in a plane crash before he could press the issue further.

There was no possibility that the Farmer-Labor Party in Minnesota would follow through on the senator's proposal. Since the party's March 1938 convention, described in the previous chapter, a series of new developments had thrown it into utter confusion.

For one thing, the failure to come out against Roosevelt's line at that March gathering had proved costly. Workers and farmers, who had been supporting the reformist party at the polls, deserted it by the tens of thousands in the November 1938 elections. As a result the governorship of the state—which the FLP had held for the previous eight years—was lost to the Republicans.

Then, two months after the November balloting, the Farmer-Labor Party held another state convention at which the right-wing machine remained in control, despite some friction between its conservative and Stalinist components. Demands by organized labor for policy changes were thrust aside, and the party continued to follow the bankrupt line that had brought about the election disaster. At that point, AFL unions began to drop out of the FLP, one after another.

In Minneapolis the Central Labor Union struck out on its own in the 1939 city elections. T. A. Eide was nominated to run for mayor on a platform drafted by the labor movement. Control of the campaign in support of his candidacy was taken over by volunteer trade union committees that sprang up in the wards. This meant that the AFL central body was acting in effect as a labor party on an improvised basis.

Thus a promising, if amorphous, political movement had arisen out of the struggle within the FLP. The new formation was solidly rooted in the working class, and it was acting under trade union control. A foundation was thereby being laid upon which to build a viable labor party, one that would provide better opportunities than had become the case in the FLP for revolutionists to promote independent mass political action rooted in class-struggle concepts.

The Trotskyist leaders of Local 544 backed the Eide campaign for these reasons. While doing so, they urged the Central Labor Union to move toward creation of a permanent labor party locally and to link up with progressive forces elsewhere in striving to build a national formation along these lines. In the last analysis, the Teamster militants stressed, effective measures to prevent war and defend labor's interests generally could be taken only through a working-class struggle for direct control of the government.

Eide's Republican opponent won the mayoralty race by a narrow margin. But that didn't tell the whole story. The close vote marked a big labor comeback after the crushing defeat suffered by the Farmer-Labor Party, just six months earlier, in the gubernatorial election.

One factor contributing to Eide's defeat was Stalinist disruption of the labor campaign. In the primaries the Communist Party sought to split the working-class vote by using its control over the local FLP to run a candidate against the trade union nominee. Eide won that contest hands down. In the subsequent run-off against the Republican candidate, the Stalinists pitched another curve. They maliciously tried to create an impression that the labor platform endorsed Roosevelt's policies, an act that created prejudices against Eide among workers taken in by the ruse.

In a postelection statement, issued on June 24, 1939, the Hennepin County Council of the Communist Party continued its attack on the political line of the AFL unions. It complained that Eide's supporters had not championed Roosevelt's objectives "in a sufficiently clear-cut manner." A labor party such as the Trotskyists proposed, the CP protested, "would be an instrument to fight against the New Deal."

Two months later, however, when the Soviet Union signed a pact with Germany, the Stalinists reversed their line. That flip-flop brought them into conflict with their former allies in the Farmer-Labor Party, who continued to collaborate with Roosevelt.

Across the next few months the CP lost many of its fellow-travelers within the FLP, and the changed relationship of forces enabled the conservative wing to take full charge of the party's June 1940 convention. There a decision was pushed through endorsing the "defensive measures" taken by the national administration, which cleared the way for a deal with the Democratic Party. An understanding was then reached that the Democrats would lend indirect aid to Farmer-Labor candidates in Minnesota, provided the FLP supported their presidential ticket.

Everything had been neatly handled by the conservative political generals, except for one matter. The convention had alienated a great many workers. In Minneapolis, especially, trade unionists were abandoning hope in the FLP, and they were

showing heightened interest in building a new political formation. Those developments indicated the likelihood that an
independent labor ticket could again be nominated in the 1941
city election, thereby giving a fresh impulse to formal organization of a labor party based upon—and controlled by—the trade
unions.

This situation was promising for the revolutionary socialists in
terms of local political factors, but we were handicapped by a
serious flaw in our approach to the upcoming presidential
election: We had no candidate to back against Roosevelt.

3. A Disagreement Over Tactics

In January 1940 my wife, Marvel Scholl, and I went to Mexico for a visit with Leon Trotsky and his companion, Natalia Sedova. I had just resigned from the organizational staff of the International Brotherhood of Teamsters in order to concentrate on political activity as national labor secretary of the Socialist Workers Party. While making the change, the party felt it would be helpful for me to talk with Trotsky, and both Marvel and I welcomed the opportunity to meet the famous revolutionary.

One of the topics we discussed with him was the coming United States elections. He offered practical suggestions in that connection, prefacing them with an outline of objective considerations involved.

Heavy pressures were being applied, Trotsky observed, to line up the labor movement in support of the capitalist government's war preparations. A dangerous situation resulted for the workers because of capitulatory tendencies within the movement, which took the general form of backing Roosevelt for reelection. Therefore, revolutionists should use every available means to counter that trend by pushing for independent working-class political action.

Projection of the latter course required, moreover, that a labor program be concretized around a set of transitional demands. Measures should be called for that would protect the workers' purchasing power and assure them job security. Labor should also demand the right to live at peace with other nations, to control production, to examine the capitalists' books and expropriate their holdings, etc. An election platform drafted along those lines would not only chart a course toward solution of the workers' immediate problems; it would prepare the way for them to learn through further experiences that their class interests could be defended only by taking governmental control away from the capitalists.

To assure that key programmatic issues were stressed during the elections, Trotsky urged, the SWP should run a candidate against Roosevelt. Parallel with that action a proposal should be made that the labor movement put up its own presidential ticket, and, to help press the point, the Minneapolis Teamsters should suggest the nomination of Daniel J. Tobin, head of the IBT, for the presidency.

When I got to the party center in New York, a special leadership session was held to hear my report on the discussions with Trotsky. On the question of electoral policy, all present agreed that his proposals were good ones, but in the existing situation other matters got in the way of carrying them out.

Demands of the kind he listed were, of course, raised in our general propaganda. That had been done consistently since the Fourth International adopted a broad transitional program at its founding congress in 1938. We did not concretize those demands, however, as planks in an election platform, due to a number of difficulties.

The SWP was small and had limited financial means. Besides that, we faced harsh discriminatory election laws, rigged against radical parties. In those circumstances the fielding of a presidential ticket required an all-out effort by the organization.

There was yet another complication. An intense faction fight had developed within the party, stemming from capitalist pressures on the war issue. A petty-bourgeois minority was demanding that the SWP abandon its policy of defending the Soviet Union, a workers' state, in case of imperialist attack. The dispute involved revolutionary principles, and a majority of the membership fought to uphold them. A deep-going split resulted in the spring of 1940.

Up to that point the factional struggle had claimed the main attention of the party leadership. Then, after the split, much effort had to be concentrated on reconsolidation of the organization, which had suffered a severe loss in numerical strength. Due to those preoccupations, the national leaders gave insufficient thought to electoral activity and failed to take the initiatives that were needed. Hence nothing was done either to develop some way of putting up an SWP presidential ticket, or to propose, through Teamster action, the nomination of Tobin against Roosevelt.

That is how matters stood the following June, when some party leaders went to consult with Trotsky about several problems. The delegation consisted of James P. Cannon, Sam Gordon, Joseph

Hansen, and myself. Three other party members—Charles Cornell and Harold Robins, who were serving in Trotsky's guard; and the veteran Antoinette Konikow, who was there for a personal visit—sat in on the talks.

When we came to the agenda point on the United States elections, Trotsky summed up the existing situation as follows: There had been no campaign in the party press for labor's nomination of a presidential candidate. Nothing had appeared in the *Northwest Organizer* on the subject. The SWP hadn't put up its own candidate, and it was too late to do so. Consequently, the party had no answer when workers asked us who they should vote for. No concrete way had been developed to insist—in trade unions where we had influence—that Roosevelt was not our candidate.

Complete abstention from the campaign, he stressed, would be highly inadvisable. Instead of taking a negative stance, we needed to apply dynamic politics. As an independent party, it was imperative that we have a line in relation to the presidential campaign.

Lacking our own slate, Trotsky continued, we had to choose between Earl Browder, who headed the Communist Party's presidential ticket, and Norman Thomas, the Socialist Party's candidate for president. Thomas was ruled out of consideration due to his ties with the social democrats who stood at the left tip of the defenders of U.S. imperialism. So that reduced our options to Browder or Roosevelt.

In presenting his recommendations on electoral policy the previous January, Trotsky reminded us, he had not proposed critical support of Browder. But he now thought we should take that course, since we appeared to have left ourselves with no other alternative. Such a step should not be viewed, however, as an opening move in a longer-range strategic policy. It should be seen as nothing more than a tactical line for the current presidential election.

By giving Browder critical support, he added, still another problem could be handled more effectively. With the signing of the Soviet-German pact in 1939, the CP leaders had begun to oppose U.S. entry into the war. A similarity had thus developed between their abstract slogans and ours. In addition, they had a larger organization, which enabled them to shout louder than us. Consequently they had become a major obstacle to the SWP in the struggle to win leadership among trade unionists opposed to

Roosevelt's foreign policy. At the same time, we had been walled off from any prospect of influencing Stalinist workers on the war issue.

However, we should keep in mind that it was only a matter of time until the Communist Party would again turn toward support of U.S. imperialism, to meet Moscow's changing diplomatic needs. When that happened, an internal explosion could be expected in the CP. The 1939 shift away from the pro-war, "people's front" line had been welcomed by workers in that party's ranks, who had become radicalized through class-struggle experiences. Many would resent the shift back to a patriotic stance, and we could introduce a wedge to start some of them moving toward us when the new reversal came. While giving critical support to their presidential candidate on the basis of the transitory coincidence in antiwar slogans, we would warn the Stalinist workers that they would again be betrayed by their leaders. Meanwhile, we would go through a common experience with those workers in the struggle against war, so as to be in a better position to attract them politically later on.

After motivating his proposal in this way, Trotsky remarked that it constituted a daring undertaking. He believed, though, that the cohesion of our party was such that we could succeed in the maneuver, which would be a short one, conducted with strong criticism of the CP.

The SWP delegation did not favor the tactic of critical support to Browder. We felt that it would run into indignation among anti-Stalinist militants in the trade unions. While reactionary prejudices would be involved to a certain extent, there was also a good deal of sincere, well-grounded hatred of the Communist Party. It stemmed from major crimes the CP had committed, such as violations of trade union democracy and betrayals of working-class struggles against the bosses.

In several industries we were building party fractions on the basis of opposition to Stalinist control. For that purpose tacit blocs had been formed with elements who could be classified as progressive trade unionists. Although weak numerically, we were strong politically; and that quality had enabled us to play a significant role in blocs of that kind, through which our forces were gradually being strengthened. Hence, we believed, adoption of the proposed tactic would disrupt our trade union work by giving anti-Stalinist militants a mistaken impression that we were moving toward collaboration with the CP.

In Minnesota, especially, the tactic would be widely misunderstood, we thought, in view of the Stalinists' criminal record. Among the counts against them were wrecking operations in the Farmer-Labor Party, disruption of the trade union movement, and sabotage of struggles against the boss class.

Under those circumstances, the SWP delegation argued, any gains registered through the contemplated approach to worker-members of the CP would be more than offset by loss of influence among anti-Stalinist trade union militants.

Trotsky replied that his proposal was intended as a means of combining two objectives: namely, to provide us, as an independent party, with a line in the presidential campaign; and to support the Stalinist workers against their treacherous leaders in the hope that some could be won over. The latter objective, he said, didn't mean that we should turn away from the progressive trade unionists. It had been a correct maneuver for us to penetrate the mass movement with their help. That phase had opened doors for us in the unions, but there were dangers involved.

As he viewed the situation, the progressives were found primarily at the top of the unions, rather than as a rank-and-file current. If we counted on success in impressing those elements politically, it could prove fatal. Officials taking a progressive stance were a reflex of the new union movement that had sprung up during the social crisis of the 1930s, but they were not a direct expression of the rank and file. Their line was determined by dual pressures: to serve the workers' needs and by fear of the Stalinists, who sought to build their own bureaucracy in the unions. The officials friendly to us were mainly seeking advice in their fight against the CP, he argued.

Playing the role of advisors to the progressive bureaucrats, Trotsky remarked, didn't promise much in the long run. Although they opposed the Stalinists, we didn't seem to be winning many of them to our party. In general they were Rooseveltians, who would turn against us when the U.S. entered the war. Our real role, he added, had to be that of a third competitor, against both the progressive bureaucrats and the Stalinists.

We agreed, of course, on the need to create our own independent forces in the contest for leadership of the working class. We took exception, however, to the implication that we acted mainly as attorneys for progressive union officials. Among the progressives, we answered, were rank-and-file unionists who had been organized by us. They were militants who had good cause to be against the Stalinists, and our main line had to be oriented toward those workers, seeking to win them politically. So far as relations with progressive bureaucrats were concerned, we insisted, nothing more was involved than a bloc over trade union policy; it was not a political bloc.

What we had outlined was a trade union policy, Trotsky responded, not a Bolshevik policy. While gains for the party had been accomplished through certain unavoidable degrees of adaptation to trade union realities, measures were needed to offset the dangers involved. Many comrades appeared to have become more interested in trade union work than in party activity; and to a certain extent we were adapting politically to the labor bureaucracy.

Bolshevik policies, he stressed, begin outside the trade unions. Although a militant worker may be an honest unionist who can develop politically, that is not identical with being a Bolshevik. Political backwardness in the workers' ranks necessitates a certain degree of adaptation by those party members engaged in trade union activity. That is why pressures from backward elements are reflected by them inside the party. It is also why trade union functionaries, especially, tend to form the right wing of the party; and symptoms of that nature had become noticeable in the SWP.

There was need for more emphasis on the party, he advised us, more systematic theoretical training, sharper maneuvering. First and foremost the comrades had to be party members and only in a secondary sense trade unionists.

After hours of discussion, it became evident that we were at an impasse on the question of critical support to Browder. At that point, Trotsky, who could be tough in an argument, gave a further demonstration of his remarkable ability to think objectively. There was no question of principle at stake. Our differences centered on nothing more than a matter of tactics, and even though the Browder candidacy was an important matter, disagreements of this kind were not uncommon in hammering out plans for day-to-day activity. Account had to be taken, as well, of the fact that we would have to carry out whatever decision was reached. So he decided not to press us further on that disputed issue.

A tactic, to be valid for a working-class party, must conform with revolutionary principles and serve strategic needs in the struggle for socialism. Trotsky's proposal, of course, met those basic requirements. But it does not follow that the step he recommended, if carried out, was certain to prove effective. Tactical maneuvers are designed to achieve limited results in concrete situations of the moment. Therefore, the potential of a given maneuver cannot be definitively ascertained unless it is applied in the specific situation for which it is intended, so that the actual results are evident. That being the case, one can only speculate today as to whether it might have been advisable for the Socialist Workers Party to give the tactic of critical support to Browder a try, as Trotsky urged.

After examining the question in retrospect, I now think we should have done so. Not because there was at the time serious danger of party comrades succumbing to the trade union milieu. They passed that test with flying colors when the SWP came under severe attack in 1941. A tendency did exist, though, to give "practical" concerns undue weight in considering our approach to political tasks in the mass movement, and I believe the Browder tactic could have been helpful in correcting that shortcoming.

Our acceptance as trade union leaders resulted mainly from demonstrated ability to fight the bosses and to cope with Stalinist disruption. While the winning of leadership roles on that basis put us in a favorable position to propagate our revolutionary views, a necessity remained to use all possible means of speeding the political development of worker-militants. Viewed in that light, Trotsky's proposal did more than present certain difficulties in our work; it afforded us a political opportunity. Although extensive anti-Roosevelt sentiment existed in the trade union ranks, the top bureaucrats—most of whom favored Roosevelt's reelection—rejected the idea of nominating a labor candidate. Therefore, if workers opposed to the warmonger in the White House were to have a concrete alternative, it had to be Browder.

Anti-Stalinist militants would, of course, have bridled at the thought of giving critical support to a candidate of the treacherous CP, but it does not seem excluded that initial reactions of that kind could have been overcome to some extent. We could have stressed the importance of distinguishing between the Stalinist hacks and workers who had been sucked in by them. Careful explanation could have been made as to just what critical support meant, why the tactic had been developed in the course of labor history, and how it could be applied in a principled way to facilitate the current struggle against imperialist war. In presenting such explanations, moreover, party trade unionists would have needed to bone up on Marxist fundamentals, thereby deepening their own political education.

Possibilities of influencing Communist Party members also seemed to exist at the time. The CP had recruited thousands of workers, especially CIO members in basic industry, and not all of them had been fully Stalinized. With the switch in party line after the Soviet-German pact was signed, many became enthused at the prospect of conducting a struggle against imperialist war. If we had solidarized ourselves with those workers in that effort, through critical support to Browder, some would most likely have taken a more open-minded attitude toward us. Besides that, they were more political than the average union militant, even though their thinking was warped by Stalinist concepts. So the prospect of having purposeful discussions with them was not excluded.

Among the subjects that might have been explored were the reasons for the Kremlin's new attitude toward the Nazis, which caused uneasiness within the CP. With a bit of adroitness the discussion could then have been steered toward a critical review of Stalinist policy as reflected in the German CP's inability to prevent Hitler from seizing power in 1933. In that way an opening could have been found—without being provocative—to predict that the CP leaders in this country would again betray the workers on the war issue, as they were to do in 1941. One cannot say with certainty that such an approach would have enabled us to win over substantial numbers of Stalinist workers. Yet it seems possible that we could have influenced them to a significant extent, and in any case the SWP trade unionists would have enhanced their own grasp of revolutionary politics in making the try.

Since the Socialist Workers Party didn't have its own candidate for president, there is another reason why I now think we should have given critical support to Browder. Our failure to take that step left us with serious problems in finding a way to differentiate ourselves from Roosevelt's supporters in the trade unions. One of the stickiest difficulties of that nature cropped up in the Minneapolis Teamsters—a subject to which I shall return later.

Concerning the outcome of the June 1940 discussion, the founder of the Fourth International showed full understanding of his responsibilities toward us as leaders of a national section. Trotsky knew how costly it could be for the movement if he lightmindedly used his great authority in a way that would undermine our ability to carry out the leadership tasks assigned to us by the SWP membership. Therefore, even though confident of his correctness on the Browder issue, Trotsky was careful to avoid doing anything that would imply a break with us. Instead, he took the initiative in proposing a compromise.

The following understanding was then reached: an approach would be made to the Stalinist workers through proposals for united front activities against the imperialist preparations for war, in defense of workers' rights, etc.; and a propaganda campaign would be conducted for the nomination of a labor ticket in the presidential election.

Soon afterward the *Northwest Organizer* raised the question of an independent labor slate for president and other governmental posts. On July 18 it published an editorial, which said: "The other day the daily press reported that a certain U.S. Congressman was frantically scribbling a plank for 'the defense of democracy' to be included in the platform of the Republican or Democratic party, we forget which party. . . .

"Democratic rights are roughly divided into three broad groups. (1) The first group consists of those special 'rights' which defend capitalist property relations. . . . (2) The second group of democratic rights . . . include[s] many of the civil liberties: the rights of free speech, free assembly. . . . (3) The third group of rights that exists under capitalist democracy are not properly 'democratic' rights at all, but rather working-class rights, as have been won in the struggle of the workers against the employers. . . .

"The one group of democratic rights that the capitalists wholeheartedly defend is the first group of rights, those guarding capitalist property relationships. The second group of democratic rights are manipulated by the capitalists to their own ends. The capitalists are actively hostile to the third group of rights, and always seek to curtail them or abolish them completely in practice. . . .

"So far as the working class of people are concerned, we have no interest in defending the first group of 'democratic' rights which protect property relations only in the interests of the wealthy monopolists. But the working class, foremost of all groups in society, has a definite interest in protecting the second and third groups of rights that constitute democracy.

"The workers cannot defend these democratic rights by supporting either of the two, old boss-dominated political parties. . . . The workers can only defend democracy by strengthening their own unions, by seeing to it that the unions themselves are democratically controlled, that they follow militant politics. And just as important and necessary, the workers must have THEIR OWN POLITICAL PARTY, a national labor party, based on and directed by the unions, to challenge the Democratic and Republican parties. . . .

"As a starter, we would like to nominate Daniel Tobin, president of the International Brotherhood of Teamsters, for President of the United States. And we would like to see the trade unions in every state nominate loyal trade unionists for every post in the elections, including the posts of United States senator and congressman, and governor."

Issue after issue, the Teamster paper continued its propaganda along the above lines, and Trotsky expressed approval of the steps taken. In a letter of August 20, 1940, written to Henry Schultz about other matters, he added: "The *Northwest Organizer* becomes more precise—more aggressive—more political. We enjoyed it very much."

Our campaign for a national labor ticket coincided with an attack on the Democratic Party from another quarter. On January 31, 1940, John L. Lewis, president of the CIO, had publicly denounced Roosevelt for "breaking faith" with the workers. Lewis, who was sensitive to the mounting discontent among trade unionists, wanted to prevent the development of a revolt against class-collaborationist politics. He began with demands upon Roosevelt for a few concessions to the workers as the price to be paid for continued trade union support of the Democrats.

During the following months, however, the White House turned a deaf ear to the pleas of the CIO leader. Then, about a week before election day, Lewis went on national radio to deliver an address that had been widely publicized in advance. He opened with a telling indictment of Roosevelt. Militant workers throughout the country listened eagerly, hoping against hope that a ringing call would follow for labor to build its own party in opposition to the capitalist two-party swindle. Instead, the CIO head concluded his talk, not with a bang but a whimper: "I recommend," he told the bitterly disappointed worker-militants, "the election of Wendell L. Willkie [the Republican candidate] as the next President of the United States."

As matters stood, the workers had no presidential candidate of their own, and they were not about to follow Lewis's advice to support the Republicans. So they wound up voting for Roosevelt, considering him a lesser evil than Willkie. In Minneapolis the AFL Central Labor Union took the same position. While backing a straight Farmer-Labor slate in the state elections, the CLU went on record in support of the national Democratic ticket.

A problem then confronted the Trotskyists, because of the formal control exercised over the *Northwest Organizer* by the Teamsters Joint Council. Apart from ourselves, the Council generally supported the CLU position on the presidential election, as did many members of Local 544. Demands came from those quarters that the Teamster paper back Roosevelt. We objected, asking that—in view of the differences over the question— nothing be said in the Council's official organ. Our request was rejected, however, due in part to pressure from Tobin. As chairman of the Democratic National Committee's Labor Committee, the IBT head insisted that all Teamster units support the Democratic presidential slate.

After considerable argument within the Joint Council, a compromise was reached. It was agreed that a factual report would be made of the position taken by the Minneapolis AFL, but there would be no editorial in favor of the Democrats. A news account of the CLU stand followed in the *Northwest Organizer* of October 31, 1940. The key paragraph in the story read: "Without concealing its differences with Roosevelt, nor its criticisms of the Farmer-Labor Party in recent years, the Minneapolis Central Labor Union feels the best interests of organized labor will be served if every union member supports the straight Farmer-Labor ticket and Roosevelt-Wallace nationally."

Since the matter had been handled in a manner that did not put us on record in support of a capitalist candidate, the compromise involved no violation of revolutionary principles. It remained advisable, though, to make doubly sure there would be no misconceptions as to our stand. Steps toward that end were taken in the next issue of the Teamster paper. Through an editorial, and in a column written by the editor, Miles Dunne, we emphasized and reemphasized our advocacy of a national labor party.

If we had extended critical support to Browder, as Trotsky advised, our problem in Minneapolis would surely have been less complicated. I do not mean to imply that a Teamster majority could have been induced to accept that tactic. In my opinion, forces in the Joint Council would still have pressed for some expression in the union paper of their pro-Democratic stand in the presidential election. But a compromise of the kind that was worked out would then have left little or no confusion. Most everyone would have clearly understood that the Local 544 leaders remained flatly opposed to Roosevelt.

In addition, some political headway might have been made among Stalinist workers, with whom the Trotskyists could have established contact through critical support of Browder's candidacy. There was nothing anticapitalist about his campaign. Insofar as the Communist Party opposed Roosevelt, it did so by giving veiled support to Willkie; and that was especially the case after Lewis came out for the Republican hopeful. Sneakily backing the CIO head's pro-Willkie line, the *Daily Worker* urged "complete support for John L. Lewis' leadership of the CIO." An opportunity thus developed to raise questions about the CP's devious methods while conversing with workers in its ranks—and to discuss principled labor politics with them. It seems likely that some could have been helped to straighten out their thinking.

Lacking a direct means of opposing Roosevelt in the elections, the Socialist Workers Party cadres in Minnesota did the best they could by running a candidate for U.S. Senator. Grace Carlson was the nominee. A technicality in the election laws barred her from appearing as the candidate of the SWP. So a successful petition drive was conducted to put her on the ballot in the name of the Trotskyist Antiwar Party.

Carlson's campaign focused mainly on war-related issues. Key planks in her platform included: against imperialist war; for trade union control of military training; trade union hours and wages on all defense and public works programs; for the thirty-hour week; for the defense and extension of civil liberties and workers' rights; for a national labor party based upon and controlled by the trade unions; defense of the Soviet Union against imperialism and Stalinism.

Copies of the platform were distributed by the thousands, mainly in the major cities of the state. With antiwar sentiment running high among the masses, the SWP campaign material was well received.

Carlson's opponents in the senatorial race were Elmer Benson, a Stalinist stooge who won the Farmer-Labor nomination in the primaries; Henrik Shipstead, a renegade Farmer-Laborite who had recently deserted to the Republicans; and John Regan, a Democrat. In confronting them, the SWP nominee stressed that war was the central issue of the campaign—that the ability of the candidates to meet the problems posed by war was the basic measure of their fitness to defend the workers and farmers against Roosevelt's pro-imperialist line.

When the November election returns came in, the combined radical vote in the state was close to 17,000—more than double the 1936 total. Party by party, the key figures broke down as follows: For U.S. Senator, Carlson, 8,761 and Carl Winter, the Communist Party's write-in candidate, 256. Among the presidential candidates, Norman Thomas of the Socialist Party got 5,454 votes in Minnesota, and Earl Browder of the CP received 2,711. Apart from those specific figures, the overall radical vote included ballots cast for other candidates of minor parties.

Carlson not only out-polled Winter. Her vote for U.S. senator was greater than the combined tally on a state scale for Thomas and Browder in the presidential contest. As the election returns showed, the SWP had become the leading party appealing to radicalized workers in the area; and many were coming closer to the organization upon learning of its program.

In the national balloting, Roosevelt was reelected to a third term, but in Minnesota the Republicans won the major contests. Shipstead got the U.S. Senate seat, and Harold Stassen was reelected governor. Labor, within the state, proved to be more united in support of Roosevelt than it was in backing the Farmer-Labor ticket.

Confronted with another defeat at the polls, right-wingers in the Farmer-Labor Party weighed the possiblity of fusing with the Democrats. The idea was not new to them. They had long been attracted politically to the Rooseveltians, with whom they had much in common. There was another factor, though, which held them off from consummating the alliance with the capitalist party through organizational unity. If anything, the Democratic machine in Minnesota was even more faction-ridden than the reformist FLP; and it was a poor vehicle for political opportunists seeking a way to ride into public office. For that reason, the FLP officials decided to confine relations with the Democrats to negotiations for horse trades in the 1942 elections.

Fusion of the Farmer-Labor Party with the Democrats had also been sought by the Communist Party during the "people's front" period. Upon making its 1939 turn in line, however, the CP temporarily backed off from that perspective, as it shifted to an anti-Roosevelt stance. The switch had brought the Stalinists into conflict with their former pro-Roosevelt allies in the FLP, who came out on top and took full charge of the state apparatus. The CP managed, nevertheless, to keep control of the reformist party's Hennepin County section. Using that as a base, it now launched an offensive against the right-wingers, seeking to profit from the demoralization caused by their losses in the November elections. .A sharp confrontation resulted at the January 1941 convention of the FLP.

Due to the hostility of the party machine toward organized labor, few trade unionists attended the gathering. By then the Minneapolis Central Labor Union had more or less severed connections with the FLP. Apart from a delegation sent by the Saint Paul Trades and Labor Assembly, which backed the party conservatives, only a scattering of small AFL locals and CIO unions were represented.

In those circumstances, the affair degenerated into a squabble between the Stalinist and conservative wings of the party. Since both factions were opportunist to the core, the contest for leadership could not be resolved through constructive debate about the political needs of the working class. It was simply a matter of determining which side had been most effective in behind-the-scenes organizational maneuvers. On that count the CP had the edge, which enabled it to dominate the convention and regain control of the party's state apparatus.

Faced with that outcome, the Saint Paul trade unionists registered their disapproval by leaving the hall. Soon thereafter the more progressive elements among them proposed that AFL affiliates in Saint Paul sever relations with the FLP and move toward formation of a labor party on a local scale. But no concrete steps were taken to put the idea into practice.

In Minneapolis, on the other hand, events soon demonstrated that organized labor remained fully determined to act independently in the political sphere. The Stalinists, having regained control of the FLP machine, used it for factional purposes in connection with the 1941 city elections. They began by scheduling a February nominating convention in the name of the reformist party's Hennepin County unit. At that point the AFL Central Labor Union intervened, asking for a brief postponement so that a joint session of the Minneapolis unions and Farmer-Labor ward clubs could be arranged. The request was rejected. A strictly FLP affair was held at which Al Hansen, a member of the city board of estimate and taxation, was nominated for mayor.

Then, early in March, the Central Labor Union named its own candidate—T. A. Eide, who had been the labor nominee in 1939 as well. He agreed to run on the platform adopted by the unions. The chief planks were: against U.S. involvement in any imperialist war; for a city administration having deep and abiding respect for democratic principles and practices; for a municipal housing and public works program to give work at union wages to the unemployed.

The *Northwest Organizer* reported that greater enthusiasm for the labor ticket existed among trade unionists than had been apparent in years. The workers felt they had a real stake in the election, as shown by the extent to which they joined volunteer campaign committees. A further stride was being taken toward creating an independent labor party, controlled by the union movement.

During the electioneering the Stalinist-run FLP put out pacifist hokum against "Wall Street's war." Almost equal prominence was given to attacks on the Trotskyist leaders of Local 544. The Teamster militants were accused of seeking to "cut the mighty F-L movement down to a narrow 'Labor Party' which would be the private property of the labor skates."

In the primaries Eide snowed under his FLP opponent, Hansen—34,492 to 6,157. On the capitalist side Marvin L. Kline edged out the incumbent mayor, George E. Leach. Both were Republicans, differentiated only by adherence to different wings of that party. Not feeling that another chance could be taken with Leach, a majority of the ruling class had opted for Kline, a member of the city council. Since Eide had out-polled Leach as well as Hansen, the run-off was between Eide and Kline.

After the FLP nominee was defeated in the primaries, the Stalinists used their control over the local CIO to call for a write-in candidate against Eide. The Socialist Workers Party, in contrast, gave critical support to Eide. In doing so it stressed the need for organization of a delegated labor party in the city and for efforts to link up with forces advocating independent labor political action nationally.

Kline, the candidate of the boss class, sought to fog the real issues by resorting to lies and slanders against the leaders of Local 544. His false allegations were made in the form of attacks on Eide. The labor nominee, Kline charged, was "the candidate of the Dunnes and the underworld." Eide buckled under the pressure and publicly repudiated the support that Local 544 was giving him.

Final returns in the June 9 balloting showed Kline the winner of the mayoralty race by a slim margin of 5,862 votes, the final figures being 80,359 to 74,497.

In its analysis of the outcome the *Northwest Organizer* said: "Eide tossed away the election in the final weeks of the campaign by his cowardly and contemptible attitude towards Local 544. Eide permitted Kline and the boss press to stampede him into a repudiation of the most progressive section of the labor movement, and that gave offense not only to the 6,000 members of the General Drivers Union, but to their families and friends. Eide's political cowardice in the face of reaction lost him the race. . . . Let the defeat of Eide be a lesson to future labor aspirants to office. You cannot ask for and receive labor's endorsement, and then kick labor in the face during the campaign, and expect anything but defeat from such duplicity. . . . With a tighter, more permanent and vigilant organization and more care in selecting its candidates, organized labor has every reason to anticipate future political victories."

More was involved than appeared on the surface in the reactionary pressures to which Eide had capitulated. For several months the FBI, acting in the interests of the ruling class, had been carrying on undercover operations to disrupt Local 544 and prepare a frame-up of its leaders.

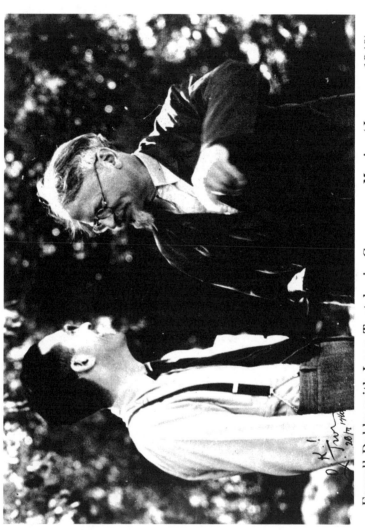

Farrell Dobbs with Leon Trotsky in Coyoacan, Mexico (January 1940)

IMPERIALIST WAR
AND TRADE UNION DEMOCRACY

4. A Moral Victory

Employer maneuvers, ranging from petty to sinister, were a constant factor in the developing assault on General Drivers Local 544. The militant Teamster organization had cost Minneapolis trucking companies millions of dollars in wage increases; it exercised firm control on the job in defense of the workers' general interests; and it was the central source of the labor movement's growing strength throughout the city and surrounding area. For those reasons the ruling class sought constantly to strip Local 544 of its power by any means necessary.

In one instance a company union, the "Associated Council of Independent Unions," was used against us. Agents of that outfit were planted in the General Drivers' ranks. Their object was to create what had the surface appearance of a membership revolt against the leaders.

Five were involved in the plot: John M. Asplund, Edward Corbett, Robert Fischer, John D. Ryan, and Adolph Svenddal. All were individual owner-operators of trucks, employed mainly on WPA construction projects. In their particular cases, investment in equipment seemed to have caused them to think of themselves as capitalists and to lose sight of their real situation as drivers who needed union protection.

On February 16, 1938, the five brought suit against Local 544's executive board in district court. They were represented by Arthur H. Anderson, a high-priced lawyer often used by the employers. During the long period of litigation that followed, there was never any explanation as to who paid Anderson's expensive fees and other costs involved in the action. Obviously enough, the plaintiffs of record didn't have that kind of money. So it was widely assumed that the boss class footed the bill.

Sweeping charges were made in the suit that officials of the local had levied unauthorized fines against members, helped themselves to union money for personal use, and intimidated rank-and-filers who sought a financial accounting. The court was asked to tie up Local 544's funds, supervise an audit of its books and appoint a receiver to take over the organization.

Under cover of that smear attack, designed to picture the executive board members as "racketeers," other employer-slanted charges were raised. We were accused of securing unemployment relief from the city for undeserving people and of conspiring in restraint of trade. A court order was requested barring "illegal" picketing, along with actions that "intimidate and coerce non-union drivers and owners." Such demands were so alien to genuine trade unionism, however, that most workers quickly perceived what was really involved. As a result the action became known throughout the labor movement as the "fink suit."

Concerning an examination of the General Drivers' accounts, the executive board had nothing to hide from legitimate trade unionists. But that wasn't the fundamental issue involved. Agents of a company union, masquerading as loyal members of Local 544, were seeking an accounting for antilabor purposes. Hence a vigorous effort had to be made to fight them off. The bosses had to be shown that their stooges couldn't gain easy access to internal union information.

In a public statement summing up the situation, the General Drivers' executive board warned: "Gigantic concentrations of capital are seeking destruction of our union. Tens of thousands are monthly spent to encompass this end. For destruction of the Minneapolis labor movement would be worth millions upon millions of dollars in wage cuts."

Sharing that opinion of the situation, AFL members throughout the area rallied to our support. Even the right-wing bureaucrats backed us up. They viewed this particular attack on the officers of Local 544 as a threat to their own trade union positions, and they saw a need to support us in order to protect themselves from similarly becoming targets of finks. By unanimous vote, both the Teamsters Joint Council and the Central Labor Union denounced the suit, as did the AFL State Federation of Labor. In addition, help was offered in securing legal counsel. Three experienced labor lawyers were retained for the defense: Gilbert Carlson and John Goldie appeared in court on Local 544's behalf; Tom Kochelmocker represented the Teamsters Joint Council.

When preliminary argument was heard before Judge Frank E. Reed, the plaintiffs' lawyer demanded access to the General Drivers' books and records. His case couldn't be prepared, he insisted, without having such material at hand. First Anderson had filed vicious charges against the union leadership; now he wanted to conduct a fishing expedition to find "evidence" in support of those baseless allegations.

In rebuttal the union lawyers asked for dismissal of the suit, contending that members of a voluntary, unincorporated association must first exhaust all avenues of relief within their own organization before turning to the courts. Besides that, they pointed out, the plaintiffs were members of a hostile formation—the company union—and could not possibly be acting in good faith.

Reed, who was notoriously antilabor, brushed aside the defense arguments. On July 28 he issued a broad order requiring Local 544 to provide Anderson its correspondence, membership lists, financial records—every scrap of information the finks' lawyer wanted. The decision was appealed to the Minnesota Supreme Court. That body refused to review the order itself; but it did say that, since the action was "of a comprehensive and blanket nature," some modification of its provisions might be considered. Reed then made a new ruling that inspection of the union files would be held up "until such time as it appears to the trial judge that such inspection is advisable." A long period of legal infighting followed, during which the opposing attorneys argued fine points of law.

Some eighteen months afterward, on January 2, 1940, the case finally came to trial before Judge Paul S. Carroll. By then several leaders of Local 544's Federal Workers Section had been imprisoned on charges stemming from the 1939 WPA strike, as mentioned in chapter 1. Anderson now sought to use that frame-up to his advantage. He did so by harping anew on assertions that the Federal Workers Section had forced the city of Minneapolis to disburse more funds than necessary for public relief. The finks' lawyer also repeated the rest of his phony charges against the union and again demanded access to its records.

Every gimmick in the smear attack on the Teamsters was made front-page stuff in the capitalist dailies. Anderson and his clients were pictured as "protectors" of the organized workers, when they were actually functioning as opponents of the labor movement. In contrast, points scored by the defense received scant notice in the boss press.

The facts were, however, that the defense lawyers got in some telling licks during cross-examination of the plaintiffs. All who took the stand conceded that they had never asked for a financial report at any meeting of Local 544, and all admitted that they had attended gatherings of the fink setup formed in opposition to the Teamsters.

While presenting his case, Anderson submitted a letter from Adolph Svenddal, a leading spirit in the company union, announcing his withdrawal from the suit. Svenddal was obviously trying to duck cross-examination. So, at the request of the defense, he was subpoenaed by the court. On the witness stand the reluctant plaintiff not only acknowledged his role in the fink union but also admitted having attended meetings of the Silver Shirts, a fascist-minded outfit, at the time it had called for an armed raid on the General Drivers' hall.

When the time came for the defense to present its rebuttal, scores of trade unionists volunteered to take the witness stand. Those called gave evidence that the plaintiffs were bitterly hostile to Local 544; that they had sought to induce Teamster members to join the company union; and that at least one of them had boasted about their being financed by "some Minneapolis business men." Testimony was also given by one Local 544 member, Douglas Raze, who had differed sharply with the union executive board on some issues. In no instance, he asserted, had any attempt been made to intimidate him, and he had always been accorded full democratic rights at union meetings.

All in all, compelling evidence was presented that the plaintiffs, acting as agents of anti-union forces, were making unwarranted charges against a democratically led labor organization. Yet Judge Carroll ruled in their favor on the immediate issue. He ordered Local 544 to throw its books and records open to the finks.

At that juncture a special meeting was held to bring the union membership up to date on developments. Speaking for the executive board, V. R. (Ray) Dunne gave an account of the clash in district court. Then he said of the plaintiffs: "These five men came from nowhere, from outside the rim of the union movement. With no funds or resources of their own, they have yet had one of the highest-priced attorneys in Minneapolis working for two solid years on this case. What we are fighting is not just some misguided men, but men who are being used as whips by the bosses. . . . We have worked as we did to make it impossible for any finks to pull this stunt again, on any union."

Robley D. Cramer, editor of the *Labor Review* of Minneapolis, took the floor as a guest speaker. "No one ever bothered looking into the books of the old [pre-1934] General Drivers Union when it had but few members," Cramer reminded the large audience. "But since Local 544 has become the keystone of the labor movement in this area, the enemies of labor are trying to cripple this union and all unionism. . . . If they succeed against Local 544, they will make the same attempt against every other effective union in Minneapolis."

Addressing the meeting as head of the Teamsters Joint Council, Miles Dunne asserted: "I always feel secure when I know our enemies are trying to beat us down, because then I know that we are doing the right things for the union. When the labor-haters quit attacking Local 544, then we will indeed know we are all in danger." That sentiment was shared by the members present, who voted to reaffirm their confidence in the union and its leadership.

Shortly thereafter, the *Northwest Organizer* began publication of a series of articles by Carlos Hudson, setting forth the truth behind the book suit. (These were later distributed even more widely in pamphlet form.) He presented a factual review of the case, along with the reasons why the suit had to be fought; and he gave a roundup of the widespread trade union support given Local 544 against the finks and their sponsors.

Turning then to background factors involved, Hudson sketched the history of the struggles through which the General Drivers Union had been consolidated in the trucking industry and its impressive power developed. He took note, as well, of the growth that resulted for Minneapolis labor generally. In 1933, for example, there had been fewer than thirty thousand trade union members in the city, whereas by the end of 1939 the total had climbed to over sixty thousand.

During the same six-year period, significant gains had been won by the truck drivers of Local 544. Their average weekly pay had risen from some $11 to about $33. Weekly hours had been cut from an average of nearly sixty to around forty-four. Those workers had strong union protection on the job, and big improvements in their working conditions had been achieved. They could now afford better housing, healthier diets, more adequate clothing, and improved medical care; and they had more leisure time to spend with their families, which added new dimensions to their lives.

All this, of course, meant lower profits for the employers. Hence their cold, calculating hatred of Local 544, their undying opposition to the local and everything it stood for. Since 1934 the bosses had kept the union under almost constant attack. Their methods had a broad range: police assaults on picket lines; the Silver Shirts' attempt to organize a foray against the union's headquarters; Roosevelt's frame-up of Federal Workers Section leaders; Stassen's "Slave Labor Law," an employer device aimed squarely at Local 544; and the murder in 1937 of Patrick J. Corcoran (then head of the Teamsters Joint Council), which had quickly been classified as "unsolvable" by the city authorities.

Now the ruling class had resorted to the fink suit, a slashing attack on all trade unionism. In describing those sponsoring the action, Hudson wrote: "Accompanying their ceaseless anti-union campaign, the employers also try to set up organizations of workers which they (the employers) can control. Such organizations are known as 'company unions.' Company unions do not fight for higher wages, or for shorter hours. . . . Instead, they take whatever the bosses give them, and they lick the bosses' boots. The Associated [Council of] Independent Unions bears all the earmarks of company unionism. . . .

"The General Drivers Union wanted to (and has made it) crystal clear that it will resist with all its strength every attempt by any fink or agent of the employers to go to a boss court in order to force an examination of the union's records. . . . After exhausting every legal possibility to prevent its books falling into the hands of labor's enemies, after two years of resistance, Local 544 has finally submitted to the court order. Even then, the union made sure the examination would take place under conditions most favorable to the union, that union officials would be in the same room with the representatives of the finks who examined the books and records."

As Hudson stressed, every effort was made to safeguard the union files. Under defense pressure, the judge ruled that inspection of the material would take place in his courtroom, which was kept locked and guarded. The only persons permitted inside were union officials, lawyers, and accountants. During the examination of the records, watch was kept for the union by Kelly Postal and Ray Dunne. (When the suit was filed in 1938, I was secretary-treasurer of Local 544. The following year Tobin appointed me to the IBT organizational staff, and Kelly was selected to replace me in the 544 post.)

Items brought to the courtroom included files of the union's correspondence, minutes of meetings, and contracts with employers; duplicates of numbered receipts for payment of membership dues, day books, and ledgers; cash books, bank statements, and copies of monthly financial reports to the membership; and records of audits made by a local certified public accountant and by representatives of the IBT.

Books and papers combined, the material weighed close to a ton. That revelation came as a shock to propagandists for the bosses. They had tried to create an impression that such records as were kept by us amounted to little more than a few scraps of paper; that the union's money was simply stuffed into a big iron box; and that the officials helped themselves to the cash supply whenever they felt like it.

The inspection began on February 6, with Anderson having hired a well-paid CPA of his own for the purpose. For weeks on end they prowled through the big stacks of union data in search of just anything that might be used against us. That went on until the judge finally grew impatient over the way they were dragging things out and ordered the resumption of court proceedings on April 2.

Anderson then opened his case by summarizing what he had found in the probe of the General Drivers' files. His presentation was described with biting sarcasm in the Teamster paper: "With the aid of Mandrake the Magician, the finks' lawyer has managed to reveal the earth-shaking facts that Carl Skoglund was born in Sweden—that the Stalinists control the Communist Party—that Local 544 had donated liberally to scores of local unions involved in battle with employers—that officials of Local 544 take vacations every few years and go where they please—that V. R. Dunne, while in Mexico, paid a visit to Leon Trotsky—that Farrell Dobbs is a member of the Socialist Workers Party—that Local 544 does whatever it possibly can to come to the assistance of its members in case of illness or death—that when 544 members are forced out on strike, the union helps the strike financially—that when 544 officials travel on union business, the union pays their traveling expenses, etc. . . . that Local 544 on December 24th, 1938, had paid out $250.18 for the Christmas party for kids given that year at 257 Plymouth avenue north!"

The finks' lawyer alleged that examination of the records had shown the local's officers guilty of encouraging threats of force and violence to attain their ends; of illegally purchasing guns, purportedly for self-defense, after Corcoran was murdered; and of illegally organizing a "standing army" on the pretext of being threatened by the Silver Shirts.

Charges of that kind were presented with a fatuous air, mainly for the benefit of newspaper reporters present. Almost daily thereafter, during testimony by witnesses for the plaintiffs, Anderson held press conferences to dish out slanted half-truths and outright distortions of facts. The practice became so vicious that Local 544's immediate parent body issued a public statement declaring: "The Minneapolis Teamsters Joint Council protests to the daily papers of this city—the *Tribune*, the *Times-Tribune* and the *Star-Journal*—that they are abetting Anderson's base work by treating his charges in their columns as good coin. . . . Anderson is seeking to try his case in the daily papers, and the daily papers are aiding him in this dishonorable aim."

Only through the *Northwest Organizer* was the labor movement able to keep abreast of what was really going on at the trial. "The best the plaintiffs could do last week," the union organ reported, "was to put on the stand a small-town boss from Red Wing, Minnesota, to testify that Local 544 caught him underpaying his driver and made him pay the driver double the back pay owed him, as provided for in the written union agreement."

Two former drivers of coal trucks were also called as witnesses for the plaintiffs. At one time those drivers had worked for less than the union wage, though both were members of Local 544. The local had collected back pay for the two from the employer and had then disciplined them for violating its by-laws. During direct examination of the pair, Anderson denounced the union's action as a crime. To his consternation, however, both workers admitted on cross-examination that they had done wrong in working for scab wages and that the disciplinary action taken against them was correct.

Testimony about various financial items was introduced through questioning of Albert E. Larson, the plaintiffs' CPA. A typical example was a payment of $2,248 to the widow of 544's former president, Bill Brown. The union membership had voted to assess themselves one dollar each for his widow after Brown was murdered in 1938, and the payment was part of more than $5,000 eventually raised and turned over to her.

Seeming absolutely certain that evidence of corruption would be found in the union's records, the bosses had carelessly relied on what appeared to be a conscientious CPA, instead of using an outright stooge. To their chagrin, Larson testified that he had found nothing wrong with Local 544's accounting system. Naturaly, that statement was not reported in the capitalist press.

As the trial proceeded, Anderson grew desperate over the failure to make a case against the union leaders. So he stepped up the demagogy. In describing motivation for the next step taken, the Teamster paper said: "Realizing that they were getting no place fast with their sputtering attacks on Local 544, attorneys for the finks last Friday pulled the old gag about 'We've got plenty of witnesses against Local 544 only they wouldn't testify in court,' the intimation being that the union would intimidate them. . . . But just try to track down such a rumor, as has Local 544, and you find that, like the Cheshire Cat in Alice and Wonderland, it fades away into the air."

Using the alleged "intimidation" as a premise, Anderson sought to widen his examination of trade union files. Specifically, he demanded that the Teamsters Joint Council be ordered to bring all its records into court. But Judge Carroll upheld the council's refusal to open its books to the finks.

After further legal wrangling, the plaintiffs rested their case. As the labor movement saw it, they had failed to prove any of the charges against the officers of the General Drivers Union. Evidence of this view appeared in the form of a resolution adopted by the Minneapolis Board of Union Business Agents. The Board voted to "go on record as condemning the plaintiffs for violating the principles of unionism by suing Local 544 in the courts, an act which can only aid all labor's enemies; and . . . join with the Central Labor Union in expressing our complete confidence in Local 544, its members and leaders."

The defense opened its rebuttal with testimony by Carl Skoglund, Grant Dunne, Miles Dunne, and Kelly Postal. They presented a documentary picture of the history, structure, and functioning of the General Drivers Union. Explanations were given of the democratic manner in which union officers were elected, of the Federal Workers Section's nature and aims, and of the criteria applied in aiding other labor organizations when they were having difficulties with employers. Anderson's attack on the local for contributing to the Farmer-Labor Party was similarly answered.

As a former officer of the union, I also took the witness stand. My answers to questions by the defense lawyers focused on our motives in developing mutual support between IBT locals, through the eleven-state structure for over-the-road drivers; and on organization of the union defense guard, formed in 1938 when the Teamstèrs were threatened by the Silver Shirts.

Anderson objected strenuously to that whole line of testimony. At one point he said: "Well, if this evidence stands, we might as well throw up our case." But the judge brushed aside his protests, commenting that the defense was presenting "a liberal education in unionism."

Ward Clarke, the CPA who had audited Local 544's accounts regularly, explained the various phases of its bookkeeping system to the court. Kelly Postal then returned to the stand to refute the finks' charges about financial matters, item by item, and to further describe the democratic procedures through which the membership controlled all union affairs. Minutes were presented of meetings where the rank and file had voted to call what the finks alleged were "illegal" strikes. An outline was given, as well, of union procedure in fining members who violated organizational discipline by working for wages below the scale set in contracts with employers.

Concerning allegations about "illegal" expenditures, Postal gave details about interest-free loans advanced to members in distressed circumstances due to sickness or death in the family, birth of a child, etc. He also outlined the factors involved in making specific loans and donations to striking unions.

Judging by the line Anderson had fed the boss press, he was eagerly awaiting this opportunity to grill the union officers under oath. When the opportunity came, though, he did a feeble job of cross-examining defense witnesses. Their rebuttal was so effective that the finks' lawyer, as the *Northwest Organizer* noted, appeared to "grow more frustrated as he watche[d] his case being reduced to scraps of rumor, lies, innuendo and distortions." Similarly, the daily papers had little to say about the facts hammered home by the defense.

After both sides had rested, the court asked for briefs containing final arguments. Anderson filed a 250-page document in which all the old, discredited charges by the plaintiffs were repeated and new, irrelevant ones were raised. Carlson and Goldie, on their part, compiled a careful summary of the defense's rebuttal, together with points of law involved. Judge Carroll then announced that he would take the case under advisement.

At that juncture a membership meeting of Local 544 was devoted to a special report on the suit. Ray Dunne recounted up-to-the-minute developments, concluding with some observations about basic issues at stake. The fight was not being made, he stressed, to vindicate a few union officers. It was a matter of defending labor's right to regulate its own internal affairs, of preventing finks and stool pigeons from working with ambulance chasers to disrupt trade unions.

Gene Larson, head of Milk Drivers Local 471, was invited to address the gathering. "The General Drivers Union," he told the assembled workers, "has been continuously subjected to attacks ever since it became a power in 1934. The attacks have been mostly on your leaders, but don't fool yourselves. The enemy attacks you through slandering your chosen leaders, in the hope of demoralizing the union and causing the members to lose confidence in the leadership. It was only through your militant leadership that you were able to build the organization and win the victories you have won. Don't think you'll have peace after this book suit is through. They will attack you for something else."

The prevailing rank-and-file sentiment was reflected in remarks by Bill Ambrose, who had been chosen by the job stewards of Local 544 to express their views to the general membership. "Our enemies," he declared, "have made us spend a lot of dough on this book suit. Now they are trying to move our leaders out of office. We've got to stop that. We've got to show the Big Shots of this town that we're behind our leaders a thousand percent."

After he spoke, a motion was made spontaneously from the floor to give the union's executive board and organizational staff a vote of confidence. It carried by voice vote, amid resounding applause.

Months later, on October 2, 1940, Judge Carroll handed down a written decision in the fink suit. "There is no evidence in this case," he ruled, "that the elections [of union officers] were not fairly held. . . . The defendants, particularly in connection with strikes and labor disputes, spent a good deal of money. They paid lawyers for legal defense. They paid bonding companies to get men out of jail and, in many instances, paid the fines for men who were arrested arising out of labor disputes. Counsel for plaintiffs seems to feel that this is an acquiescence and approval of crime. I don't think it is at all. . . .

"It seems to me that the purposes of those organizations [IBT locals in the over-the-road structure and the Farmer-Labor Party, which Local 544 had aided], as explained by Dobbs and other witnesses, could be considered well within the purposes of the particular union. . . . It seems to me that it is entirely within the purpose of this union to have an interest and support this Federal Workers Section. . . .

"Considered as a whole, the officers have not allowed themselves unreasonable salaries and allowances. . . . Nor does the court find anything to criticize in these officers buying guns in November, 1937. One of their members [Corcoran] had been murdered and they apparently thought this was the way to protect themselves." Organization of the union defense guard was similarly held to be a legitimate act of self-defense.

On balance the ruling was highly favorable to the union, but it also had some negative aspects. The judge ordered Carl Skoglund to step down from the Local 544 presidency within forty days. His action was based on a technicality. A reactionary clause in the IBT constitution barred noncitizens from holding union office, and Skoglund, who was of Swedish birth, had been obstructed by the Roosevelt administration in his efforts to obtain U.S. citizenship. There was no question of dishonesty involved. But that didn't stop the boss press from reporting the matter in an entirely dishonest way, seeking to prejudice the workers against Skoglund. The attempt failed, though, as shown by the spontaneous ovation given the victimized official at the next membership meeting of the local.

A second adverse decision involved a directive that the defendant officers reimburse the union treasury for expenditures totaling about six thousand dollars. Those items included loans made to distressed members of Local 544 and some donations to other unions. As in Skoglund's case, no wrongdoing was implied on the part of any officer. It was simply a matter of the judge, who gave no weight to concepts of labor solidarity, holding that the expenditures in question fell outside the framework of the local's by-laws.

Besides that, Local 544 was instructed to hold its upcoming election of officers under the direction of a person appointed by the court, "who is a member of a union which is affiliated with the American Federation of Labor." That order not only distorted trade union democracy, but also contradicted the judge's finding that elections within the local had been fairly held.

Those negative features of the ruling did not, however, alter its main thrust. Anderson had asked for removal of all the defendant officers and for a court-appointed receiver to take full charge of the local. The judge flatly refused to take such action, stating:

"If the members of this union desire men who are believers in the Trotsky movement, and the Dunne brothers have not denied that they are friendly with and associated with this movement, they have a right to do so. . . . The court has concluded that under the circumstances proved in this case it ought not to remove these officers [except Skoglund] and appoint a receiver."

To a certain extent, Judge Carroll's decision had cleared the air. Since 1934 the bosses had waged a continuous smear campaign against the General Drivers' leadership. Now, through the fink suit, their agents had spent months combing the union's records for evidence of "racketeering," and nothing had been found. Not a single slander was affirmed by the court's findings. Local 544 had won a tremendous moral victory, and there was jubilation throughout the labor movement over the outcome of the battle.

Even so, we couldn't afford to let our guard down. As the Teamster paper warned: "Yes, the union will be attacked again, of that there can be no doubt. The closer comes the war, the harder the attacks will be. But they won't try to pin the label of 'racketeer' or 'gangster' on 544. . . . Amid our mutual rejoicings, let's keep our eyes cocked for new attacks from quite different vantage points. The enemy never rests, and we must not rest either."

In issuing his decision, the judge had allowed a forty-day stay of execution, during which motions to amend the findings could be made. The defendants asked for three changes: nullification of the order that the officers repay $6,000 to the union; cancellation of the directive that the local's coming elections be supervised; and reference of any new complaints by the finks to trade union tribunals.

Anderson also filed a series of motions, challenging most of the findings in the suit. He reiterated demands that the court remove the entire executive board from office; prevent the spending of money for bail and defense funds; bar the union from "compelling" anyone to pay membership dues; outlaw strikes by any section of the union, unless called by vote of the entire membership; disband the union defense guard as an "alien" organization; halt the automatic mailing of the *Northwest Organizer* to union members, etc., etc.

Parallel with the renewal of such demands by the finks' lawyer, Judge Carroll was subjected to ruling-class criticisms of his decision. The pressures on him—which must have been terrific— soon began to get results, as was shown by what happened next.

Back in May 1937, Local 544 had struck a large florist shop owned by a notorious labor-hater. Nick Wagner, a trustee of the local, had been assigned by the executive board to negotiate a settlement of the dispute. In doing so he had gotten into quite an argument with the boss, and it had become necessary to use some plain trade union language in dealing with a fink involved in the controversy.

Now, over three years later, both the boss and the fink were brought before Judge Carroll by Anderson. They testified that Wagner had "intimidated" them, and on that ground the judge ordered his removal from union office.

An ominous precedent was being set against organized labor. If the action was allowed to stand, every militant union official would be in danger of removal by the courts, and the ranks would be denied the right to decide who should be their officers. Faced with that threat, the Local 544 membership voted to take the stand that Wagner remained an officer in good standing, pending appeal of the case to the higher courts. The decision to appeal the harsh ruling was strongly backed by the Teamsters Joint Council and the Minneapolis Central Labor Union.

When the regular Local 544 elections were held in January 1941, the membership returned Wagner to office as a trustee. Carl Skoglund, who had previously been ordered removed from his post, announced that he was still trying to get citizenship papers but would not run for reelection. Miles Dunne, also a trustee of the union, was chosen to replace Skoglund as president. Emil Hansen won the contest for the trusteeship vacated by Dunne. All the other incumbent officers were returned to their respective positions.

Before Wagner's appeal had been carried through the courts— and before Judge Carroll had come to a final decision concerning the order that the officers repay $6,000 to the union treasury—a new struggle erupted that was to change the entire situation. One aspect of the impending conflict stemmed from the uneven development of class consciousness in the union ranks.

5. Internal Union Developments

Variations in class consciousness within Local 544 can best be described by reviewing the union's internal history, dating back to the 1934 strikes. At that time, workers throughout the Minneapolis trucking industry were radicalizing because of severe hardships resulting from economic depression. Thousands were ready to do battle in defense of their interests, if effectively organized and competently led.

Among the older cadres were veterans of previous class-struggle experiences. A few had participated in campaigns waged earlier by the Industrial Workers of the World. Others had been schooled in militant labor concepts by Eugene V. Debs, an outstanding socialist and trade union leader of former days. There was also a component of immigrants who had come to the United States with some knowledge of Marxist ideology gained in the old country.

In the main, though, workers employed in trucking were relatively young. A majority had never belonged to a labor organization, and that circumstance put them in a contradictory position. They did not feel the inhibiting effects of defeats the AFL had suffered in the city, as did some of the older workers. But the young insurgents' ability to act was hampered by ignorance about the principles of the class struggle. They needed help in confronting the employers, both to overcome bureaucratic obstacles that stood in the way of mobilizing for such action and to avoid being misguided by class-collaborationist union officals once it got started.

The indicated vehicle for an industry-wide organizing campaign was the General Drivers Union, then operating under its original charter as Local 574. Structurally, the local was confined within narrow craft limits, and it was dominated by an incompetent business agent who controlled a majority of the executive board. He and his clique were preoccupied with building a little job trust based on sweetheart deals with a few individual employers. They had neither the desire to act in behalf of all workers in the industry nor the capacity to do so.

An opportunity thus existed for Trotskyist militants who had trucking jobs to provide the kind of leadership needed. If that was to be done, however, the tactics used had to square with the realities of the situation. Generally speaking, the rebel workers cared little about ideological discourses on the basic defects of capitalism or explanations of the revolutionary socialist road to a lasting solution of their difficulties. At that juncture they had to be approached in terms of the immediate issues over which they were radicalizing: higher wages, shorter hours, job security, and better working conditions. It was necessary to concentrate on a fight to win employer recognition of their right to organize and bargain collectively on those issues.

As a starter the way had to be opened for mass recruitment into Local 574. That was accomplished by bringing rank-and-file pressure on the executive board to go beyond the craft limits set by the IBT in accepting new members. A semi–industrial union structure was then created through a successful drive to sign up workers whose jobs were in any way connected with trucking. Meetings of the expanded membership followed, at which demands upon the employers were formulated in a democratic manner.

The above measures were instituted by an unofficial leadership component within the union ranks, which took the form of a voluntary organizing committee. It consisted of experienced revolutionists and young militants who were to learn fast during the heat of battle. As the organizing committee succeeded in mobilizing the workers—a step at a time—it led them into a series of confrontations with the bosses during 1934. These included a strike of coal workers in February, a citywide walkout of trucking employees in May, and a repetition of the latter kind of broad action during July and August.

In each instance, preparations for combat were made in a thorough way that showed the workers they were under the guidance of able captains who intended to fight. Thus encouraged, they responded heartily upon being called to battle after the bosses refused to deal with the union. When the forces of "law and order" attacked the picket lines, the workers felt that their democratic rights were violated, and they reacted angrily. Displaying great courage, they fought off vicious assaults by the police and National Guard.

From the outset the necessary discipline in combat was readily accepted. At the same time meaningful initiatives were taken by the rank and file. Even though the workers had much to learn about ruling-class methods in general, they were familiar with the petty tricks pulled by individual employers, and that knowledge enabled them to make important contributions in shaping battle tactics.

As the conflict unfolded, the strikers got an inkling, through collective action, of their inherent class power. They also began to perceive the innate viciousness of the bosses as an opposing class, including the deceptions and brutalities of which the capitalist government proved capable. In both those respects their class consciousness was raised to a somewhat higher level than had previously been the case.

For the most part the union ranks became inoculated against the virus of red-baiting. Repeated attacks of that nature, which the bosses aimed at revolutionists in the strike leadership, were more or less brushed aside. The ranks were interested in the way the leaders fought, not in their politics. Besides that, the workers had been consulted about every step taken; they believed in the policies that were followed; and for those reasons it was not hard for them to recognize the red-baiting as an attack on the union itself.

Finally, in August 1934, Local 574 emerged victorious. Significant economic gains were made in the negotiated settlement that ended the conflict; and, even more important in the long run, the union was firmly established in the trucking industry. Its members, who had tested their strength against the ruling class and won, were thus in a good position to take on the employers over day-to-day issues upon returning to their jobs.

While achieving those successes, a basis had been laid to complete the transition in leadership that had begun earlier with the appearance of the voluntary organizing committee. Carl Skoglund and Ray Dunne, both veteran Trotskyists, were the main initiators of the volunteer formation. Others who came to play central leadership roles in the strikes through that vehicle were Grant Dunne, Miles Dunne, and myself. We were backed consistently by William S. Brown, president of Local 574, and by George Frosig, the vice-president. During the course of the struggle, Moe Hork, who held an official post as a trustee, also began to play a constructive part.

The transition had gained momentum during the strikes, as the workers became increasingly dissatisfied with the performance of the business agent and his backers on the executive board. The greater the union's needs, the more the membership had turned to the unofficial leaders who were proving their worth. By the end of the third strike the ranks understood the need for a change in Local 574's officers. That made it possible to schedule an election in which a new executive board was chosen. It represented a synthesis of Trotskyist militants who had won authority in battle and incumbent officials who had conducted themselves well.

Post by post, those making up the new board were: Brown, president; Frosig, vice-president; Grant Dunne, recording secretary; Dobbs, secretary-treasurer; and three trustees—Hork and Ray Dunne, along with Harry DeBoer, who had played a big role on the picket lines.

Although Skoglund was one of the foremost leaders, he did not run for union office because of a special problem. He did not have U.S. citizenship, and we thought the employers might seize upon that circumstance in their propaganda against Local 574. Since there was no need at the moment to take such a risk, it seemed advisable for his formal status to remain that of an organizer.

Several other militants who had proven their competence in the bitter struggle for union recognition were also assigned to the organizational staff. They—together with job stewards elected at each company—formed an able body of secondary leaders. For the most part those who assumed such roles had been picket captains, and some had served on the "Committee of 100" that had been elected to lead the July-August strike. During the conflict they had sensed that the respective class interests of the workers and the bosses were so diametrically opposed that the resulting antagonisms could not be eliminated through some form of compromise. Hence, those militants realized, many battles would still have to be fought.

In some instances a still higher level of consciousness was attained. A few strikers had become aware that a revolutionary socialist program was needed to defend the workers' interests, and they had joined the Trotskyist movement.

There was also another, less favorable, side to the local's internal situation. A broad layer of the membership remained at a quite elementary stage of class consciousness. Workers in that category tended to interpret the concessions won in the strike settlement as an indication that the employers, having been defeated in battle, would thenceforth bargain with them in good faith. They expected to make additional gains in the future, a step at a time, without further conflicts of a serious nature. As a consequence those union members were prone to assume a conciliatory attitude toward management upon returning to their jobs.

Workers holding such mistaken views needed patient guidance, carefully attuned to the flow of events, in order to widen their knowledge of the class struggle. The effort had to begin at the level of their limited grasp of trade unionism. Then, as they accumulated further experience, the fact that there could be no lasting peace between the union and the employers would become clearer to them. That, in turn, would open the way toward acquisition in transitional stages of an increasingly high degree of consciousness.

Proceeding accordingly, the executive board started with an explanation of the real score about post-strike relations with the trucking firms. They would reconcile themselves to the local's existence, the board stressed, only if allowed to continue riding roughshod over their employees. But it was precisely to halt such practices that the union had been organized; and so long as it acted in keeping with that objective, the bosses would search for some way to cripple it. Therefore, Local 574 would still have to fight off major attacks from time to time in the days ahead.

Not only that. Disputes over various issues would arise almost daily on the job. In handling them, the board advised, complete freedom of decision should be kept in the workers' hands. Rulings on such matters should not be entrusted to arbitration by so-called neutral parties, who would tend to favor the employers. The unqualified right to strike should be safeguarded, and the membership should stand ready to use it when necessary. Persistent efforts were in order, as well, to establish the widest possible union control on the job, which should be exercised strictly in the workers' interests. There was no room for "statesmanlike" concern about the opposing interests of the ruling class.

Before long the employers provided confirmation of the prediction that they would remain hostile to the local. That brought a change of mind among members who expected them to be more reasonable. Many began to accept the validity of the policies advocated by the union leadership, and in putting those policies into practice they regained much of the militancy shown during the earlier struggles. As will be seen later, though, not all of them proved to be capable of understanding the true causes of new conflicts that arose.

There was one important action, on the other hand, for which almost everyone in the ranks of Local 574 had become prepared through experiences during the strikes. Broad agreement existed that the local should help those who had supported it in time of need. Several moves designed to further intensify the unfolding class struggle throughout the area were thus made possible.

Among those was the establishment by the General Drivers Union of an auxiliary formation, which all the city's unemployed were invited to join. It was designated the Federal Workers Section. From then on the new body received solid backing from the local as a whole in battling city relief administrators and WPA officials.

Steps were also taken to back other trade unions in conflicts with employers elsewhere in industry. In that connection Miles Dunne was assigned to help workers' organizations outside Minneapolis, starting with Teamster Local 173 in Fargo, North Dakota. Assistance was likewise extended to various AFL locals within the Twin Cities by other members of our staff.

Then, just as this campaign was getting well under way, Tobin revoked Local 574's charter for alleged violations of the IBT "law." After that he set up a paper outfit, designated "Local 500," with the object of using it to displace the real General Drivers Union. Virtually every member of Local 574 reacted angrily to this unjustified attack, and we launched what turned into a long, fierce struggle to win reinstatement into the international union.

While the fight with Tobin was raging, the time came in January 1936 for the local's annual election of officers. All the incumbents accepted renomination, standing on the program carried out in the past year. Those holding the offices of president, vice-president, recording secretary, and secretary-treasurer were returned to their posts without opposition.

Only the three trusteeships were contested. The new candidates running against the incumbents were: L. Abroe, R. F. De Pew, Lee Oscar Gardner, Axel Soderberg, and Curt Zander. Each ran a separate campaign, conducted in relatively low key. None of the new contenders challenged the basic policies of the central leadership. It was essentially a matter of individual militants seeking a somewhat larger role in the organization through election to what was considered a secondary post.

A feeling seemed to prevail in the ranks that no change whatever was needed in elected personnel. Little interest was displayed in the campaign, and only a small fraction of the membership participated in the voting. The returns showed that the incumbent trustees—Ray Dunne, DeBoer, and Hork—had been reelected by about a two-to-one majority.

Later in 1936 the General Drivers Union won reinstatement into the IBT under a new charter as Local 544. Tobin was forced to take the local back intact, except for some changes in the official leadership. A new executive board was set up in modified form. It consisted of three representatives from former Local 574, three from former Local 500 and one from the Teamsters Joint Council. With membership approval, specific posts were alloted as follows: president, Bill Brown (574); vice-president, Jack Smith (500); recording secretary, F. Dobbs (574); secretary-treasurer, L. A. Murphy (500); trustees, Carl Skoglund (574) and Nick Wagner (500). One of the customary trusteeships was discontinued for the moment, and Pat Corcoran (the TJC representative) was designated to serve temporarily as chairman of the seven-member board.

There was a definite reason for our change in policy concerning Skoglund's official role. Because of his extensive knowledge about organizational infighting, it was considered vital for him to play a direct role in the formal executive apparatus, where our delicate situation as a minority would present unusual difficulties. So we decided to take a chance regarding problems that could arise from his lack of citizenship papers.

After a few ups and downs, constructive collaboration was established in the new board. Significant progress followed in shaping the basic policies of the reorganized official leadership. In that connection Corcoran, Murphy, Smith, and Wagner were influenced by our demonstrated ability to fight the employers. Therefore, they were more or less inclined to let us take the initiative in developing an effective union-building course. We did so, proceeding to launch a militant organizing campaign on an area-wide scale.

Then, in the fall of 1937, tragedy struck the movement. Corcoran was murdered, under mysterious circumstances having the earmarks of a plot to blunt the new Teamster expansion drive. While pressing the authorities to search for Pat's killers, it was also necessary to fill the vacancies in the leadership structure caused by his death. The problem was soon compounded, moreover, when Murphy resigned from his position in Local 544.

Corcoran had held two posts in the Teamsters. He was both a member of the General Drivers' executive board and secretary-treasurer of the Joint Council. Before long the council voted to select Miles Dunne as Pat's successor in that body. In Local 544's case, though, a more complex problem had been created. Therefore, the choosing of replacements for Corcoran and Murphy was left for decision through the local's regular elections at the end of the year, in which all executive posts would be up for consideration.

At that time Brown, Smith, Skoglund, and Wagner were nominated to succeed themselves in the respective offices of president, vice-president, and two of the trusteeships. I became a candidate to replace Murphy as secretary-treasurer, and Grant Dunne was put forward to fill my former post as recording secretary. The arrangement for a chairman of the executive board was discontinued, and Miles Dunne was nominated to replace Corcoran on the board, running as a candidate for the usual third trusteeship.

Only the office of president was contested in the elections. None of the other nominees listed above faced any opposition, a situation that was especially significant concerning the standing of Smith and Wagner from former Local 500. It indicated the extent to which their loyal participation in the new leadership team had won them approval in the ranks.

In the case of the presidency Lee Oscar Gardner ran against Brown. As in the 1936 elections, the contender raised no programmatic differences with the incumbent leadership. His action was new only in the sense that he now sought a top union office, not the lesser post of trustee as had been the case before. He campaigned primarily on a claim that he could do a better job than Brown in carrying out established union policy.

This time a heavy vote was cast. The turnout at the polls seemed to be the membership's way of indicating rejection of slanderous charges against the union leadership made by capitalist propagandists after Corcoran was murdered. It also appeared that a good many had strong opinions as to who would make the better president. Brown was reelected by a majority of nearly three-to-one.

Just five months later another killing took place. Bill Brown was shot to death, and Arnold Johnson, a member of the union's organizational staff, confessed the crime. Johnson, who was a good friend of Brown's, appeared to have acted in a fit of temporary insanity. When he was finally put on trial—after protracted attempts by the authorities to use the case as the basis for new smear attacks on the union—Johnson pled that he was in a mental fog at the time of the murder. Seeming to accept that defense, the jury found him not guilty.

Once again it had become necessary to fill a vacancy in union office under tragic circumstances. As a safeguard against false charges that the slaying of Brown was politically motivated, the executive board recommended that a special election be held to choose his successor. Four candidates were nominated: Carl Skoglund, Peter Harris, Frank McArdle, and Thomas McCue. Skoglund was elected president by a majority of all votes cast.

Action then had to be taken on the trusteeship previously held by Skoglund. With membership authorization the board appointed Kelly Postal, who had been prominent in the secondary leadership since 1934, to complete the unexpired term in the post.

There was ample cause for the careful procedure followed to replace Brown. Ever since Corcoran's assassination the ruling class had been conducting a vicious propaganda assault on Local 544. Outrageous accusations were leveled against the union, such as one insinuation that Pat's death resulted from a falling out among "labor czars, levying tribute through violence." On phony premises of that kind, the boss press called for "civic action" to rid the labor movement of "gangsters and racketeers," and plans were announced to raise a big fund for the purpose.

Steps were also taken to initiate a company union. Agents of that outfit were then planted in the General Drivers Union for the purpose of counterfeiting a rank-and-file revolt against the leadership. The fink suit, mentioned previously, served as the vehicle. Charges made in the suit centered on allegations that union officers used threats of force and violence—against workers and employers alike—to attain their ends; and that they helped themselves to the organization's funds for personal use.

When Brown's murder followed in May 1938, propaganda against "labor gangsterism and racketeering" rose to feverish heights, and the sustained boss offensive finally began to have an impact within Local 544. For the first time since the change in official leadership after the 1934 strikes, an organized opposition developed inside the union. Formation of a "Committee of Fifteen," purporting to speak for the ranks, was announced. They demanded special measures to establish day-to-day supervision over all executive board policies and activities. Their demand, which was obviously intended to placate the employers, reflected a conservative mood that had in some instances resulted from gains made thus far by the organization.

New concessions had been won from the trucking companies upon each successive renewal of the local's contracts with them. Sharp antagonisms in worker-employer relations, which had been generated by the bitter conflict that took place earlier, thus became eased to a certain degree. This was especially true in the case of union members whose class consciousness had remained at an elementary level. Despite the continuing attacks on the local by the boss class, those workers mistakenly believed that they could have both an effective organization acting in their interests and peaceful relations with the employers—if union activities were conducted "responsibly." But the lasting peace they hoped to establish hadn't materialized. So a notion arose in such quarters that the union leadership must be "provoking" management.

Although conservative views of that nature were primary to the development of the oppositional formation as a whole, it also showed traces of another characteristic. Some in the setup manifested ambitions to advance their personal careers. They had the makings of petty bureaucrats, who would readily adopt the class-collaborationist policies of the IBT officialdom. It was to take somewhat longer, though, before opportunists of that stripe would get the outside help they needed to become practicing "business agents"—that is, the polar opposite of genuine labor organizers.

In the union elections held the following December the Committee of Fifteen ran four candidates: R. F. Hornig for president, Frank McArdle for vice-president, Harold Haynes (sometimes spelled Haines) for recording secretary, and Pete Harris for trustee. (Douglas Raze, who had a record of fronting for the Communist Party, also entered the contest as a candidate for secretary-treasurer. Although he had no direct connection with the Committee of Fifteen, it appeared that a tacit under-standing existed concerning avoidance of competition for the same office on the part of oppositionists.)

Hornig, McArdle, Haynes, and Harris campaigned on a platform containing two key planks. One of these demanded that a "representative group of rank and file members be elected annually to constitute a control board." The proposed board would be authorized to review "the general policy of the executive board, the activities of the individual members of the staff . . . and the general financial management of the affairs of the Union."

A second plank demanded that "personal political activities of all present officers be divorced from their official duties as representatives of the Local." The leadership was charged with "negligence of routine duties in pursuit of political policies inimical to the best interests of the organization." Proof of the alleged misconduct was held to be "truly self-evident on the basis of the political creed known to be professed by those involved."

On the surface it appeared that the Committee of Fifteen's candidates intended to curb their own authority to lead, if elected to the posts for which they were running. In reality, though, something else was involved. They didn't expect to win the contest, and for that reason they felt free to use the "control board" angle as a way to generate distrust of the existing leadership within the union ranks. Pressure could thus be exerted, they hoped, for a reversal in basic union policy. That was the purpose, as well, of the red-baiting attack on Trotskyist members of the executive board. It was our class-struggle course that the opposition considered "inimical to the best interests of the organization," because that outlook stood in the way of collaborative relations with the bosses.

As against the opposition's line, we defended the militant policies and democratic organizational norms through which the union had developed its impressive capacity to serve the workers' interests. On that basis all but one of the officers whose terms were expiring ran for reelection. The incumbent vice-president, Jack Smith, announced that he could no longer serve in that office because of ill health. For that reason he nominated George Frosig, who had been vice-president of former Local 574, to replace him.

In the balloting the Committee of Fifteen's candidates received 32 percent of all votes cast. (Raze got around 12 percent of the overall tally for secretary-treasurer.) The incumbents' slate won by a majority averaging about two-to-one. Considering the complexities of the existing situation, the election outcome represented an impressive rank-and-file endorsement of the leadership's policies.

A few months afterward I was appointed to the organizational staff of the IBT. Kelly Postal was selected to complete my term as secretary-treasurer of Local 544; and Curt Zander, a leader of the Independent Truck Owners section of the local, was chosen to fill the trusteeship vacated by Postal.

Although the oppositionists had not contested those changes in executive personnel, they were working quietly to build up support in the ranks and to raise campaign funds for the next general election of officers. An indication of the methods they used appeared in an official statement printed in the *Northwest Organizer* of October 26, 1939. It said in part: "The attention of the Executive Board has been called to the fact that several Union members have arranged meetings of members of Local 544 away from the Union Headquarters and without consulting and receiving authority of the Union. . . . The Board also has information which indicates that funds are being solicited from business firms in the name of the Union. The Union has not authorized anyone to solicit funds in its name."

When the next election of officers took place in January 1940, the Committee of Fifteen again put up a slate of candidates. The incumbents ran for reelection, except for Grant Dunne, who was in poor health. Grant nominated Ray Rainbolt to replace him as recording secretary. Rainbolt, like Postal, had been prominent in the secondary leadership since 1934.

Voting took place just as the fink suit was filed to spearhead a new smear attack on the officials of Local 544. The turnout at the polls was the largest up to then in the local's history, and the balloting left no doubt as to where the members stood on the issues in dispute within the organization. All candidates on the incumbents' slate were elected by thumping majorities of three-to-one.

Faced with this crushing defeat, some of the oppositionists became determined to use whatever means they could—no matter how foul—to oust the union leadership. Two among them, Lee Oscar Gardner and Harold Haynes, demonstrated that attitude by appearing later as witnesses for the finks in their court suit.

The action by Gardner and Haynes took place prior to the January 1941 union elections. In preparation for that contest the Committee of Fifteen again ran its own slate, and the incumbents whose terms were expiring, except the debarred Skoglund, were renominated. Miles Dunne was put forward to succeed Skoglund. Emil Hansen was nominated, in turn, to replace Miles as a trustee. Hansen, a revolutionary socialist, had long been a member of the local's organizational staff.

Every trick the opposition could think of was used during the campaign. An illustration can be given by citing a statement of Skoglund's that appeared in the *Northwest Organizer* dated January 2, 1941. He referred to "many rumors circulating among the membership as to why I am not running for president of the union, and other rumors about dissension and disagreements among the board and staff." Concerning the presidency, he said: "As it will be several months before I receive my final citizenship papers, I decided not to run." In refutation of the gossip about dissension in the leadership, Skoglund added: "Ever since our trying struggles in 1934, the unity of the board and staff of our union has been and is one of the main reasons for the success and advancement of this organization and its members' welfare."

Unfortunately for the scandalmongers, their insinuations paled to insignificance in the face of the sweeping victory the union had won in the fink suit. Judge Carroll had refused to credit a single one of the many slanders against the executive board. The union officers had won moral vindication, and most of the members were proud of the fact, as they proceeded to demonstrate at the polls. All incumbents who were up for reelection were returned to their posts by a landslide, receiving some 80 percent of the huge vote cast. The executive body which had received such a strong membership endorsement consisted of Miles Dunne, Frosig, Postal, Rainbolt, Wagner, Hansen, and Zander— and that team was soon to have the task of guiding Local 544 in battle against the most formidable array of enemies it had yet faced.

In the struggle about to develop, the union leadership would be confronted with a new type of internal opposition that had begun to crystallize toward the end of 1940. The organizers of the new formation were opportunists to the core. They were motivated entirely by ambitions to get ahead personally in the labor officialdom, and their conduct was, therefore, utterly unprincipled.

Even though a strong local had been built, which could and did serve the membership effectively, those individuals were not satisfied. They coveted the official posts held by others. It was not a matter of simply believing in all sincerity that they could do a better job of leading the organization. Specious arguments of that nature were used, of course, to gain the ear of anyone having a grievance against the executive board. But their real objective was to have the union's power and prestige bring them personal benefits through the acquisition of official positions. Before that could be attained, however, the incumbents had to be removed. So a clique was organized to conduct a fight against the existing officeholders, and the attack centered on red-baiting of Trotskyists in leadership positions.

Tommy Williams was chosen to head the new opposition. He had played a militant role in the union earlier, especially during the 1934 strikes, and that background was now stressed in the group's propaganda. Another gimmick was employed in choosing a label. The clique called itself the "Committee of 100," so as to create a mistaken impression that a broadly representative body, like the Committee of 100 elected in 1934, was again being created to protect the rank and file from bureaucratic misleaders. On that phony basis a campaign was launched to gather supporters among politically backward elements in the local.

At the time of the January 1941 elections the Committee of 100 had not challenged the union leadership in its own name. A changed situation arose, however, when the Committee of Fifteen's ticket was badly defeated—for the third time—in the 1941 balloting. The latter formation began to disintegrate. Some of its adherents then went over to the Committee of 100, and that outfit proceeded to open an all-out offensive against the executive board.

It did not follow, though, that the opportunistic clique was about to gain significant influence in the union ranks. From 1934 on the leadership had been red-baited by both capitalists and AFL bureaucrats. Most of the workers had thus become more or less immune to that type of propaganda, recognizing it as the device of those who opposed militant working-class policies. So the Committee of 100's new attempt at red-baiting didn't get very far.

Finding itself unable to gain significant influence in the membership of Local 544, the Williams group began a campaign to have Tobin intervene in the local's internal affairs. In doing so they seemed to have gotten an idea from Judge Carroll's use of the IBT constitution against Skoglund. A demand was pressed for enforcement—against all Trotskyists—of yet another reactionary clause in the Teamster document, which denied "Communists" the right to hold union office.

The little clique of opportunists didn't care a whit that they were violating the democratic principle of majority rule in calling for outside help to oust a leadership chosen by the rank and file. Their only concern was to find some way of getting into union office; and, sensing that sharp differences over the war issue would result in an attack by the Teamster hierarchy on the militants of Local 544, they were angling for the IBT franchise against us.

6. Friction with Tobin

The promoters of the Committee of 100 seemed to believe that Tobin was looking for a pretext to intervene in Local 544's internal affairs and that he would leap at the chance they gave him. In reality, though, the situation could not be defined in such simple terms. Antagonisms existed between the IBT head and the Trotskyist leaders of the local, but these did not stem from a crude power struggle, as superficial analysts were prone to assume; nor did they generate uninterrupted hostilities. The antagonisms were rooted in fundamental differences over program, and the relationship that resulted was conditioned by the phases through which the class struggle was passing. Periods of open conflict alternated with periods of limited cooperation, depending on the flow of objective processes.

At the outset, in 1934, we had an edge over Tobin because of the radicalization taking place among the workers. The prevailing militancy enabled us to organize thousands of trucking employees in Minneapolis. It was then possible to guide that force onto a class-struggle course through which an effective fight was conducted against the employers.

Basic to our success was defense of the workers' right to decide what demands would be made upon the trucking companies and to determine how the battle for those demands would be carried on. Democracy, we stressed, meant more than the right to have one's say; democracy also meant the right to act in keeping with the will of the majority. By proceeding in that principled manner it became possible to exercise local authority in defiance of attempts by the general president of the IBT to intervene dictatorially.

During the struggles against the boss class we strove to help the union rank and file learn political lessons from their experiences. The need was explained for the workers to break completely with capitalist politics, to form their own mass party on a national scale, and to fight for state power in labor's name. At every opportunity we also pointed out why outlived capitalism had to be replaced by a socialist society. Through such efforts those workers who became most advanced in their political thinking were recruited into our revolutionary socialist party. Within the party they received further education in the program, strategy, and tactics needed to defend the interests of the working class. Cadre training along those lines served, in turn, to provide the local union with a hard core of class-conscious fighters capable of standing up against all external pressures, no matter from what quarter the pressures came.

In all the foregoing respects our concepts and methods were the opposite of Tobin's. He was a class collaborator through and through, devoid of any ability to rely on the power of the workers. His notion of trade unionism was to seek a "partnership" with the employers concerning labor matters. Politically, he was a Roosevelt Democrat, eager to serve as a White House flunky in advancing the national and international interests of the ruling class. To justify that course he pointed to his ability to wangle an occasional small favor from the government concerning IBT affairs. Fancying, moreover, that his personal role gave the union the best possible "image," thereby enabling it to act most effectively, he expected the members to show their appreciation by loyally obeying his commands.

Organizationally, the IBT head sought to confine union building within narrow craft bounds, focusing attention on the more skilled workers and disregarding the rest. With only the relatively privileged employees thus involved, small concessions could more readily be gotten from the employers. In that way reformist concepts of maneuvering to make gains a tiny step at a time could more effectively be put into practice—with "statesman-like" attention to management's side where disputes arose. As a safeguard in the latter connection strict control was maintained over strike action. Wherever possible, governmental mediation or arbitration by "neutral" parties was substituted for use of the union power. As a corollary, of course, the workers were pressured to accept whatever contract terms the employers were willing to concede.

An altogether different attitude was taken, however, concerning the personal interests of Tobin and his top servitors within the IBT bureaucracy. In their cases the emphasis was on high salaries and open-ended expense accounts. Being no less discriminatory in their associations, these worthies held contact with the union membership to a minimum, preferring to mingle with employers and capitalist politicians. Economically, they knew more about investment portfolios than they did about the workers' needs; and what the IBT bureaucrats had learned best of all was how to protect their privileged positions. Standing constantly on the alert against possible threats to their rule, they dealt viciously with dissidents in the ranks. Anyone who challenged "official" policy or resisted dictatorial control over union activities could expect to be "disciplined" with an iron hand.

Under those conditions our 1934 campaign in Minneapolis was bound to bring about a head-on clash with the Tobin gang. It was necessary, therefore, to minimize friction with the union hierarchy until sufficient rank-and-file forces could be mobilized for a showdown. For that reason we avoided any implication that we were challenging the incumbents for official leadership when we initiated a drive to expand the membership of what was then Local 574. Steps were taken, instead, to pressure officers of the local into support of the union-building effort.

Similar care was exercised in the beginning to follow normal IBT procedures insofar as possible. Those were modified only through a crossing of established craft lines in signing up new members; and since union growth did not in itself arouse suspicions among the top Teamster bureaucrats, a strong, semi-industrial formation was built locally before they realized what was happening.

It was then possible—through careful timing—to get well under way in a fight to win concessions from the trucking firms before a collision with Tobin developed. The union-employer confrontation began with the February 1934 strike in the coal industry. Prior to that action the local had formally requested approval of its intended course from the IBT headquarters, but after considerable delay the request was denied with the advice that help be sought from government mediators. By that time, however, the workers were about to win the strike, which had already started. Their victory caused trucking employees throughout the city to join the local in large numbers, and at the same time the IBT head lost prestige because of his failure to help the coal workers.

Those developments enabled us to bypass the formality of asking IBT approval before launching the citywide walkout in trucking that took place in May. A request of the kind could in this case have precipitated bureaucratic intervention to prevent such a bold move. So action was taken strictly on Local 574's initiative. In the struggle that followed, the strikers defended their picket lines in hand-to-hand combat with the cops; and Tobin, who was thrown into a panic by this rude violation of his class-collaborationist norms, ordered the local to seek arbitration of its demands. But sufficiently large forces had been set into motion—and enough struggle momentum had been developed—to put the situation beyond his control. His order was ignored. The workers fought on and forced the employers to negotiate a settlement with the union.

Not long thereafter Tobin began to red-bait the Trotskyists in his official magazine, demanding our expulsion from the labor movement. The opening diatribe was so vicious that the employers gleefully used it in their propaganda as they proceeded to force the local into another strike. Tobin's disloyal act angered the embattled union members, who publicly denounced his conduct and demanded that he stand aside while they finished their fight with the trucking bosses. In no uncertain terms, the strikers were asserting their right to have local autonomy; and, as matters stood at the moment, the IBT head could do nothing about it.

A few months later, though, he was able to take advantage of a situation that we couldn't avoid. Local 574's charter was revoked on formal grounds of delinquencies in the payment of per capita taxes to the IBT. We had previously acknowledged the obligation, giving assurance that it would be met in full as soon as the organization could recuperate sufficiently from the heavy drain on its finances during the earlier strikes. But Tobin chose to ignore the pledge. Being eager to get rid of the local because it was upsetting his class-collaborationist line, he was quick to use the tax delinquency as the excuse for doing so. The intended permanence of his action was shown by the speed with which he chartered "Local 500" to assume the General Drivers jurisdiction in the city.

Establishment of the new IBT unit, which existed only on paper, was accompanied by a decree calculated to decimate the forces mobilized by Local 574. Workers whose jobs placed them outside the narrow craft bounds laid down by Tobin were to be denied further affiliation with the Teamsters. Those who survived the intended purge were to be reorganized into separate craft formations. Militants who had played leading roles in the 1934 strikes were to be excluded from membership, no matter what their occupations. Besides that, the new setup was to remain under the direct control of the international union; there was to be no local autonomy, and no democratic rights whatever were to be accorded to the rank and file. So harsh was the decree, so potentially destructive of the gains for which the workers had shed blood, that its very promulgation aroused the wrath of trade union members throughout the city.

We responded to the attack with a demand for reinstatement into the IBT with full democratic rights. In keeping with that approach, Local 574 continued to act as though it remained part of the AFL. Jurisdictions of other unions were respected, and our powerful organization gave them help in their struggles against the bosses. In return we received a large measure of cooperation in kind, along with extensive support of our reinstatement demand. Under those circumstances Tobin's agents in Minneapolis, who were trying to carry out his disruptive tactics, found themselves unable to make headway against us.

As had been the case in 1934, objective trends remained quite favorable to our cause. By the spring of 1936 major strikes were beginning to erupt in basic industry, and the CIO was coming into existence as a new, dynamic labor formation. Finding itself faced with that challenge, the AFL bureaucracy could pay little attention to Tobin's need for help against us. Within Minneapolis, meanwhile, his agents were becoming increasingly discredited; and Local 574, helped along by the rising tide of labor militancy, was gaining steadily in strength and prestige. Finally, in the summer of 1936, the situation became so bad for the local Tobinites that they initiated negotiations for a settlement of the internal union conflict. A compromise was then reached in which our organization was reinstated into the IBT as Local 544.

Concessions were forced from Tobin which left the local basically unchanged. Its autonomy was safeguarded. Internal democracy continued to prevail in deciding policy. All the members and leaders were included in the reinstatement, without exception; and as that development indicated, the organization was allowed to retain its semi-industrial form. In short, new leeway was being allowed officially for local initiatives and changed jurisdictional concepts—a turn in line that would ultimately lead to significant readjustments in the IBT itself.

On our part it was necessary to concede Tobin's representatives a four-to-three majority on Local 544's executive board. He obviously assumed that such an arrangement would give him firm control over the membership, but things didn't work out that way. Class-struggle trends, both nationally and in Minneapolis, continued to reflect an expanding labor upsurge. Thanks to that situation we were able—with solid support in the ranks—to steer the local Tobinites onto a constructive union-building course. More than that, we got their help in extending Local 544's influence into wider IBT circles. Workers in trucking elsewhere in the area were anxious to emulate the example set by the Minneapolis Teamsters. In addition, officials of various IBT locals recognized the need for changes in the existing policies. Those forces were ready to collaborate with us in getting a broad organizational drive under way, and it soon became possible to draw them together in a body called the North Central District Drivers Council (NCDDC).

Tobin looked upon the new formation with great suspicion. He was incapable of viewing it objectively as a necessary vehicle for effective union building. To him the emergence of the district council represented a threat to his dictatorial rule over the local unions and possibly even a step toward creation of a national caucus for the purpose of challenging him for the presidency of the IBT. So he issued an arbitrary order that the council be disbanded forthwith.

What happened next came as a shock to the IBT head. A group of angry delegates from various locals participating in the NCDDC confronted him at his headquarters. He tried to intimidate them with a lecture on the "laws" of the organization, which were based on outmoded concepts. But they stood firm, insisting that changed conditions in the industry made it imperative for the locals to act collectively on a broad geographic scale. Tobin finally realized that either he had to allow some readjustments in policy or a major revolt might develop against his rule. Therefore he agreed to the establishment of an area-wide body to coordinate union activity in long-distance hauling. With that breakthrough the way was opened to introduce militant policies into broader spheres of the Teamster movement.

A massive organizing campaign was then launched among over-the-road drivers, extending across the upper Mississippi Valley, from the Alleghenies to the Rockies. The action was led by a newly formed area committee made up of representatives from key local unions. Since the committee was charting a new course for the IBT it was in a position to lay down its own rules of procedure, and that circumstance permitted the development of a democratic atmosphere in which the union fighters were able to function at their best.

Demands upon the trucking firms were formulated so as to reflect the needs and desires of the workers in the industry. As a result, militants behind the wheels of trucks enthusiastically carried word of the campaign down every highway and byway, helping the Teamster organizers line up new members. Road drivers began to join the union by the tens of thousands, and before long a major component of the bosses yielded peacefully to the mounting pressure. They signed an eleven-state contract which for the first time established uniform wages and conditions for over-the-road trucking on an area scale. It was also the biggest contract ever negotiated by the IBT up to that time.

Tobin was quite impressed by the area committee's accomplishments, especially in terms of gains to be measured by *his* yardstick. New members were pouring into the union at an ever-increasing rate. Per capita tax payments mounted, swelling the international union's treasury; and the organization experienced an unprecedented leap in power and prestige. All this had been done, moreover, without having to go on strike, which was most pleasing to the class-collaborationist head of the IBT. Having become convinced that we were acting "responsibly," he promised to back the area committee in forcing every long-distance outfit in the eleven states to sign the area agreement.

The promise of help from the international union was made good when it became necessary to conduct an extensive strike in the Missouri Valley region, mainly in Omaha and Sioux City. Financial backing was received. Heads of Teamsters Joint Councils, who tried to interfere in some cities, were ordered to stay out of over-the-road affairs, and full authority in that sphere was given to the area committee, with assurance of continued official support until the battle was won.

Valuable though such assistance was, the outcome of the struggle depended in the last analysis on the truck drivers involved. They gave a good account of themselves, picketing militantly and resisting all strikebreaking attempts with grim determination. After almost six months of fierce conflict the workers emerged triumphant. Long-distance trucking firms throughout the Missouri Valley region were forced to sign the area contract, and, in a mopping-up action that followed, the remaining holdouts across the entire eleven states were brought to book. That advance, in turn, stimulated a wave of local organizing drives, city by city. Immense potential had thus been created for the IBT to develop into a first-rate powerhouse acting in the service of the working class—if it was properly led.

Tobin responded happily to the Omaha–Sioux City victory and the new expansionary impulses that ensued. Hailing the union's gains in the May 1939 issue of the IBT magazine, he said: "I have never known a better conducted strike or better union men than those that were engaged in this conflict."

But this tribute to the militants who had fought the union's battle reflected nothing more than jubilation over the results of their victory. It did not signify any change in the Teamster president's basic line. He continued to think in terms of acting in "partnership" with the ruling class; if anything, his personal ambitions in that respect were soon to become more decisive than ever.

In July 1940 the White House announced that Tobin was to be appointed to Roosevelt's staff of administrative assistants. Eager though he was to grab the post, the IBT head coyly asked that his appointment be withheld until after the Democratic convention, at which he was to be delegate-at-large from Indiana. Meanwhile, he undertook to lay what he considered a proper basis for acceptance of the White House assignment, through measures introduced at an IBT convention that took place in September 1940.

A new clause was added to the section of the union's constitution dealing with the duties of the general president. The amendment read: "It is understood, however, that this shall not prohibit or prevent him from accepting a call to service by the President of the United States; and if such call is made and he believes that it is in the best interests of the International Union to accept, this position and remuneration as now outlined in the constitution shall not be interfered with and shall continue."

Acceptance of the White House appointment was not to prevent the Teamster president from continuing to exercise dictatorial authority within the organization; nor was it to interfere with collection in full of his handsome salary and lavish expense allowances.

By that time Roosevelt's preparations for war had come to

include naked strikebreaking in the fake name of "protecting the national interest." So Tobin, anticipating his primary function as a White House lackey, asked the convention for authority to ban strikes by IBT units. Concretely, he proposed that the general president be empowered to order arbitration of disputes with employers; and, to put teeth in such orders, local unions refusing to comply were to have their charters revoked. Miles Dunne of Local 544 led a fight against the proposal from the convention floor. Something previously unheard-of resulted, thanks in large part to the effective manner in which the strike weapon had been used during the 1938-39 over-the-road campaign. The delegates overrode Tobin, voting by a big majority to refer the matter back to the constitution committee. There the proposed new clause was rephrased, making it optional with the local unions to accept or reject arbitration of industrial disputes.

The convention was also asked to authorize a raise in the general president's salary to $30,000 a year (in 1940 dollars). Once again the Minneapolis delegates expressed opposition, taking a stand as a bloc. But the increase was granted on a roll-call vote of 950 to 186.

Local 544's role in blocking Tobin's attempt to impose compulsory arbitration of disputes with trucking bosses irritated him, of course, as did the opposition to his salary hike. Factors of that nature were largely offset, however, when shortly after the Teamster convention Judge Carroll rendered his decision in the fink suit. As described previously, the judge absolved the local's executive board of all charges made by the finks. Since IBT units everywhere had been watching the case with apprehension that a precedent might be set for use against them, our victory gave us added prestige throughout the international union. Even Tobin was affected. Referring to the fink suit in the May 1940 issue of the IBT magazine, he had said: "There is no greater curse than to have an individual member who wants to take the local union into court." We had now beaten off such an attempt, thereby rendering an important service to the whole movement, and the general president had to show respect for our success.

As a consequence, our relations with the IBT head remained relatively stable insofar as strictly trade union matters were concerned. Evidence to that effect appeared toward the end of the year in connection with the Minneapolis Teamsters Joint Council's celebration of its twenty-fifth anniversary. Tobin was invited to participate, but he was tied up with other matters. So he sent Dave Beck, then the leader of the Western Conference of Teamsters, to speak for him.

Beck's remarks were reported in the *Northwest Organizer* of December 12, 1940. "While I was in New Orleans with President Tobin," Beck said, "he requested that I come to Minneapolis and represent him on this occasion, and talking with him this afternoon on the telephone, he again asked me . . . to say to you that our International office commends the local organizations at Minneapolis . . . on the splendid progress that has been made."

Then, after expressing his own "great interest in the progress of the Minneapolis Teamsters," Beck urged that "we change the old system of union organization and get caught up with developments in transport."

Clearly enough, Local 544's union-building methods were evoking a sympathetic response, to one degree or another, in many quarters of the IBT. In those circumstances Tobin, who had himself been influenced somewhat by our role in the over-the-road campaign, had no realistic premise for the initiation of hostilities on purely trade union grounds. Nevertheless, friction was again developing between us, stemming from an entirely different cause.

The IBT head was committed to unconditional support of Roosevelt's foreign policy. Local 544, on the other hand, had been campaigning since 1937 against U.S. imperialism's preparations for war; a large part of the Minnesota labor movement had been won over to that position; and the *Northwest Organizer*, the official organ of the Minneapolis Teamsters Joint Council, was alerting the workers against every jingoistic move that emanated from the White House. Tobin wanted to stifle that opposition, so that he could exercise monolithic control over all Teamster expressions on the war issue. Yet he hesitated to start a new fight with us because we had defeated him in previous clashes and now had more influence than ever within the international union.

As events would soon show, however, a decision was about to be forced upon the IBT head. The federal cops were masterminding a plot to maneuver him into an all-out attack on Local 544.

7. FBI Disruption

As Roosevelt prepared for war against imperialist rivals abroad, he launched an assault on the working class here at home. The aims were to gag opponents of his foreign policy and to prevent industrial disputes from escalating into production stoppages. Towards those ends, all agencies of government were mobilized for a crackdown on the more aggressive sections of organized labor.

On the industrial front, repressive measures were instituted through a presidential decree barring "strikes against the government." This proscription extended beyond public employees and WPA workers. It was used to justify attacks on picket lines generally, through phony "government seizure" of struck facilities in private industry. Roosevelt could go only so far in acting as an outright strikebreaker before incurring serious political risks. So he stepped up governmental interference inside the trade unions, the object being to assure domination of the labor movement by bureaucrats who supported his line.

Vicious attacks followed on the political rights and civil liberties of militant workers, especially those opposed to Washington's foreign policy. They were subjected to intensive red-baiting, as a propaganda cover for the actions taken against them. An assortment of presidential orders and legislative measures served as weapons in the assault. Among these was the notorious Smith Act. Labor's "friend" in the White House signed that thought-control instrument into law in June 1940, despite widespread protests from labor and civil liberties organizations.

A key role in the unfolding witch-hunt was assigned to J. Edgar Hoover, director of the Federal Bureau of Investigation. Roosevelt gave Hoover free rein to use his forces as political police. The top federal cop proceeded with great zeal in carrying out the assignment, and the president winked at the illegal methods Hoover employed in flagrant violation of the Bill of

Rights. Undercover activities were carried on to infiltrate and disrupt trade unions and workers' political parties. FBI operatives spied on labor organizations, functioned as agents provocateurs, planted or recruited informers in the workers' ranks—all to engineer frame-ups of militants. Those who became targets of the political cops were prosecuted in a brutal manner, usually on charges of "conspiring" to violate one or another federal law.

In most instances the proceedings began with secret indictments on the stiffest possible counts. If the issuance of indictments was made public, the names of those involved were likely to be concealed. Surprise arrests followed, taking place as a rule in the small hours of the morning. The victims, who didn't know they were wanted by the FBI, were dragged off to jail in a manner that enabled the boss press to dishonestly picture them as dangerous criminals. Once they had been put behind bars, outrageously high bail was set for their release pending trial.

New twists came into play when the cases were tried in the federal courts. Trumped-up evidence was presented by FBI agents and by stool pigeons who had been coached as government witnesses. When defendants took the stand to rebut the false testimony, U.S. attorneys subjected them to savage cross-examination and deliberate character assassination. Such acts of intimidation were accompanied by legal ploys devised to obstruct counsel for the defense. Then, at the end of the kangaroo proceedings, the cases went to rigged juries, which usually brought in "guilty" verdicts, and the victimized militants wound up serving time in prison.

More was involved in this diabolical process than efforts to make sure that those indicted were jailed. These tactics were intended to serve a broader purpose. They were designed to generate fear throughout the labor movement of the dire consequences that would result for anyone who got out of line with Roosevelt and Company.

Operations of this kind were thus begun against the midwest Teamsters during 1938, in the aftermath of a bakery strike conducted by IBT Local 383 in Sioux City, Iowa. During the walkout a truck was allegedly burned near the Iowa-Minnesota line—far from Sioux City, where the actual struggle took place. The boss press tried to put the blame on Local 383. Local officers denounced the smear attack and suggested that a company had deliberately burned one of its rigs in a bid for public sympathy. In the end, the union won the fight. Peaceful relations were resumed with the bakery firms, and the incident was forgotten by everyone—except the federal police.

In the fall of 1939 the FBI arrested seven leaders of Teamster locals in Des Moines, Omaha, and Sioux City. All were charged with conspiracy in connection with the alleged truck-burning a year earlier. Since the Des Moines and Omaha locals had not been involved in the Sioux City dispute, there could be only one reason why officers of those unions were included in the roundup. The "burning" episode was being parlayed into an attack on the IBT's main strongholds in the Missouri Valley, so as to weaken the organization throughout the entire region.

Preparation of the frame-up had begun soon after the bakery strike was settled. An elaborate survey was made of the highway at the state border, to cook up a phony claim that the 1938 incident was an interstate matter. That put the case under federal jurisdiction. Standard operating procedures were then followed— as described above—to secure indictments, make the arrests, put the defendants on trial, and railroad them to prison. All seven of the victimized Teamster leaders had to serve two-year terms.

The next attack, which stemmed from the 1939 WPA strike, was made upon Local 544's Federal Workers Section. Police action centered on the FWS because it had conducted the most effective struggle during the national WPA walkout. In total, 166 workers were indicted. They were accused mainly of conspiring to deprive the government of workers' services.

A newspaper report of FBI activities at the time indicates the manner in which "evidence" was gathered for the grand jury. This revealing item, published in the *Minneapolis Tribune* of July 24, 1939, referred to a bloody assault the local cops made on pickets at a WPA project. It said in part: "The Federal Bureau of Investigation agents, about twenty-five of them, were in a good position to learn what took place. . . . Wearing overalls and other articles of workmen's clothing, the agents, posing as pickets and onlookers, mingled with the crowd surging around the project building."

Another quotation will serve to describe the tone set in the criminal proceedings against jobless workers who had resisted Roosevelt's policy of cutting federal relief in order to increase the military budget. The remark is taken from a speech to the jury by Victor Anderson, the prosecutor. "Minneapolis, so long as I am here," he brayed at the top of his voice, "is not going to become the Moscow of America."

Protests against the WPA frame-up became so extensive, there was such pressure from organized labor nationally, that Roosevelt deemed it expedient to drop many of the indictments without bringing the accused to trial, and some of the defendants who had been convicted were merely put on probation. But sixteen who were leaders and outstanding activists of the FWS got prison sentences of as much as a year and a day.

After the WPA strikers were jailed, the FBI continued its undercover operations against Local 544, extending them beyond the Federal Workers Section. Knowledge of what was being done became public only two years later. At that time twenty-eight people who played leading roles in either the union or the Socialist Workers Party were tried in federal court on charges of conspiring to overthrow the government. Among those who testified against the twenty-eight were FBI agents and members of the Committee of 100. Admissions forced from them during cross-examination by defense counsel provided significant information about dirty tricks that Hoover's cops had been using against us.

For a considerable period, we learned during that trial, the FBI had been accumulating files on Trotskyist militants in Minnesota. Then, toward the end of 1940, its operations were broadened to include prying into the affairs of Local 544. Two special agents, Roy T. Noonan and Thomas Perrin, concentrated on the project. They had dual objectives: internal disruption of the local and preparation of a witch-hunting attack on its leadership.

Noonan and Perrin soon established contact with the Committee of 100, and one aspect of that outfit proved quite attractive to them. Some of its adherents had once belonged to the Socialist Workers Party. Their affiliation had not been motivated by socialist convictions, however; they had taken the step for strictly opportunist reasons. Since top leaders of Local 544 were party members, these ambitious individuals had followed suit with the expectation that it would help them to carve out personal careers in the union apparatus. When things didn't work out that way they quit the SWP, turning against it with an apostate's hatred.

Excellent prospects thus existed for the FBI to convert such types into police informers. They could then be used to finger whatever union militants they chose, as alleged Trotskyists, and to bear false witness against the SWP as an organization.

Proceeding with those aims in view, the political cops made their services available to Tommy Williams, head of the

Committee of 100. Williams was on Local 544's organizational staff at the time, and he used that post to draw others into the undercover operation that was being set into motion. Workers were invited to his home, for example, to be fed red-baiting tidbits about leaders of the union, which had been supplied from FBI dossiers.

During this process Sidney Brennan and James Bartlett began to play leading roles, along with Williams, in the developing scheme. Brennan was a job steward in Local 544. Bartlett, who was president of Warehouse Employees Local 359 of the IBT, had no direct connection with the General Drivers Union. Williams, Brennan, and Bartlett had all been members of the SWP for brief periods.

In February 1941 the three sponsored a caucus meeting, held at the Nicollet Hotel. Perrin was allowed to sit in for the FBI. Only twenty-five members turned out for the affair, which left the clique quite a bit less than a Committee of 100. Discussion at the meeting centered on a campaign to have Tobin remove Local 544's executive board from office. Pretending to raise the demand as a loyal opposition inside the union, the Williams-Brennan-Bartlett cabal hid the fact that it was acting in collusion with the antilabor political cops.

As efforts continued to strengthen the fink setup, a particularly odious tactic was used in one instance. Perrin suggested it. Henry Harris, a member of the Federal Workers Section who had joined the plotters, did the dirty work. Harris was sent to offer Carl Skoglund help in getting his citizenship papers if he came over to the Committee of 100. Skoglund denounced the offer as an insult to his integrity.

Williams, too, was operating in a most reprehensible manner. His methods had, in fact, become so disruptive that the union took action in self-defense. He was fired from the organizational staff for indiscipline and disloyalty. Williams protested his discharge in writing, sending a copy to Tobin. Local 544's executive board then held a further hearing on the matter, in which John Geary and T. T. Neal participated. Geary was an IBT vice-president who resided in Saint Paul. Neal had been appointed to replace me as general organizer in charge of over-the-road activities, following my resignation from Tobin's apparatus. After getting the facts, neither Geary nor Neal made any effort to have Williams returned to the post he had held.

Shortly thereafter the Committee of 100 pressed red-baiting

charges against Local 544's leadership in the Minneapolis Teamsters Joint Council. But they didn't get to first base. Most delegates to the council saw through their calculated attempt to split the Teamster ranks, and the charges were summarily rejected.

Meanwhile, the disrupters had scheduled another secret meeting for March 1, again at the Nicollet Hotel. This time, however, Ray Rainbolt got wind of the affair, and he sent a loyal union member to cover it. Knowledge of what went on was thus obtained, as follows: About 115 were present at the start of the meeting, but a number walked out when Williams launched into a red-baiting diatribe against officers of the union. Those who stayed decided later in the session to demand that Tobin "step into Minneapolis and clear up an intolerable situation." They also chose an executive committee "to further the cause of Americanism within the union."

Then, on March 10, Tommy Williams suffered a heart attack while climbing the headquarters stairs to attend a membership meeting of Local 544. He was rushed to the hospital, where he died soon after arrival.

With leadership of the clique now falling entirely upon Bartlett and Brennan, they changed its name to the "Committee of 99." Their object was to paint Williams as a "martyr," seeking thereby to whip up a lynch spirit against Trotskyist militants in the union. The climate that resulted was described by Geary in a letter to Tobin on March 14, 1941. "This committee of 100 representing the Williams and Bartlett outfit is still raising Cain," he wrote. "I have been told that they are bringing men around the headquarters carrying guns. . . . The funeral yesterday [for Williams] was very large. The officers of the local Union did not attend as they were warned not to attempt to go to the funeral—if they did there would have been trouble."

Geary's report also mentioned that he had talked with Miles Dunne about the situation in Local 544. Tobin's reply of March 17 dealt only with that aspect of the report. "I think you should not have too much to say to Brother Dunne and others," he warned, "on the subject matter about which we talked here in the office."

Two new developments followed on the heels of this exchange. Brennan asked the IBT head for guidance in filing charges against the Trotskyists in the union, and the political cops went to work on Geary.

"Another wrangle that appeared this week," Geary wrote to

Tobin on March 22, "was the F.B.I. stepped into the game. How they got started, I don't know. One of their men came over to see me. Brother Neal was there with me when he came in. He wanted to know what we were going to do. I told him we didn't want any F.B.I. men in our affairs and we were well able to take care of them when the right time arrived and didn't have any information to give him. . . . He is interested mainly in digging up the record of the men that are affiliated with the Socialist Workers Party."

Tobin replied on March 24: "In answer to your letter . . . first let me say to you that you must not show any disrespect for the representatives of the F.B.I. They have many things in their minds that we do not know anything about. As far as I know, they have always been friendly to the International Brotherhood of Teamsters. Show them respect and answer their questions without, of course, committing anybody or saying anything to injure anyone. They know what they are doing."

While giving Geary this scolding, Tobin also sent formal notices to Local 544's executive board and to the Committee of 99 that a hearing on the local's internal situation would be held in Chicago on April 8, 1941.

Upon receiving the notice, Bartlett and Brennan moved quickly to rig up "evidence" against leaders of the local. It took the form of affidavits signed by individuals in their clique who had once been in the Socialist Workers Party. Pretending to have accurate information obtained during their sojourn in the party, those individuals named many of Local 544's officers, organizers, and job stewards as members of the SWP. After that piece of stool-pigeonry had been prepared—to the apparent satisfaction of Noonan and Perrin—the affidavits were rushed to the IBT headquarters.

At that time we didn't know about the FBI's use of the Committee of 99 to bring pressure on Tobin. We were aware, however, that the Teamster president was feeling his way toward development of the "communist" issue as a weapon against us. So the party called a special meeting of the comrades in the union to decide how the problem should be handled.

In sizing up the situation we began with an appraisal of changing objective conditions. It seemed certain that the ruling class was on the verge of plunging the country into World War II. Once that came about, the current rise of reactionary political trends was bound to become intensified. Under those adverse circumstances, we felt, an attack by Tobin based on charges of affiliation with the SWP would put our IBT comrades in a bad spot, for there was virtually no chance that the right of formal membership in a revolutionary party could be successfully defended in the wartime political climate that was rapidly developing.

Therefore, we reasoned, formalistic defense of the constitutional right to freedom of choice in political affiliations would be self-defeating. More was involved in that connection than the improbability that such a fight could be won under the given conditions. We, too, would be bringing the question of party membership into central focus, thereby helping Tobin divert attention from his real aims. What he wanted, we already had good cause to assume, was to strip Local 544 of its autonomy. His purpose in doing so would obviously be to strangle internal union democracy and impose his class-collaborationist line upon the membership. That being the case, our emphasis had to center on warning the rank and file not to be taken in by "subversive" charges against their leaders, which would be merely a smoke-screen to conceal the IBT head's actual objectives. It was necessary to drive home the fact that the workers' hard-earned gains, achieved during seven years of bitter struggle from 1934 on, were in jeopardy.

For the above reasons we decided that comrades holding executive posts in the local should drop their formal membership in the SWP and assume the status of party sympathizers. No change in political beliefs was involved. It was only a matter of making tactical readjustments found necessary in view of the scheduled hearing.

The Chicago proceedings were conducted by John M. Gillespie, assistant to the IBT president. His announced purpose was to examine charges that officers of Local 544 were "communistic, alien and grossly negligent and inefficient." The "alien" angle involved Skoglund, who had already been removed from union office by Judge Carroll. It could only have been thrown in for window dressing, as were the ridiculous charges that officers of the local were "negligent and inefficient." Gillespie's real intent, of course, was to explore the "communistic" issue, and the deliberations centered entirely on that count.

Bartlett and Brennan appeared for the Committee of 99. Their testimony amounted to nothing more than a rehash of red-baiting smears—manufactured in large part by the FBI—which they had previously been peddling in the Minneapolis Teamster movement.

Local 544 was represented by Miles Dunne, Postal, and Rainbolt. As had been decided in advance, they refused to let themselves be thrust into a defensive posture. Allegations that officers of the local held formal membership in the SWP were denied for the record. Then the official delegation blasted the Committee of 99, detailing the Bartlett-Brennan clique's unprincipled conduct in order to show that it could not possibly have the best interests of the union in mind.

At the end of the hearing, Gillespie called for a truce in the conflict within Local 544. But we viewed the proposal as a fake. It seemed likely that he was merely trying to throw us off guard and that the "truce" would last only until the bureaucratic hierarchy decided how to intervene in the local.

Our estimate of the situation was soon verified. In the May 1941 issue of the Teamster magazine, Tobin publicly denounced "Trotskyists" in the Minnesota movement, without naming specific individuals. Citing a provision in the IBT's constitution barring Communist Party members from the organization, he asserted that the Socialist Workers Party was the same as the CP. Therefore, he demanded, the alleged SWP members had to be thrown out of the union. It was an open declaration of war, and we weren't the only ones to take note of that fact.

The Minneapolis employers, who had been conducting an unceasing offensive against Local 544, were quick to use Tobin's hostility toward us for their own purposes. His diatribe in the IBT organ was picked up by the capitalist press and given concrete interpretation as a demand for the ousting of the local's executive board. In similar vein increased attention was paid to the Committee of 99's red-baiting role. If it proved impossible to behead the union, the ruling-class strategists appeared to think the Bartlett-Brennan gang could in any case be relied upon to precipitate a phony split in the workers' ranks.

Along with those moves, as we were soon to learn, a behind-the-scenes maneuver was launched by the trucking bosses. Their aim was to hold up renewal of Local 544's contracts in the industry, most of which were to expire on June 1, 1941. Toward that end, arrangements were made for Governor Stassen to invite Tobin to negotiate sweetheart deals with the employers, behind the backs of the union membership. The IBT head responded to the overture, and from then on he collaborated with the ruling class in blocking the local's efforts to obtain new contracts.

A vicious Minnesota statute enacted in 1939, which the workers called "Stassen's Slave Labor Law," was used as the main obstructive device. It required a union to give ten days' notice of a desire to negotiate with the employees and a further ten days' notice before a strike could be called. An additional delay of thirty days could then be imposed by the governor if a labor dispute was held to be "affected with a public interest." All told, a strike could be ruled out for at least fifty days after a union first served notice of a desire to open negotiations.

In 1941 the law was being administered by Alfred P. Blair, an ultraconservative official of the Brewery Workers Union, who had recently been appointed state labor conciliator. He was given the position as a reward for political services rendered to the Republican Party.

Since Blair could be expected to invoke all provisions of the Stassen law against Local 544, steps were taken to open contract negotiations well in advance of the June 1 expiration date. No progress was made, however, in the talks with the employers that followed. The union found itself up against a conspiracy to stall the bargaining sessions, and evidence soon appeared that heavy-handed discipline was being used in boss circles to impose that line.

In an effort to get meaningful negotiations going, the local filed strike notices against some 370 trucking companies. These were worded in language that had been accepted on previous occasions without challenge. Yet Blair now rejected all but 19 of the notices as "irregular." He was trying to prevent the union from calling a major strike, in order to buy time for the bosses to consummate a deal with the IBT hierarchy.

At that point Local 544 held a special membership meeting to take stock of the situation. It was a massive gathering, that overflowed into the streets outside the union headquarters. A fighting mood prevailed among the workers present, and their sentiments were reflected in a huge banner stretched across the front of the union hall, which read: "Revive the spirit of 1934." Ray Dunne gave the main report. In blunt fashion he described the parallel attacks by the employers and Tobin, denounced attempts being made to split the organization, and called for unity in the ranks. Extensive discussion followed, after which the workers voted to empower the executive board to take whatever action was needed to win the contract demands.

Almost simultaneously an order came for the local to send an official delegation to appear before the IBT executive board in Washington, D.C., at the beginning of June. Upon receiving the news Jim Cannon, then national secretary of the SWP, and I hurried to Minneapolis from the party center in New York. George Novack, a prominent member of the party's national committee, soon followed. Our purpose was to help the Teamster militants on a day-to-day basis in the battle that was about to begin.

Since the conflict was bound to unfold swiftly, the political committee of the SWP provided the necessary authorization for us to act with maximum flexibility. Members of the party's national committee on the scene—Ray Dunne, Skoglund, Cannon, Novack, and myself—were designated to serve as a steering committee. That body acted in close consultation with the Teamster fraction, which consisted of all party members in the union. Collectively, we were empowered to make policy decisions as necessitated by the flow of events.

It was also deemed advisable for me to again function within the union. At the time I left my IBT post Tobin had urged me to continue paying dues into Local 544. That, he said, would facilitate my return to his staff later on, if I should wish to do so. Having followed his advice on that particular point, I remained a member in good standing in the local and was thus able to take a direct hand in the fight against him.

Our first task was to think out a strategic course and then shape tactical steps within that framework. Although we had bested the Teamster hierarchy in previous clashes, it did not follow that we could win again by using methods that had succeeded before. The 1941 conflict was developing under changed objective conditions, which were growing increasingly unfavorable for us. Therefore, we had to devise a new plan of battle in keeping with the needs of the day. The earlier trends had given us an advantage over Tobin. Workers employed in trucking, like their counterparts throughout industry nationally, were then looking for leaders ready and able to guide them in militant struggle against the bosses. In those circumstances we managed to set large forces into motion in defiance of the union bureaucrats. So powerful was the struggle momentum, in fact, that the Minneapolis General Drivers Union blocked an attempt by Tobin to exclude it from the Teamsters international, and after that it played a key part in an expansion drive that transformed the IBT itself.

Now, however, Local 544 was falling victim to the failure of organized labor elsewhere in the country to sustain comparable fighting ability. Although CIO strikes were taking place in auto, coal, and steel during 1941, these were essentially rearguard actions. The momentum of the general union upsurge of previous years had been broken, due to leadership defaults in the movement nationally. Politically, the workers remained entrapped in the Democratic Party; the capitalists were unhindered in using the governmental power against labor; and that power was being employed to crush all opposition to the imperialist drive toward war.

Emboldened by the reactionary trends, conservatives in the trade unions were growing increasingly aggressive. Opportunists were switching their allegiances in conformity with the general drift to the right. Bureaucratic control was becoming stabilized in both the AFL and CIO; and the top union bureaucrats—except for a handful around John L. Lewis—were knuckling under to Roosevelt's demand that the interests of the working class be subordinated entirely to capitalist militarism.

Owing to those developments a major change was occurring in the relationship of forces between ourselves and Tobin. His hand was being strengthened. Local 544, in contrast, was being thrust into isolation; it had numerous enemies and few reliable allies.

Special measures were, therefore, needed to gear the local for battle. To begin with, the leadership structure had to be expanded. Since the struggle would be highly political, guidance of the union forces could not remain entirely within the relatively narrow framework of the executive board and organizational staff. The SWP fraction in the Teamsters—representing the most politically conscious workers—had to be used as the instrument through which to mobilize the broadest possible leading contingent around a clearly defined program.

Toward that end an intensive schedule of activities was outlined to step up recruitment of new members into the party fraction and at the same time to set about the building of a strong left-wing caucus in the union. All who belonged to the party were drawn into the work to the fullest possible extent; strict discipline was maintained, and regular attendance at fraction meetings was required. As has always been SWP procedure, equal decision-making rights were extended to all party members involved, including those who held no official posts in the local as well as the ones who did.

In no time at all the party comrades organized several hundred workers into a broad caucus. It was named the Union Defense Committee, and membership in the formation was based upon readiness to support the following program:

"1. Revive the spirit of 1934.

"2. Strike action against any and all employers who reject the union contracts for improved wages and working conditions.

"3. Support the democratically elected leadership of the union in this fight against the bosses.

"4. Support the leadership in the fight against disrupters inside and outside the union.

"5. Defend the democratic right of the union to select its own leaders. No appeasement of any would-be dictator.

"6. We made Minneapolis a union town. Let's keep it that way."

The forces mobilized around the above program were seasoned fighters, who had participated in earlier battles with the bosses and the IBT overlord. They knew through experience that the new attacks from those quarters had to be beaten off or every gain the workers had made would be endangered. These cadres were quite well equipped, in both consciousness and training, to face up to coming events. They could be relied upon to serve as the firm backbone of the local, to rally the rest of the membership in its defense, and to campaign aggressively for support from other Minneapolis unions.

While building up this expanded leadership formation, steps were also taken to prepare the union membership generally for what was coming. We would be up against a three-pronged assault—from the IBT bureaucracy, the trucking bosses, and the capitalist government. To put that complex situation in a perspective that the workers would best understand, we decided (as the Union Defense Committee's program indicated) to direct the main fight against the bosses. In that way the ranks could be mobilized most effectively for action, the treachery of Tobin and the Committee of 99 could be more fully exposed, and the workers would be more apt to see whatever actions the government took against us in their true light—as strikebreaking, union-busting moves.

Proceeding accordingly, the *Northwest Organizer* of May 29, 1941, presented a roundup of the situation. An account was given of the employers' refusal to consider contract demands presented by the workers. The roles of Stassen and Blair in maneuvering to prevent strike action were also described. Referring to those developments, the union paper added editorially that "the uniform tactic of all the major employers' groups in stalling the Local 544 negotiators indicates a determined and well organized plot to open a new drive upon the General Drivers Union. . . . Yes, the employers of Minneapolis, seizing upon the criticisms of Local 544's leaders being made by cliques and individuals in and out of the labor movement, think they see an opening to crush the General Drivers Union."

The same issue of the union paper carried a statement by the local's executive board. Referring to Tobin's attack on "Trotskyists" in the Minnesota movement, the board declared: "The present leadership of Local 544 has been elected by the membership in a free and democratic election . . . . Nobody can change this leadership, in whole or in part, except the membership which placed its confidence in them and elected them to their posts. Local 544 believes in trade union democracy. It is opposed to personal dictatorship."

So that there would be no misunderstanding about our determination to stand firm on all questions of principle, an editorial on Roosevelt's foreign policy was also published. It said in part: "We have waited long and patiently for the leaders of labor to speak out against this war and the war-makers. The time is growing short. Let's hear the heads of the American union movement stand up on their hind legs and denounce the war and the government strike-breaking."

Bundles of the May 29 issue of the *Northwest Organizer* were mailed to every local union in the IBT. Our purpose, of course, was to seek allies in the impending conflict with Tobin. More precisely, we were laying the groundwork to appeal later on for the support of other Teamster units in carrying out yet another contemplated move.

As matters stood, Local 544 was in desperate need of national trade union backing. It was important, therefore, to explore the possibility of getting into the CIO. Things were different now in that connection than they had been in 1936, when we had made a similar request after Tobin revoked the local's IBT charter. At that time the CIO had been concentrating entirely on an organizational drive in basic industry. It had had no desire to become involved in the trucking sphere, and its leaders had advised us to continue our fight for reinstatement into the AFL Teamsters.

Since then much had changed. By 1941 the industrial union movement was showing a general tendency to expand in all directions. It had even begun to challenge the jurisdiction of the IBT, especially in Michigan, where the United Auto Workers Union was a powerful force. Those developments pointed toward a favorable response to Local 544's contemplated overture.

If the CIO accepted us, we assumed, it would probably be necessary to settle for merely a local charter at the outset, but our longer-range aim would be to get a general charter encompassing trucking nationally. In that way Tobin's attack could be met with an all-out counterattack.

To be successful in an attempt of this kind, we had to proceed carefully in making the charter application. The president of the CIO was now Philip Murray, who had replaced John L. Lewis in that post at the end of 1940. Murray was a staunch Rooseveltian. Therefore, he was unlikely to grant our request for a charter or to give us any real backing in a fight with Tobin.

Lewis, on the other hand, seemed more likely to respond to our appeal. He had continued to oppose Roosevelt after the 1940 national elections. He was pressing Murray to break with the White House because of the national administration's attacks on labor. And of special importance concerning our problem, the Lewis forces were in the thick of the clash with the IBT in Michigan. That left no question as to whom we should approach.

Shortly after we came to that conclusion, the Local 544 delegation left for the IBT hearing in Washington. It consisted of Ray Dunne, Kelly Postal, and Ray Rainbolt. They had instructions to take an uncompromising attitude toward Tobin, to inform him that any demands he made upon the local would have to be referred back to the membership for decision, and to see Lewis about the possibility of getting a CIO charter.

8. Local 544 Goes CIO

Although Tobin centered his propaganda on what was vaguely termed "Trotskyism," he actually had something very concrete in mind. He was concerned about the growing influence wielded by the leaders of Local 544. They were playing a decisive role in shaping the policies of the Minneapolis Teamsters Joint Council and in setting the editorial line of the *Northwest Organizer*. Through those media a successful campaign had already been conducted to put the entire AFL of the city on record against U.S. involvement in the imperialist war; strong antiwar sentiment was being generated throughout the Minnesota labor movement; and in the process, the Socialist Workers Party was gaining increased influence among radicalized workers on a regional scale. It was this expanding role as organizers of mass opposition to Roosevelt's foreign policy—not the matter of political affiliations as such—that made the officers of Local 544 targets of the Teamster hierarchy.

The IBT president wanted desperately to squelch the antiwar movement that had arisen in the Minneapolis section of the organization. But the leaders of the movement were capable trade unionists who had earned the respect and confidence of the workers during clashes with the employers. If he tried to discipline them, they would resist with strong rank-and-file support; and since the outcome of such a battle could not be predicted with certainty, he hesitated about proceeding from the propaganda assault to direct orgainzational measures.

There was yet another complication, however, that made it hard for Tobin to shy away from decisive action. He was under heavy pressure from the FBI, which had gone beyond pressing charges against the leaders of Local 544 through the Committee of 99. The political cops were now sending contrived "evidence" against the Trotskyists directly to the Teamster president.

Additional needling was also being brought to bear on him through such media as *Fortune*, a magazine published by and for big business. Its editors pointedly called attention to the Trotskyists' role in Minneapolis and chided the IBT head for tolerating such a situation.

In an effort to work his way out of this bind, Tobin scheduled the Washington session of the international union's executive board. He had apparently decided to have the board rubber-stamp the following course of action: reaffirm unconditional Teamster support of Roosevelt's foreign policy; outlaw "Trotskyism" from the union; but temporarily accept the dropping of formal membership in the SWP by officers of Local 544, provided they allowed him to dictate policy for the local and gag the editors of the *Northwest Organizer*. A further purpose of the board meeting was, of course, to line up his bureaucratic machine in support of the foregoing tactics.

These were the circumstances under which Local 544's delegation appeared at the Washington hearing. What happened during the proceedings was described later by Ray Dunne in a report to the membership of the local. His description can be summarized on the basis of accounts carried in the *Northwest Organizer* of June 12, 1941, and *The Militant* of June 14, 1941.

Both the official representatives of Local 544 and a delegation from the Committee of 99 were called into the IBT board meeting on the afternoon of Tuesday, June 3. During the session that followed, Tobin was the main one to speak for the board. The rest of its members did nothing more than throw in an occasional innocuous remark.

A committee from the Minneapolis Teamsters Joint Council had also traveled to Washington with an authorization to speak for that body in support of Local 544's leaders. It consisted of Harold Seavey, Clair Johnson, Joe O'Hare, and Larry Davidson. Upon entering the board room they were kept standing by Tobin, who arrogantly said to them: "You know you were not invited here. Why did you come? Why did you put the council to that expense? But as long as you are here, what have you got to say?"

Each member of the council's committee spoke. They told the board, in effect, that the officers of Local 544 were honest people who had helped to build the union movement. When the four had finished their remarks, Tobin insolently waved them out of the room.

As though to add insult to injury, the IBT president was most cordial toward James Bartlett, who headed the delegation from the Committee of 99. Bartlett was allowed to present a fresh set of affidavits charging that the leaders of Local 544 were "supporters of the doctrines of Trotsky" and "members of the Socialist Workers Party." He was also extended the privilege of addressing the board at length on those "subversive" charges.

After that, Tobin began reading aloud from the new affidavits and from a bulky report the FBI had sent to him. Later he gave the press some quotations from the FBI document, one of which was printed in the *Minneapolis Star Journal* of June 13, 1941. It stated:

"The main specific task of the Socialist Workers Party is the mobilization of the American masses for struggle against American capitalism and for its overthrow. . . . Our information is that apparently one of the strongest and most militant sections of the party is located in Minneapolis. This group is referred to as General Drivers' union No. 544. Local 544 is led by the Dunne brothers, Miles, Vincent and Grant, and has developed a wide reputation for strikes and disorders. The radical element is organized into a 'defense guard.' The defense guard is based around squads of five men, four men and a captain. They are supposed to wear gold badges."

When he had finished reading, Tobin launched into a rambling speech about the international situation and the war. He stressed the need for the labor movement to support the government and to make sacrifices, to give up gains that had been won.

During this long discourse he also admitted that the leaders of Local 544 had some good points. They had helped to build the Teamster movement and win improved wages and conditions for the workers. They were good organizers who knew how to fight antiunion employers. But we can't have them in "our" international, he said, because they are radicals and members of the Socialist Workers Party. They attack the government in the *Northwest Organizer.*

Then, addressing himself to the board and members of his organizational staff who were present, the Teamster president added: "These men are fighters. Are you going to fight to back your international union?"

At that point he abruptly declared the session over for the day and informed the board it wouldn't be needed for the next stage of the proceedings. It was his intention, he said, to have a private talk with Local 544's representatives. That was agreeable to our delegation, and the following morning a session of that kind took place.

During the private meeting, Tobin claimed that Local 544 had been protecting an "enemy of the International"—Jack Smith. Upon hearing that absurd charge, Rainbolt angrily reminded Tobin that he had sent Smith into Minneapolis from Chicago in 1936 as part of the gang that tried to crush former Local 574 at that time.

"I didn't," Tobin protested.

"You did!" Rainbolt shouted, pounding Tobin's desk to emphasize the point. The patently false charge against Smith, Rainbolt added heatedly, was of a piece with the rest of the lying assertions contained in the Committee of 99's affidavits.

The IBT overlord was obviously shaken by this episode. He wasn't accustomed to having a union member stand up to him that way, and, like most bullies, he felt offended when someone dealt harshly with him. Besides that, he now realized it had been a blunder to make the assertion concerning Smith.

"Well," he said, after a pause to regain his composure, "we'll throw out the affidavits, but I've got plenty of other evidence to convict you."

Tobin then brought out a memorandum which he wanted Local 544 to accept. It contained a proposal that the executive board of the local ask him to appoint a receiver, who would have the final say in its affairs. He stressed that the receivership would be operative mainly in determining the policies of the local and the line of the *Northwest Organizer* on "national issues." There would be minimal control, he implied, where strictly trade union matters were concerned.

The Teamster head pressed eagerly for an immediate decision on his proposal. He wanted our delegation to agree then and there that Local 544 would accept it. They refused, explaining to him that the local operated democratically, that they could only bring his proposition back to the executive board and the membership for a decision.

He next asked that the rest of the Local 544 board be contacted by telephone in order to obtain their answer at once. When that procedure was also rejected, he urged the committee to fly back to Minneapolis, get the executive board's acceptance of his memorandum, and return to Washington to work out the details of the proposed arrangement. Again he was told that such a course couldn't be followed, and it finally dawned on him that there would be no quick reply to his proposition. An understanding was then reached that the delegation would take the matter up with the local's executive board upon returning to Minneapolis, and the board's decision would be telephoned to him the following Saturday, June 7.

While Dunne, Postal, and Rainbolt were in Washington they sought an interview with John L. Lewis. He arranged, instead, for them to talk with his brother, A. D. Lewis, who was chairman of the United Construction Workers Organizing Committee of the CIO. Since it was vital to obtain help from the Lewis forces, the UCWOC chairman was given a full and precise account of Local 544's situation. Our delegation also emphasized the potential that existed for a general Teamster revolt against Tobin and urged that a national CIO charter be issued for truck drivers. A. D. Lewis said that such a step was possible but he would have to consult other CIO leaders before a definite answer could be given. He promised that Local 544 would be notified of the decision within a couple of days.

Tobin, meanwhile, had made further preparations to move against us. On June 5 he sent a telegram to Roosevelt in the name of the IBT's executive board. As reported later in the *Minnesota Teamster* of July 25, 1941, it declared: "We, who are Americans, and members of one of the largest labor organizations in America, or in the world, do solemnly pledge that we will follow out and put into practice any procedure outlined by you and your associates who are handling this most dangerous world situation which is now confronting civilization. . . ."

The IBT board then voted to classify the Socialist Workers Party as a "subversive, revolutionary party," whose members were to be barred from the union. Adoption of that decree was followed, in turn, by a move to lay the groundwork for the next step. Shortly after the board meeting adjourned, Dave Beck was sent to line up support within the Minneapolis Teamsters Joint Council for the imposition of a receivership upon Local 544.

Although we didn't know about those actions at the time our representatives returned from Washington, their report showed that an attack was imminent. Clearly enough, the war issue had intensified the antagonisms between Tobin and ourselves to a point where he was ready either to impose his control over Local 544 or to destroy it in the attempt. Toward that end he was using a tactic based on a clause in the IBT constitution which read: "If the General President has or receives information which leads him to believe that any officers of a local union are dishonest or incompetent, or that the organization is not being conducted for the benefit of the trade, he may appoint a Trustee to take charge and control of the affairs of the local union."

Under that sweeping authorization Tobin could resort to any course he might choose. The trustee—that is, the receiver he wanted us to ask for—would be a sub-dictator assigned to carry out orders issued by the general president. This receiver could be used to veto the membership's decisions, remove democratically-elected officers from their posts, and expel "troublemakers" from the union.

At the Washington hearing the IBT head had sought to create an impression that the receivership would be confined to handling matters of "national policy," namely the war issue. But if a single concession was made to him concerning local autonomy and democratic control of the union by the membership, he would soon become more demanding. His next objective would be to undermine the local's class-struggle policies generally. In the end the organization would lose virtually all its capacity to defend the workers against the bosses.

As a process of that kind unfolded, moreover, those who managed to retain official posts in the local would become compromised. They would lose the respect of militant workers— and rightly so—because they would be playing fast and loose with principles on the vital issues of imperialist war and trade union democracy.

Under those circumstances we had no alternative but to mobilize Local 544 for an all-out fight against the IBT dictator. A special notice was, therefore, printed in the *Northwest Organizer* of Thursday, June 5, urging maximum attendance at the regular membership meeting the following Monday. "Reports of considerable importance to every union member will be submitted to this meeting," the workers were advised.

Then, as had been agreed in Washington, a call was put through to Tobin on Saturday to inform him that the local's executive board had rejected his receivership proposal. His only response was to express disappointment in a cold voice and abruptly end the conversation.

The same day A. D. Lewis notified us that the CIO would not issue a general charter for truck drivers. There was no point in arguing with him on that particular question, so we merely urged him to at least find some way to grant Local 544 a CIO charter as a vehicle for its fight against Tobin. Lewis said he would try to give us a quick answer on that request.

While awaiting his further reply, we called the Union Defense Committee into session. About five hundred of the local's best fighters responded to the summons. After being brought up to date on developments, they agreed unanimously with the policy course we recommended. There was no alternative, these militants recognized, but to resist Tobin's attempt to take over the local and to seek CIO backing against him. The UDC forces also undertook the responsibility of pressing for support of such a course among other union members.

Just a few hours before the general membership meeting on Monday, June 9, Lewis notified us that a charter was being issued in the name of the United Construction Workers Organizing Committee. The specific designation was to be Motor Transport and Allied Workers Industrial Union, Local 544, CIO. And with that explicit information now at hand, the executive board quickly drew up a resolution making precise recommendations to the rank and file.

Close to four thousand workers turned out for the meeting that night. They listened with rising anger as Ray Dunne told them about the Washington hearing and explained why the receivership demand should be rejected. The executive board had already informed the IBT head that it refused to ask for a dictator-receiver, he added, and "that was the last Local 544 heard from Tobin. Since then Tobin contacted members of the Teamsters Joint Council. He talked with Governor Stassen and his man Blair. He talked with newspaper reporters. But he has not talked with us. . . . Tobin and Stassen and the bosses are getting in a position to negotiate contracts behind the backs of Local 544's membership, and Tobin wants to confront us with the ultimatum that our union accept his contracts or face expulsion."

Ray then described the cooperative attitude A. D. Lewis had shown toward Local 544. He also stressed the importance of grasping the opportunity that Lewis had opened for the local to get CIO support in its fight for autonomous rights.

After that I gave a talk sounding the call to battle, and Miles Dunne then presented the executive board's resolution for discussion and action. It asserted:

"In view of the unwarranted attacks directed against our union by President Daniel J. Tobin, and his arbitrary and dictatorial threats and actions which have been prejudicial to the interests of our membership, and giving aid and comfort to the employers in their refusal to renew our contracts, it becomes necessary for General Drivers Union, Local No. 544 to end this intolerable situation.

"Therefore be it resolved . . . that we hereby disaffiliate from the International Brotherhood of Teamsters, Chauffeurs, Warehousemen and Helpers, AFL. . . .

"Be it further resolved that we accept the invitation of the Congress of Industrial Organizations (CIO) to become a constituent part of that great progessive body of labor, and we do hereby so affiliate.

"Be it further resolved that the Executive Board of the General Drivers Union, Local 544 is hereby instructed to take all the necessary measures accordingly." (It had been explained to the workers that this last proviso was intended to prevent Tobin from grabbing the local's funds, and the steps that would be taken had been described.)

During the discussion from the floor only one speaker opposed the recommendations of the executive board. A member of the Committee of 99, Axel Soderberg, said: "This is what happens under Trotskyist leadership. Here we have got an example of a revolution."

When the question was called, an overwhelming majority voted to quit Tobin's setup and join the CIO. Only a very thin scattering of dissenters recorded disapproval of the action.

Word of the local's decision spread quickly as thousands of workers appeared on their jobs the following morning proudly displaying union buttons with the imprint "544-CIO." That afternoon's edition of the *Minneapolis Star Journal* reported: "Still echoing in every corner of state labor circles today was the explosion of the bomb dropped when powerful 544 voted to drop the AFL and join the CIO." There were also immediate national repercussions.

A. D. Lewis sent us a message stating: "Local 544-CIO is the spearhead of what must soon develop into a great popular movement of transport and allied workers on a national scale. . . . We have assigned Brother Frank Barnhart [regional director of the UCWOC] to assist you on the ground and will give you all necessary further support and cooperation as the campaign develops."

Telegrams pledging solidarity with Local 544 poured in from

CIO bodies around the country, including international unions, state and city councils, and local units. Among the internationals thus responding were those in auto, rubber, subway transport, furniture, die casting, leather, and distilling.

Philip Murray was reluctant, however, to follow suit as president of the CIO. He, like Tobin, had been indoctrinated against "subversives" by the Roosevelt administration, and he didn't want to take any responsibility for those whom the IBT president had denounced as "reds." But the Lewis forces pressed Murray to take positive action, and he finally sent Barnhart word that the UCWOC's chartering of Local 544 was "in complete accord with the policies of the CIO." Barnhart then issued a statement calling Murray's message "the authoritative signal for the whole great movement of the CIO from coast to coast to come to the support of Local 544-CIO in Minneapolis and put all its power behind the drive to organize the nation's transport and allied workers into a progressive, modern industrial union, affiliated with the UCWOC."

Objectively, the Minnesota section of the CIO should have been among the first to follow the course recommended by Barnhart. But its apparatus was dominated by Stalinists, who reacted factionally to the entrance of the dynamic Teamster local into the otherwise relatively weak CIO movement in Minneapolis. They saw this development as a threat to their dominant position in the industrial union officialdom of the city and state, so they decided to publicly attack the leaders of the rebel IBT force.

Leonard Lagemen, state CIO secretary, told newspaper reporters: "As far as the membership of 544 is concerned, we welcome them into the CIO. However, the leadership of 544 will have to carry out the policies of the CIO or they will have to be removed." A further press statement, issued this time in the name of the Hennepin County CIO council, said: "It is our opinion that the Dunne brothers' leadership, which has been thoroughly discredited in Minnesota, will hinder our progress and will not be of benefit to the CIO. . . . and it now appears that because of their present position in the AFL they have taken advantage of the sentiment of the workers in an attempt to maintain their control and to carry on their disruptive policies." Luverne Noon, secretary of the Hennepin County body, then added that "it becomes reasonably evident that this is not a battle between the CIO and AFL, but is rather a showdown fight between the Beck-Tobin forces and those of the Dunne brothers of 544." As the

Stalinists no doubt intended, these snide cracks were soon picked up by Tobin's propaganda machine.

· In refreshing contrast, an altogether different attitude was taken by some local units of the CIO. Unions of foundry and hosiery workers, which had received help from the General Drivers Union in strikes, welcomed Local 544 into their movement, as did the Newspaper Guild chapter. The greeting from the hosiery workers said: "Branch 38 still remembers the militant assistance given us by your union when the chips were down and no holds were barred. Your union played a major part in making Minneapolis the Union Town it is today."

Meanwhile, sentiments for and against Local 544's action were being manifested within the Minneapolis Teamsters Joint Council. Some of its officers, led by Harold Seavey, who was basically a loyal Tobinite, tried to block publication of the June 12 issue of the *Northwest Organizer*, which reported our change in affiliation. This problem was resolved through a compromise that was reached just a few hours before the paper was due to go to press. The council sold the *Northwest Organizer* to Local 544 for "one dollar and other valuable considerations," with a provision that it could be repurchased within thirty days. In that way the paper was brought out on schedule as the official organ of 544-CIO.

By then some units of the Joint Council were following our lead in the revolt against Tobin. On June 10 the day-labor section of Ice Drivers Local 221, the basic component of its membership, voted to join 544-CIO. Shortly thereafter part of Warehouse Local 359 (whose president was James Bartlett) took the same step, acting under the leadership of three officers of the local—Don Penwell, Bob Tibbets, and Erling Nelson. Elsewhere in the region, IBT Local 778 at Austin, Minnesota, applied for and quickly received a charter from the United Construction Workers Organizing Committee. IBT Local 116 in Fargo, North Dakota, scheduled an early meeting to consider doing likewise. And a number of Teamster units elsewhere in the country asked A. D. Lewis for information about the new CIO movement in motor transport.

In the midst of those developments Dave Beck arrived in Minneapolis. He called to request a talk, and Grant Dunne and I were assigned to see him. Beck said he had been sent to inform us of Tobin's decision to accept the dropping of formal membership in the Socialist Workers Party by local union leaders, provided the local was placed in receivership. Tobin wanted him to be the receiver, Beck added, but he would take the assignment only if we agreed to it. We told him the local had no intention of returning to the IBT, and with that our discussion ended.

Beck also consulted with officers of the Teamsters Joint Council and leaders of the Committee of 99. A report of his findings was then relayed to Tobin. After that he issued a statement that the IBT "won't tolerate any subversive actions" and left town.

Tobin, himself, had already been trying to block Local 544's admission into the CIO. A. D. Lewis was asked to withdraw the charter granted to the "reds," and he was questioned as to whether Philip Murray had approved the step. Lewis replied that the UCWOC didn't need Murray's approval of its actions, that radicals were not barred from the CIO, and that the charter he had issued to us would be allowed to stand. Tobin next sought Murray's intervention on his behalf. Although Murray "understood the situation," the IBT head told the press, he could do nothing about it.

A statement was then issued from the Teamster headquarters in Indianapolis, Indiana. As reported in the *Minneapolis Star Journal* of June 13, it provided quotations from dossiers on the Trotskyists, which the FBI had given to Tobin, along with fervent declarations of IBT "patriotism." The statement also said: "Over 100 of our good union men in Minneapolis preferred charges against the radicals in Local 544. . . . The general executive board decided to send a representative to Minneapolis to lay the entire situation before them and to ask them to abide by the laws by withdrawing from the subversive Trotsky organization named above. There were no penalties placed on them unless they refused to comply with the request of the board, based on the constitution and laws of the international union."

Tobin was wrapping his reactionary brand of trade unionism in the flag, and he was lying about there being "no penalties" if the leaders of Local 544 withdrew from the "Trotsky organization." His aim was to draw attention away from the demand that the local accept the rule of a dictator-receiver. At the same time he was trying to make our guidance in the fight for union democracy appear to be nothing more than an attempt to use the local for "subversive" purposes.

A quick decision was also made in Indianapolis to pretend that the IBT charter for Local 544 remained viable, using the handful of "good union men" in the Committee of 99 for the purpose. T. T. Neal was named as the receiver Tobin had sought to impose upon the local, and Joseph A. Padway, general counsel for both the AFL and IBT, was sent to assist him. Plans were then laid for a legal attack on 544-CIO, and as a step toward all-out collusion with the boss class, the trucking firms were notified that the IBT would "protect its contracts."

Padway brought along one of his law partners, I. E. Goldberg. In addition he retained the services locally of the legal firm of Nichols, Mullin, and Farnand. These well-paid shysters proceeded to file a suit in district court for the purpose of tying up 544-CIO's funds and grabbing its property. To all intents and purposes the new court action superseded its cousin, the 1938 fink suit, which was still under appeal to the Minnesota Supreme Court.

Neal and Padway also brought heavy pressure to bear upon the Teamsters Joint Council and managed thereby to force through a vote to support the IBT against 544-CIO. As matters stood at the time, however, it was a rather hollow victory. On June 16, three days after the vote, Padway sent a letter to Tobin complaining that "officers of the Joint Council are very friendly to the Dunnes."

Even before getting that disturbing news the Teamster president had begun to panic. He appeared shaken by the extent to which the new CIO movement was attracting the interest of truck drivers nationally. To serve Roosevelt's needs, Tobin had undertaken to crush opposition to the imperialist war program within the IBT, and the move was starting to boomerang. His attempt had set into motion uncontrolled forces that threatened to deprive him of the trade union base upon which he had built his personal career. So Tobin, who had gotten into deep trouble because of his efforts to serve Roosevelt, now appealed for action from the White House to rescue him.

Roosevelt's response was reported in the *New York Times* of June 14, 1941. His secretary, Stephen Early, told the Washington press corps: "Mr. Tobin telegraphed from Indianapolis that it is apparent to him and to other executives of his organization that because they have been and will continue to stand squarely behind the government, that all subversive organizations and enemies of our government, including Bundists, Trotskyists and Stalinists, are opposed to them and seeking to destroy loyal trade unions which are supporting democracy. . . . When I advised the

President of Tobin's representations this morning he asked me to immediately have the government departments and agencies interested in this matter notified and to point out to you that this is no time, in his opinion, for labor unions, local or national, to begin raiding one another for the purpose of getting membership or for similar reasons."

A. D. Lewis immediately denounced Roosevelt's interference in internal union matters and announced the scheduling of a conference in Chicago on June 15 to plan further steps in the CIO campaign to organize motor transport workers. Those who came to the Chicago gathering, over which Lewis presided, included Lee Pressman, general counsel for the CIO; Frank Barnhart, the UCWOC regional director; a group of CIO organizers; and leaders of several IBT units in the area.

Ray Dunne and I attended the session as representatives of Local 544. We tried to impress upon Lewis that the fight in which we were engaged was an all-or-nothing situation. Tobin realized how high the stakes were, and that was why he had run to Roosevelt for help; that was why he was preparing to concentrate his forces against us in Minneapolis, seeking thereby to nip the revolt in the bud. To prevent such endangerment of Local 544, which represented a vital CIO base in motor transport, it was necessary to use all possible means of broadening the UCWOC campaign, so as to draw the IBT into battle on a series of fronts. A deliberate course had to be charted toward the complete smashing of Tobin's rule over organized trucking employees, or he would be able to crush the rebellion that we were spearheading.

There were valuable assets that could be drawn upon, we urged, in launching a full-scale UCWOC campaign. The Lewis wing of the CIO—especially its central leader, John L.—had great standing in the eyes of the workers generally. In addition Local 544 had earned the goodwill of many truck drivers in the country. Those workers despised the Teamster dictator, and large potential thus existed for the CIO to assimilate the most progressive sections of the IBT, thereby swiftly developing a struggle momentum that Tobin would be unable to reverse.

Unfortunately, Lewis failed to grasp the tempo of the battle. Apparently thinking that Tobin could readily be beaten off in Minneapolis, he decided to move slowly elsewhere. It was his view that Local 544 should be used as the base from which the UCWOC could gradually extend its influence in trucking nationally, concentrating at the outset on efforts to inch across the midwest area.

Proceeding accordingly, Lewis assigned Frank Barnhart to open an office in Minneapolis from which the UCWOC campaign was to be directed. Two local figures—Walter Brock, a one-time secretary of the Hennepin County Industrial Union Council; and Frank Alsup, a former director of the packinghouse workers' union in South Saint Paul—were employed as special representatives of Barnhart. In addition, financial aid was provided so that Local 544 could add several new organizers to its staff from the union ranks. To help us on the legal side, attorney William Thomas of Cleveland, a member of Pressman's staff, was sent to Minneapolis.

Although such measures were beneficial, they fell way short of the action required. The formidable array of enemies we faced was left free to concentrate on the fight within Minneapolis, and in the given circumstances that made our prospects rather bleak.

We had many sympathizers within the local AFL movement, but very few of them who held leadership posts could be expected to stick their necks out once the serious infighting started; and so far as the CIO officialdom in the city was concerned, the Stalinists would use their dominant position in it to attack us at every opportunity.

Within Local 544 itself, a great majority of the members deeply resented Tobin's dictatorial conduct, and they had respect for the national CIO. These workers were to be badly hampered, however, in the use of their full power for self-defense. For one thing, the trucking firms were pretending to be "caught between two fires in the AFL-CIO fight," and on that pretext the boss courts had already begun to issue restraining orders against strikes. The court orders showed, moreover, as did the stands taken by Roosevelt and Stassen, that preparations were being made at all levels of government to crack down on the "subversives" who had rebelled against the Teamster overlord.

It was in that setting that Tobin now mobilized his entire bureaucratic machine for a vicious assault on Local 544.

UNION-BUSTING CONSPIRACY

Daniel Tobin

9. IBT Invasion

In 1934 the Minneapolis bosses had used a private army of their own against the General Drivers Union, camouflaging it as auxiliary police. This time, however, the IBT provided the mercenaries, and the operation was given an aura of legality by President Roosevelt, Governor Stassen, and Mayor Kline. As a propaganda cover for the offensive against Local 544, Tobin contended that the fight was not between the AFL and CIO, "but simply between the AFL and the Trotskyites with their un-American following"; that the local's break with his setup was "merely the resignation of the leadership and some members."

Later on, this canard was further developed by Joseph M. Casey, an IBT representative from San Francisco, who was placed in command of Tobinite operations in Minneapolis. In a statement carried by the *Minneapolis Tribune* on June 24, 1941, Casey alleged: "Gathering together with a group of non-members, also imbued with the idea that this American way of life as we practice it in this city was far inferior to that of Germany and Russia, the order was sent out for a special meeting which was attended by less than 750 members out of more than 5,000 which make up the roster of Local 544. The outside Trotskyites thereupon mingled with the membership present and were the most vociferous when the Dunnes and Dobbs stampeded the meeting, and with a complete disregard for any parliamentary procedure, proceeded to take a pressure vote, finally announcing that the membership of 544 had declared themselves in favor of deserting the AFL."

Casey's statement was a tissue of lies. Attendance at the caucus of the Union Defense Committee on June 8 was deliberately misrepresented to be the total number of workers present at the regular membership meeting on June 9. No less false was his allegation that the leadership had packed the meeting with "outside Trotskyites" and had forced the question of leaving the IBT to a vote without allowing discussion from the floor. The purpose of these untruths was, of course, to pretend that 544-CIO represented only a small gang of "un-Americans" and that most members of the local remained loyal to the Teamster dictatorship.

Tobin, meanwhile, had called for all-out war against Local 544. "We have $6 million in our defense fund," he boasted, "and if we have to spend it all to keep our locals in the AFL, we are going to do it." Spend he did, indeed, for that antidemocratic objective.

A strong-arm force of more than three hundred was rushed to Minneapolis. The main contingent consisted of Tobin's organizational staff, plus an assortment of payrollers from joint councils and local unions, who were eager to win advancement in the IBT bureaucracy. Another category was made up of outright hoodlums in the employ of the Tobin machine. There were also a few local union officers and organizers, who became involved because they had been misled as to what the fight was about. This invading force came from various cities—Chattanooga, Denver, Indianapolis, Milwaukee, Nashville, Seattle, and elsewhere. There was an especially large number from Detroit.

In addition, a detachment of AFL organizers was sent by William Green, the AFL president, to aid Tobin in Minneapolis. They were headed by Meyer Lewis, who had previously fought the General Drivers Union in 1935-36. International representatives of virtually every AFL union with locals in the city also arrived to join in the fight against us, and officers of the Minnesota State Federation of Labor promised the IBT full support.

These AFL bureaucrats, acting in combination with Tobin's gang, soon forced the Minneapolis Central Labor Union to denounce Local 544 as "Communist-led" and pledge loyalty to the Teamster overlord. An effort was then made to promote an AFL boycott of CIO drivers.

Within the AFL officialdom locally, right-wingers greeted the bureaucratic invaders with open arms and gave them full support. The opportunists began face-saving maneuvers with the object of doing the same. Other union officers, who remained friendly to Local 544, merely stood aside in most cases on the ground that they were not parties to the conflict. But the attitude of rank-and-file AFL members was altogether different; a great majority sympathized with our struggle for union democracy, and they helped us in every way they could.

Parallel with the campaign to whip the Central Labor Union into line, steps were taken to create the impression that Tobin's paper union, Local 544-AFL, actually had substance. Officers were named for the setup, but not through elections. Neal, the receiver, simply appointed them. For president he chose Leonard Brady, one of the IBT invaders from Detroit. The remaining posts were allotted to members of the Committee of 99 as follows: George Williams, vice-president; Steven Nehotte, recording secretary; Sidney Brennan, secretary-treasurer; Edward Blixt, George O'Brien, and Fritz Snyder, trustees. Several others from the Committee of 99 were hired to serve in the IBT's strong-arm force.

A "mass meeting" of 544-AFL was then held. It was attended mainly by Tobin's crew, other AFL bureaucrats, and members of the Committee of 99. Few were there who didn't have a personal ax to grind. This contemptible assemblage responded enthusiastically when Casey announced in his speech that he was launching an "intensive organizing campaign" by "able-bodied organizers."

The "organizing campaign" took the form of a terrorist attack upon the membership of 544-CIO. Goon squads began cruising the city—many in cars with out-of-state license plates—accosting truck drivers on the streets and inside workers at their places of employment. The purpose was to make the motor transport workers sign cards pledging support to 544-AFL and at the same time to forcibly collect membership dues. As instruments of persuasion Tobin's thugs used clubs, blackjacks, chains, knives, and guns. CIO members were beaten up, some after having been dragged from trucks and others while working on loading docks or inside warehouses. Similar tactics were used in assaults on 544-CIO road drivers at freight transfer points throughout the region around Minneapolis.

Within the city itself the terrorists acted with confidence that their conduct had the approval of the public authorities. In fact, Padway sent a report to Tobin on June 16 that he had "met with District Attorney [Ed J.] Goff, the Chief of Police, and the Captain of Detectives, who promises us all protection and cooperation possible. . . ." The promise was followed by the deed. In several instances caravans of IBT goons arrived at truck terminals and warehouses escorted by police squad cars. The cops then looked the other way when 544-CIO members were slugged. They moved in only when groups of angry workers sought to deal firmly with the Tobinites.

The authorities also sought to lay traps for the rebel union, with the object of framing its leaders. A typical incident involved Nick Wagner, a member of 544-CIO's executive board. As Wagner got out of his car in front of his home one night, he was attacked by five IBT hoodlums, who beat him to the ground and kicked him. A neighbor called the police. They let the assailants go free, but Wagner—who had a black eye, swollen lip, and other bruises—was arrested on a false charge of menacing the bullyboys with a pistol.

Like the cops, the bosses were also helping the Tobinites. CIO members were threatened with loss of their jobs unless they returned to the IBT. In some cases employers refused to issue paychecks to the workers until they signed AFL pledge cards. Several CIO militants who defied such demands were fired. All of this took place, moreover, under cover of malicious propaganda tricks in the capitalist press, which were designed to put 544-CIO in the worst possible light and to picture the Teamster overlord as a sterling champion of the workers.

Due to the vast scope of this union-busting conspiracy, we could not put a halt to the terrorism by fending off the IBT gangs in direct combat. The bosses and their government would have intervened against the CIO militants, using every conceivable device to victimize them, and such a confrontation could have resulted only in our being defeated at heavy cost. For that reason we initiated protective measures in different form. It was decided at a membership meeting that workers threatened by the goons would sign the AFL pledge cards, and if necessary pay dues to the IBT, doing so under protest. Temporarily, they would have to carry two union buttons: the detested one which was being forced upon them, and the real emblem signifying their loyalty to 544-CIO.

At the same time we managed to obtain a court order enjoining the Tobinites from "interfering with the free and uninterrupted use of the streets, methods of transportation, and from obstructing places of employment or attempting through force or violence to compel workers to join the AFL union." The language our lawyers used in drafting this order for the judge's signature was borrowed from the Stassen law.

In issuing the decision, however, the court insisted on a further provision that it "shall not be construed so as to prevent the defendants from lawfully attempting to induce individuals to join the defendant union."

As the latter gimmick indicated, none of the authorities had any intention of interfering with IBT activities. Yet there was a useful purpose in the step we had taken. It helped publicize the fact—concealed by the daily papers—that a mass movement was being attacked by gangsters. We were thus enabled to further impress upon workers throughout the city that we needed support in our fight for union democracy.

Both the resort to passive resistance by individual union members and the securing of a restraining order against the goons were secondary tactics. Our central effort was directed toward the use of mass action, pointed squarely at the bosses. In that way we could come to grips with the main enemy, and open interference by the Tobinites would brand them as outright strikebreakers. Before we could embark on such a course, however, an opening had to be sought in the network of antistrike injunctions with which the employers were hemming us in. An answer was found in the few exceptions Blair had made the previous May when he had rejected Local 544's strike notices as "irregular." Among the notices he had validated was one involving the furniture stores. This group of employers, like all the rest, had refused to negotiate with us in a meaningful way; the "cooling off" period had in this instance expired; and even under the Stassen law we were free to take action.

So a meeting of 544-CIO's furniture section was held, and after hearing an explanation of the situation the three hundred-odd workers involved voted to go on strike. The walkout began on the morning of June 17. It was so solid, the shutdown so effective, that the companies didn't even try to operate their delivery facilities. By virtually unanimous action the workers were giving the lie to the employers' alibi that they "didn't know whom to bargain with"; also to the IBT's claims that it represented the trucking employees.

Instead of acting in accord with the demonstrated will of the workers, however, the bosses proceeded to help the Tobinites open a new attack on the union chosen by the ranks. It involved a plot to strip 544-CIO of its material resources and to lay a basis for framing up leaders of the local on criminal charges.

On the morning the furniture strike began, the court ruled in Tobin's favor on the civil suit that had been filed against us, thereby opening the way for him to grab the local's assets. An order was issued by Judge Luther Youngdahl authorizing Neal, as IBT receiver, to seize all monies, properties, and records previously held in the name of Local 544. Later the same day the cops invaded the union's headquarters at 257 Plymouth Avenue North and turned it over to Neal, along with books and files found there. Thanks to precautions taken by the executive board under instructions from the membership, no cash was grabbed other than the day's receipts. An accusation was thereupon made by Neal that officers of the local had "secreted and distributed large sums of money to diverse persons unknown, for the use and benefit of the defendants and the rival and dual labor union which they contemplate organizing."

Having expected such an attack, we had already lined up an alternative headquarters at 1328 Second Avenue North, just a couple of blocks from 257 Plymouth. The operations of 544-CIO were quickly transferred to that location, including arrangements for facilities needed by the furniture strikers.

Meanwhile, the furniture bosses had rushed to court for a ban on picketing. They still pretended that they didn't know whether to deal with the CIO or the AFL, adding a further allegation that in any case the strike was "illegal." Judge Youngdahl accommodated them with a restraining order, which was issued toward nightfall on the first day of the walkout. Copies of the order were served on individual pickets the next morning, but it took time to complete the service because new detachments of workers kept taking over the patrolling of struck firms as each previous contingent was handed the court order. While that was going on, the bosses gave the strikers written notice that they would be fired if they didn't return to work by June 19, and the IBT announced that it was opening contract negotiations with all employers who had been under agreement with Local 544.

Central to those developments was the court order against picketing. It could not be resisted effectively by the furniture strikers alone, because they didn't have sufficient numbers for that purpose. If the ban was to be defied, mass action had to be expanded on an industry-wide scale. But many other firms had already gotten antistrike injunctions against 544-CIO; we were further handicapped by legal fetters imposed through the Stassen law; the entire governmental apparatus was looking for pretexts to move against us; and we were under heavy attack from inside the labor movement. In such circumstances, a move to broaden the strike would have resulted in little more than the immediate jailing of the best union militants on contempt charges. That could have proved fatal to the organization.

For those reasons we had to abandon our efforts to block the conspiracy against 544-CIO by bringing production to a halt. But the danger still remained that the IBT's terror campaign could sap morale within the local. Even though the militants who comprised the Union Defense Committee could be relied upon to fight to the bitter end, there was a limit to the staying power of the membership as a whole. On one point, however, the ranks were unanimous. If provided a democratic opportunity to express their wishes, the workers would vote for the CIO.

Under these circumstances our next step had to be a demand for collective bargaining elections to determine what union should represent the trucking employees. Once raised, that demand was bound to have several favorable effects. It would demonstrate 544-CIO's confidence in the real sentiments of the workers; it would strengthen our case in the eyes of AFL members throughout the city; and it would further expose the Tobinites as a gang of usurpers, since they were bound to oppose a democratic solution of the conflict.

After reaching those conclusions in the leadership, we explained our thinking to a meeting of the furniture strikers. They accepted the steps we recommended and voted to return to their jobs pending the holding of collective bargaining elections. A statement was then issued by the executive board of the local, which the *Minneapolis Star Journal* of June 20, 1941, quoted as follows:

"The question of what union really represents the workers can be rightfully decided only by the workers themselves. They have already expressed their choice by voting in overwhelming majority in a free, democratic and regular meeting, for Local 544-CIO.

"The workers' choice of Local 544-CIO has been challenged by the employers as well as by the imported agents of Daniel Tobin's international union affiliated with the AFL, who are conniving with the employers to thwart the will of the workers and force employer-dictated contracts upon them.

"These imported agents of Tobin are already attempting to circumvent the democratic choice of the workers by violent interference with the operation of trucks by 544-CIO.

"Local 544-CIO proposes to meet this challenge by calling for a general election. . . .

"In view of the campaign of violence started by Tobin's imported agents against the Minneapolis truck drivers, it is quite obvious that any delay in holding these elections we propose would put upon Governor Stassen and other public officials a grave responsibility."

As was to be expected, Casey promptly issued a public declaration against the proposal for a democratic poll of the workers concerning what union they wanted to represent them. "The elections," he arrogantly declared, "are taking place already." He was referring, of course, to the compulsory registration of motor transport workers as AFL members through acts of coercion, and those methods were even further intensified in response to our demand for elections. Casey also made frenzied efforts to speed up his negotiations for sweetheart contracts with the trucking bosses, so as to confront us with a *fait accompli* in collective bargaining.

Local 544-CIO, meanwhile, had made formal application to the state labor conciliator, Blair, for immediate industry-wide elections by secret ballot to ascertain the workers' choice as their bargaining agent. Specific petitions were also filed for elections at the furniture stores and at other establishments concerning which the local's earlier strike notices had not been ruled "irregular." Letters were sent at the same time to all employers, warning them not to sign contracts with the AFL before the workers balloted on the question of union representation.

Since the CIO petitions could not be ignored without flouting the Stassen law, Blair announced they would be heard in proceedings to begin on June 30. Those to be taken up first, he said, would involve the furniture, concrete block, and wholesale grocery industries.

Upon learning that public hearings were being scheduled on the question of giving the workers a democratic choice of their bargaining agent, Tobin again panicked. He knew that employee elections would reaffirm the decision made by the members of Local 544 when they voted on June 9 to leave the IBT and affiliate with the CIO. So the Teamster president once more sought help from the White House, and he got quick action. Although preparations for the steps about to be taken by the federal authorities at his request had obviously been going on for a considerable time, the new moves bore the earmarks of having been hastily set into motion.

10. Roosevelt Backs Tobin

During the afternoon of June 27—three days before the hearings on union representation elections were to begin—FBI agents and U.S. marshals raided the branch headquarters of the Socialist Workers Party in Minneapolis and Saint Paul. Large quantities of literature were seized, along with two red flags and a picture of Leon Trotsky.

Sensational accounts of the foray appeared in the next day's papers. Reporters and photographers had been invited to accompany the raiders, and they provided stories embellished with pictures of "evidence" grabbed by the political cops. Scare headlines were used, as well, to show that the attack on the SWP was also aimed at the Teamster rebels. Among these was one on the front page of the *Minneapolis Tribune*, which read: "Announcement links some 544-CIO chiefs to group under fire." The *Saint Paul Dispatch* was even cruder about the whole thing. Its banner headline simply blurted out: "U.S. to prosecute 544."

Unquestionably, our conflict with Tobin was central to the timing of the federal onslaught, but the matter of timing was only a secondary factor. The primary motive for the government's action lay in the fact that the trade union fight had developed over national issues. Tobin's immediate needs coincided with Washington's long-range plans. Roosevelt was asking the labor bureaucrats for help in silencing protests against his steps to regiment the workers for war; and in that connection he had urged the gagging of Local 544, which was a focal point of mass opposition to the administration's foreign policy.

The Teamster overlord had sought to comply with the president's wishes, but it had proven impossible for him alone to tame the Minneapolis General Drivers Union. His terrorist measures had not succeeded in cowing the workers. Attempts by the local authorities to assist the IBT head in drawing 544-CIO into the type of confrontations that would lead to its entrapment had been sidestepped, and we had launched a countercampaign for a democratic solution of the conflict through employee elections. Since our policy endangered Tobin, the federal authorities had struck a new blow on his behalf. Their action had a double purpose: to help one of Roosevelt's closest labor lieutenants in the internal IBT conflict then taking place, and to show other trade union bureaucrats that support of the imperialist foreign policy would earn them governmental backing against dissidents in the union ranks.

The timing of this move on Tobin's behalf was not the most favorable from the ruling-class viewpoint. As matters then stood, insufficient war hysteria had been developed to stampede the masses against radicals in the labor movement on patriotic appeals alone. Instead, the government had to bear the onus of taking sides in what appeared on the surface to be nothing more than a dispute between two union factions. And on both those counts we were given something of an edge in securing labor and liberal support of our defense against the impending frame-up.

Despite such disadvantages, Roosevelt deemed it imperative to take quick action against us, and the FBI had already laid a preliminary foundation from which to begin. So the assault was opened with dual objectives in mind. These were to prevent the SWP from promoting the antiwar movement nationally and to strip 544-CIO of its strong moral position in the Midwest through criminal prosecution of its leadership.

As the first step, Henry A. Schweinhaut, a special assistant attorney general, was sent from Washington to represent the Department of Justice on the local scene. He was the one who supervised the raids on the SWP, and a propaganda cover for the move was provided by Attorney General Francis Biddle. As reported in the *Minneapolis Star Journal* of June 28, Biddle issued a statement from the national capital, declaring: "The principal Socialist Workers Party leaders against whom prosecution is being brought are also leaders of Local 544-CIO in Minneapolis. This prosecution is brought under the criminal code of the United States against persons who have been engaged in criminal seditious activities, and who are leaders of the Socialist Workers Party and have gained control of a legitimate labor union to use it for illegitimate purposes."

In the same issue the *Star Journal* quoted an announcement by Victor E. Anderson, the U.S. district attorney. He said that grand jury indictments would be sought accusing SWP leaders of "seditious conspiracy to advocate the overthrow of the government of the United States by force and violence."

Schweinhaut then carried the government's propaganda campaign a step further. According to the *Minneapolis Tribune* of June 30: "A hint that startling revelations on subversive activities in the Twin Cities would be forthcoming was dropped last night, as governmental officials moved under a tight lid of secrecy in preparation of their case against leaders of the Socialist Workers Party." Henry A. Schweinhaut, the newspaper reported, "said last night he believed the government had evidence of Socialist Workers Party activities in the Twin Cities which goes far beyond public knowledge."

This ominous talk about having uncovered secrets which went "far beyond public knowledge" appeared in the papers on the day Blair opened the hearings on the CIO's petitions for elections. The allegation was a barefaced lie. Literature of the kind seized by the FBI as "evidence" was carried on local newsstands, and it was available in the public libraries. But that fact was deliberately ignored by Schweinhaut, for it didn't square with the scheme to frame us as "conspirators."

At that stage no mention was made of specific individuals who were to be prosecuted, but even that policy was given a twist intended to smear us. When reporters asked U.S. Attorney Anderson if there would be arrests before indictments were returned by the grand jury, he replied: "Not unless some of the boys try to get away."

Reactions both favoring and opposing Roosevelt's conduct were at once manifested within the labor movement. The IBT forces, of course, hailed the federal attack on us. They claimed it justified Tobin's charge that "these fellows were engaged in subversive activities."

Similar enthusiasm for the actions of the witch-hunter in the White House was expressed by the Stalinists. About a week before the FBI raids, Germany had invaded the Soviet Union, thereby definitively scrapping the Stalin-Hitler pact. While that pact had remained in force, the Communist Party had opposed U.S. entry into the war, using as its slogan: "The Yanks are not coming." In the changed situation, however, the Stalinists reversed their line, moving virtually overnight into a campaign for the U.S. to open a second front against Hitler.

A new CP offensive was launched simultaneously against the

Trotskyists, centered on condemnation of our continued opposition to U.S. involvement in the war. We were denounced as "Nazi agents," the government's steps to prosecute us were applauded, and efforts were intensified to line up the Minnesota CIO against its new affiliate. In the latter connection Leonard Lagemen, state CIO secretary, told the *Star Journal* on June 28 that the move by the federal authorities "justifies our action in refusing to have anything to do with the Dunnes."

An opposite stand was taken within the CIO nationally. A statement from A. D. Lewis's office in Washington put the question: "If the leadership of 544 was good enough for the Teamsters union of the AFL for many years, why is the justice department action taken now instead of earlier?" Messages of solidarity with 544-CIO were sent from many CIO sections elsewhere in the country. Liberals and civil libertarians, too, voiced protests against the course Roosevelt was following against us.

Frank Barnhart, regional director of the UCWOC, issued a statement which was reported in *The Militant* of July 5, 1941. "Before granting a charter to local 544," he said, "the CIO made a careful investigation of the union and its leadership. As part of this investigation, representatives of the CIO consulted the Minneapolis Police Department and were informed by them that the leaders of Local 544 had no criminal record and were not in any sense classed as labor racketeers. A further irrefutable evidence of the honorable record of the leadership of Local 544 is contained in the finding of Judge Carroll during the court hearings which involved an examination of all the books, records, minutes, contracts, financial transactions, etc., of Local 544."

Speaking jointly with the executive board of 544-CIO, Barnhart also declared: "Unable to bend the workers to his will by the other vicious tactics which he has employed, Dan Tobin has persuaded Roosevelt to carry out this action in payment of his political debt to Tobin for past services rendered. . . . A great majority of the membership of the AFL Teamsters Union is opposed to Tobin's high-handed methods and moth-eaten organization policies. There are also many who are opposed to the war, especially in the Northwest area. This is not Hitler Germany. The United States is still a democracy. The people of this country still have the right to express their opinions about the politics of both Tobin and Roosevelt. . . .

"The CIO will continue to press its fight to win for the motor transport and allied workers of Minneapolis their democratic right to belong to an organization of their own choosing—the CIO."

Relatively few within Local 544 were shaken by Roosevelt's assault. Even though all who played leading roles within the local were potential targets of the federal witch-hunt, not a single individual flinched in the face of that danger. A comparable stand was taken in the ranks. Since the workers had accurate knowledge of their leaders' actual policies and conduct, they were generally prone to dismiss talk of "seditious conspiracy" as an obvious frame-up. Strong backing thus existed for the fight against the actual conspirators—the bosses, their government, and the Tobinites—who were hurling false accusations at their intended victims.

Such was the local's internal situation when the Blair hearings opened as scheduled on June 30. First on the agenda was 544-CIO's demand for elections to determine the bargaining agent in furniture delivery. Our case was presented by attorneys Gilbert Carlson and William Thomas.

Carl Skoglund and Kelly Postal appeared as lead-off witnesses. They explained how the Tobinites, acting in collaboration with the employers, had used threats and intimidation to force IBT buttons and pledge cards on workers. A large number of CIO pledge cards were then submitted, which had been freely signed by employees throughout the industry. This evidence, our representatives stressed, justified 544-CIO's contention that it spoke for the workers, but an election was urged, nevertheless, to definitively settle the question of bargaining agent.

I. E. Goldberg served as chief mouthpiece for the Tobinites. He opposed the CIO's election petitions, arguing that most workers in the industry had never left the IBT. In an effort to buttress that phony line, he launched into a tirade about "Trotskyite trickery" at the June 9 membership meeting, where Local 544 voted to switch its affiliation to the CIO. That action, he insisted, was "illegal."

Throughout this confrontation Blair dealt with our representatives as though they had already become convicted criminals. To Goldberg, on the other hand, he extended the most gracious treatment.

After the opening presentations 544-CIO began putting workers on the stand to testify about specific acts of intimidation committed against them. That move had scarcely gotten under way, however, when the hearings were abruptly postponed for a week. The delay could have only a malicious purpose. Blair, who took orders from Stassen, was plainly giving the IBT a further chance to terrorize workers and conduct secret contract negotiations with the bosses. Time was also being allowed for the federal authorities to make further preparations for the impending conspiracy indictment.

On the same day that Blair postponed the hearings—July 1— the national CIO sponsored a rally in Minneapolis to demonstrate solidarity with Local 544. It was held at the Lyceum Theater with some fifteen hundred workers in attendance. Frank Barnhart presided. Visiting speakers included Cecil Owen, publicity director of the UCWOC; Lee Pressman, CIO general counsel; and Allen Heywood, of the CIO's national organization department. John L. Lewis wired personal greetings to the gathering, as did Philip Murray. Ray Dunne, Carlos Hudson, and Ray Rainbolt spoke for Local 544.

In the course of his remarks Owen said: "Your coming over to the CIO created a sensation in Washington. For a few days it appeared that the national administration had dropped its campaign of 'Aid to England' for a campaign of 'Aid to Dan Tobin.'"

Pressman took up a key question. "When a single local union like 544 joins the CIO," he asked, "why is there all this excitement? Why have you become a national issue? . . . The story dates back to 1934 when you teamsters, under your present leadership, decided to build a strong, militant union and succeeded against great odds. The tradition behind your local union leads right to the origin of the CIO. . . . Your 1934 strikes gave meaning to the need of the workers for strong unions. The CIO has carried out concretely on a national scale what you started in 1934."

In sorry contrast to these manifestations of national support for the rebel Teamsters, representatives of the Hennepin County CIO council were conspicuous by their absence. The Communist Party had effectively organized a local boycott of the rally held to express solidarity with Local 544. It had also succeeded, however, in arousing the anger of the Lewis forces in the CIO. Strong pressure was brought upon the Stalinists from those quarters, and they soon found themselves forced to put the Hennepin

County body on record in formal support of our demand for employee elections in the trucking industry.

At this juncture a dramatic local action in support of the rebellion against Tobin came from an AFL quarter. It involved Henry A. Schultz, who had played a significant role in the third General Drivers strike of 1934 and had since become an international representative of the International Brotherhood of Electrical Workers, AFL. He resigned from the IBEW post to join 544-CIO's organizational staff. In his letter of resignation, published in *The Militant* of July 12, 1941, Schultz said:

"Last night I attended a meeting in Minneapolis under the auspices of Tobin's International Union of Teamsters, AFL. What I saw there was enough to turn the stomach of any loyal union man. . . . Tobin and his perfidious gang had a real mobilization. Paid organizers and officials located in places from Pennsylvania to San Francisco were mobilized on the platform in battle array against the workers in Minneapolis. The front rows were packed with state and local Minneapolis business agents, who could never be dynamited off their chairs to take part in a picket line against the bosses. The whole meeting stunk to the heavens, as a mobilization of reactionary labor officeholders against the legitimate rights of rank and file workers to determine the union of their choice. . . . A bitter fight is raging in Minneapolis and I consider it my duty to take my place on the side of the workers, as I did in the workers' strikes of 1934."

Meanwhile, a federal grand jury had been convened to consider "evidence" against the Socialist Workers Party. Information about the proceedings was then leaked to the boss press in a manner calculated to create the impression that a sinister underground organization was about to be exposed.

Literature seized in the melodramatic raids on the SWP headquarters in the Twin Cities was presented to the jury through testimony by FBI agents. Members of the Committee of 99 who had previously submitted affidavits to Tobin, were called in to lie about "subversive manipulation" of Local 544 and to name alleged members of the SWP in the union. All this was accompanied, moreover, by a prediction from Assistant Attorney General Schweinhaut that there would be "startling disclosures" when indictments were returned and those named were arrested.

U.S. Attorney Anderson also contributed to the smear campaign against those about to be indicted. He claimed that members of the Committee of 99 had been threatened with reprisals if they cooperated with the grand jury. Anderson said the FBI told him it had gotten reports of such threats.

While this was going on, state labor conciliator Blair resumed the hearings on 544-CIO's election petitions. Carlson and Thomas thereupon called in more workers to testify about the brutal manner in which they had been forced to sign up with Tobin's paper outfit. Job stewards were also put on the stand to verify that employees on their jobs had voluntarily signed the pledge cards which the CIO had submitted to the labor conciliator.

Goldberg claimed in rebuttal that the AFL had "proof" of support by a big majority of the workers involved. Besides, he contended, 544-CIO had lost the right to ask for an employee election by calling an "illegal strike" in the furniture industry.

Pretending that Goldberg's arguments had merit, Blair ordered both sides to prepare briefs on the election question. Again he was stalling, and, as soon became evident, his reason had nothing to do with the subject of the hearings. Blair was marking time while a series of new blows were struck at us, one following another in rapid succession.

On the morning of July 14 we got word that two of Tobin's agents were testifying before the Hennepin County grand jury. They were T. T. Neal, the IBT trustee, and F. D. Brown, an auditor for the Teamsters international. This development could have only one meaning. Criminal proceedings were about to be initiated over the matter of a few thousand dollars in Local 544's treasury which had been taken along when the local went over to the CIO.

So attorney Gilbert Carlson and Steve Glaser, a member of the 544-CIO staff, rushed to the county attorney's office. The object was to arrange for Glaser to appear before the grand jury and refute the Tobinite allegations on the financial question. The money involved, he was prepared to show, had been placed in safe hands in accordance with a membership decision at the June 9 meeting of the local, and an accounting had since been given to the ranks, in keeping with democratic union procedures. The IBT claim to these funds, on the other hand, had no basis whatever in terms of actual representation of the workers. Only twenty-nine were present at a membership meeting of 544-AFL held that same day.

The grand jury got around that hurdle of truth by simply refusing to hear Glaser's testimony. Instead, it took immediate action on the false premise that Local 544's assets belonged to Tobin. Beginning on the afternoon of July 14, several indictments were voted against four leaders of the local—Miles Dunne, president; Kelly Postal, secretary-treasurer; Nick Wagner, a trustee; and Moe Hork, an organizer. They were charged with "embezzlement" and "grand larceny."

After being arraigned, the four were released on bond, and the setting of trial dates was postponed repeatedly. It seemed that the ruling class wanted further steps in this frame-up held in abeyance for the time being. In that way the indictments could be used to smear the victims, through propaganda designed to make accusations appear tantamount to proof of guilt.

On July 15—just twenty-four hours after the "embezzlement-larceny" attack was launched—the federal grand jury indicted twenty-nine of us. We were charged with conspiracy to overthrow the government by armed revolution whenever the time seemed propitious, conspiracy to advocate the overthrow of the government by force and violence, and conspiracy to foment insubordination among the armed forces.

Although the real reason for these sensational charges was our antiwar views, the word *war* appeared nowhere in the federal indictment. That was the case because it would have been unpopular at that juncture to persecute us as opponents of imperialist foreign policy. Therefore, as the *Northwest Organizer* pointed out, a smokescreen was provided through allegations of a "revolutionary conspiracy" aimed at "overthrowing the government." The charges were contrived, moreover, so as to involve 544-CIO, a mass organization which stood in the vanguard of the antiwar movement.

Militants in the Socialist Workers Party and in union organizations alike were accused of "conspiracy against the government," when the real conspiracy was against the democratic right of the Minneapolis transport workers to have a bargaining agent of their own choosing. We were branded conspirators, when the actual conspirators were Tobin, the Committee of 99, Roosevelt and his political cops, Stassen, Kline, and the Minneapolis employers.

Those under indictment fell into several categories. Fourteen were officers, organizers, or job stewards of 544-CIO, or on the editorial staff of the *Northwest Organizer*. Included were Jake Cooper; Harry DeBoer; Grant, Miles, and Ray Dunne; George Frosig; Walter Hagstrom; Clarence Hamel; Emil Hansen; Carlos

Hudson; Kelly Postal; Ray Rainbolt; Carl Skoglund; and Nick Wagner.

Six were officers or outstanding activists in the Federal Workers Section: Max Geldman, Carl Kuehn, Roy Orgon, Edward Palmquist, Oscar Schoenfeld, and Harold Swanson.

Four were national leaders of the Socialist Workers Party: James P. Cannon, Farrell Dobbs, Albert Goldman, and Felix Morrow.

The remaining five comprised a rather loose category made up of Grace Carlson and Oscar Coover, who played leading roles in the Minnesota SWP; Dorothy Schultz, Twin Cities secretary of the Workers Defense League; Rose Seiler, business agent of the Minneapolis Office Workers union; and Alfred Russell, a former officer of Teamster Local 554 in Omaha, Nebraska.

This time the federal authorities agreed to negotiate pretrial arrangements, instead of starting with surprise arrests in the wee hours of the morning. In that way the twenty-nine were able to surrender themselves voluntarily on July 18 to be booked, fingerprinted, and released on bond. Initially the government demanded stiff bail of $5,000 each, a total of $145,000. But rapid organization of a protest movement led to some reduction in those figures.

A quick response to our appeal for support came from Labor's Non-Partisan League, the national political arm of the CIO. The LNPL issued a statement denouncing the federal indictment as "a menace to fundamental civil liberties and to labor's basic rights." Acting with comparable promptness the American Civil Liberties Union and a number of prominent liberals also condemned the witch-hunt tactics used against us by the Roosevelt administration.

Under those pressures the authorities backed off from the original demands concerning bail. Significantly enough, though, the amount finally set for sixteen defendants belonging to 544-CIO was reduced only from $5,000 to $3,500 each; whereas the sum for the remaining thirteen was cut to $2,500 per person. Funds to provide bond for all 544-CIO members involved were wired to Minneapolis by the CIO. Help was obtained from the ACLU and other sources in arranging for the release of the other defendants.

As had been done in the "embezzlement-larceny" cases, no firm trial date was set. Here again it appeared that our enemies hoped to gain sufficient propaganda ammunition for the nonce from the mere fact of the federal indictment.

Although Carl Skoglund was among those for whom bond was made in the "sedition" case, he alone failed to escape immediate incarceration. Earlier he had applied for U.S. citizenship, and up to the winter of 1941 the request had simply been pigeonholed. At that time, Perrin of the FBI had arranged to offer Skoglund help in getting his citizenship papers if he went over to the Committee of 99. Skoglund had repudiated that cynical attempt to convert him into an FBI informer, and nothing further was done about his personal situation until Local 544 broke with Tobin. Then, on July 18—the day the twenty-nine were booked as "seditious conspirators"—Skoglund was arrested on a deportation warrant issued by the U.S. Immigration and Naturalization Service. he was thrown into jail, and bail on this charge was set at the monstrous figure of $25,000.

Skoglund was held behind bars for a week, during which the city was plagued by a terrible heat wave. Finally, after nationwide protests had flooded into the White House, his bail was reduced to $3,500, and that sum was posted by the CIO. I then went to arrange Carl's release. When he got out I took him to a nearby saloon for some cold beer, but the poor man was so dried out from the stifling heat inside the jail that it was like pouring the refreshing liquid onto the sands of the Sahara at high noon.

In speaking later about the attempt to deport him, Carl said: "There is one citizenship they cannot deprive me of, and that is citizenship in the working-class movement. I took out those papers back in Sweden when I was sixteen or seventeen years old, a member of the Young Socialists and of the union in the paper mill where I worked. Throughout the years, I think I have served that movement faithfully and to the best of my ability. The time is coming when governments all over the world will recognize loyalty to the interests of the working people as the highest form of citizenship."

Parallel with this several-sided assault on us at that juncture, a move was started to strip 544-CIO of a key defensive weapon, the *Northwest Organizer*. Tobin's sensitivity about the paper's service to the rebel cause was reflected in an item that appeared in his official magazine, directing all Teamster units to "return the Dunnes' poisonous literature." As was typical of him, though, he had no intention of allowing anyone freedom of choice in this matter, and steps were taken to save the curious from temptation.

On July 9 Tobin's mouthpiece in Minneapolis, Goldberg, telegraphed the IBT headquarters that he was "arranging with postal authorities for cancellation of *Northwest Organizer* mailing permit." Shortly after that, Goldberg got a court order restraining 544-CIO from publishing its paper or using the mailing lists involved. At the same time the Tobinites came out with a paper of their own, called the *Minnesota Teamster*.

Taking this new blow in stride, 544-CIO simply changed the name of its official organ to the *Industrial Organizer*. The first issue under the new designation appeared on July 17, just seven days after the *Northwest Organizer* ceased publication. Despite Tobin's efforts, there had been no hiatus in the weekly paper's regular appearance; and that accomplishment was of exceptional importance in view of the new sequence of events that was about to unfold.

With the smear campaign against us now escalated on a massive scale, a new form of attack was launched. The specific aim in this instance was to strip 544-CIO of its legal right to bargain for the workers. As an opener the Tobinites began filing strike notices against various trucking firms, especially those already involved in hearings on the CIO's election petitions. One purpose was to pretend that 544-AFL had the workers' support in dealing with the employers, but there were other considerations involved. These were reflected in a complaint that appeared in the *Minnesota Teamster* of July 25, 1941.

It read: "The America-haters are facing indictment; the unions have been purged of false leaders; all looked harmonious but. . . ." But what? To the dismay of the IBT gang, "Now comes the employer to do a bit of contract chiseling, believing that the time is ripe to set up his own idea of wages, hours and conditions. . . ."

The bosses, of course, were doing precisely what was to be expected—demanding that "harmonious" labor relations be established on their terms; and that put the Tobinites in a bind. If they allowed too many of Local 544's hard-won gains to be taken away, it would be extremely difficult for them to exercise control over the workers, no matter how much help they got from the ruling class. So Tobin's agents felt compelled to assume a pseudo-militant posture in their propaganda, hoping that it would induce the employers to act more "responsibly."

At that point state labor conciliator Blair began to take a direct hand in the new plot against 544-CIO. First he used the Stassen law to decree a "cooling off" period, acting as though the IBT really planned to call a strike. Then Blair offered his services as a "conciliator" in the behind-the-scenes negotiations between the Tobinites and the trucking companies.

Those moves were followed, in turn, by the filing of two AFL motions at the hearings on the CIO's petitions for collective bargaining elections. One called for dismissal of the CIO petitions. As grounds for the request, Goldberg argued that 544-CIO leaders were "guilty of unlawful conduct as officers or members of a labor union." The second motion asked that 544-AFL be certified—without elections—as the industry-wide bargaining agent. In presenting that brazen demand Goldberg claimed that over four thousand of the workers involved were paying dues to the IBT. He neglected to mention, though, the methods used to collect that money.

Blair immediately called for briefs from the two sides on the new AFL motions. There would be no further hearings on our election petitions, he then announced, until action had been taken on the requests submitted by Goldberg.

A few days later, on August 2, Blair ruled against the holding of collective bargaining elections at the furniture stores. In doing so he charged that 544-CIO was guilty of an "unfair labor practice." The furniture strike, he claimed, had been called without giving proper notice as required by state law, and therefore the union was not entitled to an election.

There wasn't a grain of truth in his allegations. We had been careful to comply with all requirements of the state law. Notice had first been served of a desire to negotiate with the furniture bosses. When the ten-day waiting period involved at that stage had passed without any progress in such negotiations as took place, strike notices had been served. Blair had accepted them as valid, after which he imposed a "cooling off" period, using the "public interest" gimmick. At no time had he informed the union that there was anything "irregular" about those particular strike notices, and the furniture workers had walked out only after the full "cooling off" period had been scrupulously observed.

To get around those iron facts, Blair resorted to a contrived legal interpretation based upon a flimsy technicality, and it was applied retroactively. He now ruled that the notices filed in advance of the furniture strike had become invalid when Local 544 changed its affiliation from the AFL to the CIO. This crooked decision did more than outrageously violate the workers' democratic rights; Blair was giving the IBT an open invitation to continue the collection of membership dues by terrorist methods.

We resisted this new attack as best we could under the given adverse circumstances. As the first step, 544-CIO filed new strike notices against the furniture employers. An effort was then made to have the courts reverse Blair's decision. Nothing came of that, however, other than a bit of publicity of value to us. We also filed two new petitions with the state's so-called labor conciliator. One of these demanded that 544-AFL's request for certification as bargaining agent be denied because its strong-arm tactics violated a provision of the Stassen law. As our lawyers pointed out, a clause in that law specifically made it an "unfair labor practice" to "threaten any person while in pursuit of lawful employment." The other petition demanded on similar grounds that 544-AFL be disqualified from any further participation in hearings on the question of elections in other sections of the industry. Blair said he would take these demands under advisement.

Viewed formally, the ruling against the furniture workers did not preclude elections being allowed in other sections of the trucking industry. Actually, though, there was no longer any real prospect that such would be the case. The employer-governmental-Tobinite conspirators figured they now had 544-CIO set up for the kill, and they proceeded accordingly.

11. Governmental Hatchet Job

By this time the strong-arm gang Tobin had sent to Minneapolis was undergoing a change in composition. Among the initial contingents were officers and organizers from IBT locals in other states. They had come to the city believing that the membership of Local 544 really favored the AFL Teamsters and that a "subversive minority" had resorted to trickery in order to switch its affiliation to the CIO. Such elements had soon discovered, though, that they were attempting to destroy a progressive organization which had the workers' solid support, and once aware of that fact, the genuine union fighters among them had begun returning to their home locals on one or another pretext.

The remaining invaders consisted almost entirely of IBT hacks and outright plug-uglies, who were supplemented locally by the Committee of 99. Moreover, the criminal activities of some of these unsavory characters were beginning to extend beyond the tasks assigned to them by Tobin.

On July 20, 1941, four of these hooligans—George O'Brien, Robert Brennan, Axel Soderberg, and Frank Bochniak—got into a shooting scrape in a rural community. The press reported that guns were pulled on a farmer, Walter Doree, in a personal dispute over the ownership of a truck. Doree rushed to get his hunting rifle, and, in the fight that followed, Brennan was killed. A coroner's jury decided that Doree, who was badly wounded, had fired in self-defense.

Then, on August 7, Kenneth Buckley of Kansas City, Missouri, and John Beeler of Galveston, Texas, were arrested on charges of invading the bedroom of a nurse in the Nicollet Hotel, where the IBT had set up its Minneapolis headquarters. Press accounts of the incident said hotel officials responding to the woman's screams were blackjacked by the two Tobinites, who were subdued only when the cops arrived.

A couple of days later the police booked Buckley and Beeler, together with Henry Smith of Kansas City, on new assault charges. They were accused of beating up Alderman Desmond F. Pratt and his brother, Dr. Gerald H. Pratt, in a Minneapolis cafe. The doctor's jaw was fractured.

Since the cops looked the other way when 544-CIO members were slugged, Tobin's thugs seemed to feel they had immunity for their personal indulgences as well. But it became too much for the Kline administration to overlook when a nurse was attacked, hotel officials beaten, an alderman assaulted, and a doctor's jaw broken. So in those instances arrests were made, after which the culprits got off with light fines.

Even the IBT had to take action. The *Minnesota Teamster* of August 15, 1941, announced: "Kenneth Buckley and Henry Smith have been discharged as organizers for Local 544-AFL because of the recent attack on a Minneapolis alderman in a tavern last Saturday." An attempt was made at the same time to resolve the Beeler problem by simply disclaiming any responsibility for him.

Such was the Tobinites' public image when their moves for a sweetheart deal with the trucking employers were brought fully into the open. For weeks negotiations had been going on behind the scenes. During that period Blair, who was a party to the plot, had recommended that new labor agreements be signed on the basis of a six-cent raise in hourly pay and "readjustment" of various stipulations previously won by Local 544. He made the proposal only to the bosses and to the AFL, concealing his action from the CIO. Then, on August 9, Joseph M. Casey announced that the IBT had accepted the Blair terms and was preparing accordingly to sign contracts with ninety major trucking firms.

Casey's announcement had a dramatic impact upon the workers, but not of the kind he intended. Earlier the attendance at 544-CIO rallies had tapered off considerably as the Blair hearings dragged along. Now, however, there was a sudden reversal of the trend. On August 11 close to a thousand workers turned out for a meeting at the CIO hall, a figure that stood in marked contrast to the total of fifty-six who participated in a 544-AFL session held the same evening.

With scarcely an exception, the workers were outraged by the IBT's treacherous deal with the bosses. Their mood was shown both by the exceptional attendance at our membership rally and by the extent to which more and more of them resumed the wearing of CIO buttons on the job, in open defiance of Tobin's goons.

Coordinating its action with this resurgence of worker militancy, 544-CIO chose that time to petition the National Labor Relations Board for the collective bargaining elections Blair had denied the furniture store employees. But our request was pigeonholed with the excuse that the matter needed "careful study."

We also served additional strike notices on the firms preparing to sign contracts with the IBT, and that move brought a quick response—against the workers. Stassen promptly invoked the "public interest" clause in the state law. Our notices were thus automatically referred to special commissions for review, and a further thirty-day strike ban was imposed upon the CIO.

Immediately thereafter Blair thrust aside all our petitions for employee elections. He gave precedence, instead, to a blanket hearing on the IBT's request for industry-wide certification as bargaining agent. By its very nature, this step indicated that a decision was to be made without the workers having any voice whatever in the matter. Moreover, the procedure now followed was rigged to fog the real issues with a further propaganda smear of the 544-CIO leaders.

Tobin's lawyer, Goldberg, was allowed to make charges at the hearing that officers of the rebel local were "subversive." As "proof" he cited the federal indictment for "seditious conspiracy." In addition Thomas McHugh of the Committee of 99 was put on the stand to tell about seeing a red flag in the General Drivers headquarters during the 1934 strikes. What he had actually seen was the local's official banner. Its border was blue and the number *574* appeared in white against a red background. All McHugh could remember, however, was the red.

Testimony was also taken from Sidney Brennan of the Committee of 99. With comparable duplicity, he presented a rehash of the anti-Trotskyist affidavits he and others had prepared under FBI tutelage the previous April. As usual, such crap was played up in the boss press.

This red-baiting was followed by submission of "evidence" to show that the Tobinites represented a majority of the trucking employees. It consisted of a report by certified public accountants who had merely added up names contained in 544-AFL ledgers. The figures thus compiled were accepted by Blair as a true report of IBT strength in motor transport locally. He chose to ignore the fact that the members in question had been signed up by terrorist methods.

Local 544-CIO protested Blair's flagrant misconduct, demanding that he be removed from his post as "unfair, partial, unqualified and incompetent." Governor Stassen's response was reported in the *Minneapolis Tribune* of August 14, 1941. "I'll keep in touch with the situation," the governor cynically replied to us, "but I don't think you have made any showing thus far of any unfairness on Blair's part."

Just twenty-four hours later the trucking companies began signing contracts with 544-AFL. Since this was done before an official decision had been made on the issue of bargaining rights, Blair tried to cover up the fact that the step was meant to set the stage for official recognition of the Tobinites. "It does not necessarily follow," he said in a lying statement to the press, "that this union has been certified as bargaining agent for employees in these industries." Like Blair, the bosses also sought to cushion the shock effect upon the workers of this callous violation of their rights. Checks were issued with unprecedented speed to cover back pay on the six-cent-an-hour raise involved, which was made retroactive to June 1, 1941.

Since the signing of contracts on the foregoing basis constituted an outright violation of federal law, 544-CIO demanded that the National Labor Relations Board take action against the ninety firms involved. Blair thereupon rushed an "explanation of the facts" to the NLRB, and it used his intervention as a pretext for ignoring the whole thing.

Casey meanwhile called a drumhead meeting of 544-AFL, at which his contract with the bosses was presented for "ratification" by the few members present. He gave an oral report of the terms, which had been negotiated behind the workers' backs, and flatly refused to read the text of the agreement. A motion was then made to approve his report, and, despite protests from the floor, the motion was declared carried. After that the daily papers were informed that the workers had voted to accept the Tobinite deal with the trucking employers.

By that time we had managed to obtain a copy of the IBT's contract with the wholesale grocers, the basic terms of which were typical of those contained in pacts with other companies as well. The full text of the grocery agreement was published in a special bulletin issued by the *Industrial Organizer* on August 8,

1941. The first printing of two thousand copies was distributed within two hours. An additional four thousand copies were then run off, and these too were quickly grabbed up by workers eager to get the facts about Casey's behind-the-scenes deal.

An analysis of the IBT-employer swindle was also contained in the special bulletin. The grocery workers had demanded a 17½-cent raise in hourly pay, it was explained, and Casey had settled for six cents, ignoring urgent problems created by rising living costs. Concessions were made to management on overtime schedules and vacation rights. Guarantees of job protection were eroded. Compulsory arbitration of grievances was stipulated, with the decision-making "neutral" party to be recommended by a "priest, minister, reverend or rabbi." The latter requirement was especially costly to the workers. It left the bosses free to chisel away at will, thereby making a mockery of Local 544's long-established policy of enforcing contract terms to the letter.

Once those facts became known, the workers reacted angrily to the Tobinite betrayal of their interests. Over twelve hundred packed the 544-CIO hall at the August 25 membership meeting, eager to battle collectively in defense of their rights. It was, in fact, the largest meeting since the local had voted on June 9 to leave the AFL. The ranks were again rallying massively in support of the union of their choice, uninhibited by the circumstance that its leaders faced criminal charges ranging from embezzlement to seditious conspiracy.

Stickers were passed out at the meeting bearing the slogan, "Don't let the bosses shove Casey's contract down your throat." These were pasted up at every place of employment the following morning, and angry workers engaged in heated arguments with Tobin's "organizers" whenever they appeared.

Casey tried to counter this trend by shouting about "Americanism" and denouncing "infectious propaganda spread by the CIO." At the same time he promised that 544-AFL would have elections of officers "in the near future," and that steps would be taken to establish sick and death benefits. But the workers knew that Tobin would not allow union democracy, and they were too well schooled in class-struggle tactics to be taken in by a scheme to substitute "fringe benefits" for higher pay, shorter hours, and the unqualified right to strike.

It was in those circumstances that 544-CIO proceeded to rebut the IBT's claims on the certification issue. Workers, not ledgers, were produced at the hearing as sources of evidence about what had actually been taking place. Scores of witnesses from every section of the industry came forward to turn the affair into a public forum.

Worker after worker described the brutal methods used by Tobin's goons in compelling them to remove CIO buttons and sign applications for AFL membership. Accounts were given of severe beatings administered to employees who refused to sign with the AFL, sometimes with bosses looking on. Those testifying explained why they had left the IBT, why they backed the CIO; and all demanded that Blair order democratic elections to determine their bargaining agent.

At the beginning of 544-CIO's presentation a number of Tobin's thugs were on hand as spectators. But when our witnesses pointed them out as assailants, they suddenly disappeared from the hearing room. Goldberg, too, found it tough going. He tried to bulldoze the first few giving CIO testimony, and the attempt boomeranged. After that he had little to say, because it had proved chancy for him to cross-examine these angry workers.

This phase of the hearing was, of course, played down in the boss press. But extensive accounts were carried in the *Industrial Organizer,* and in that way a full understanding of what was going on became available to the entire Minneapolis labor movement.

Blair, like the editors of the capitalist dailies, seemed nervous about this stage of the proceedings, and immediately upon completion of the CIO's presentation he declared a short recess. His action was apparently dictated by the need of the union-busting conspirators to initiate countermeasures designed to get around the strong case we had made for the holding of employee elections; and steps of that kind were taken forthwith.

As a safeguard against the workers' anger exploding into industrial stoppages, hasty decisions were made by the commissions Stassen had appointed to consider 544-CIO's latest series of strike notices. The findings were essentially the same in each case, all the notices being dismissed as "invalid" for contrived reasons.

We were accused of violating Minnesota law on two counts: failing to make new written demands upon the employers before filing new strike notices; and serving the notices before Blair "had an opportunity to act" on the certification of a collective bargaining agent. While we were thus branded "lawbreakers," not a word was said about the strike notices filed earlier by the

Tobinites. Instead, we were berated for intending to strike firms that had already signed contracts with the AFL. The purpose of this perverted logic, plainly enough, was to falsely picture 544-CIO as a "dual union," which sought by illegal means to violate the IBT's "established" jurisdiction over trucking.

As soon as the first of these commissions announced its findings, the employers involved rushed to court and got new restraining orders against strike action by 544-CIO. These orders were issued on the grounds that we had violated the state's labor relations act. The other commissions thereupon added the court orders to their reasons for dismissing the remaining CIO strike notices, and in each instance judicial restraint was further used to tie the workers' hands in every section of the industry.

While this shell game was going on, Tobin had been pressuring AFL president Green to intensify his crackdown on the Minneapolis Central Labor Union. Although the CLU officers had declared themselves in support of the IBT's fight against 544-CIO, rank-and-file resistance had prevented them from backing up their words with deeds. So the Teamster dictator now labeled them "Communist sympathizers" and demanded their official heads.

Green responded by appointing an investigating committee, led by Matthew Woll, who was among the most reactionary of the AFL vice-presidents. It would have the power, Green announced, to revoke the CLU's charter. This threat began to have an effect even before the Woll committee arrived in town. Steps to purge Tobin's opponents from AFL affiliates were initiated by the local bureaucrats, and a ban was declared on handling of building materials delivered by CIO drivers.

By then Blair had scheduled another session to hear final arguments on the representation question. In summing up the CIO's case, our attorneys centered on the compelling evidence submitted by workers who had testified in favor of employee elections. Tobin's lawyers merely repeated their red-baiting line, stressed the alleged membership totals contained in the CPA's report, and closed the IBT's case without having called a single rank-and-file worker to the stand. After their pitch was finished, Blair adjourned the proceedings with an announcement that he would "take under advisement" the AFL's request for certification as industry-wide bargaining agent.

At that point we raised a public demand that Mayor Kline and the Minneapolis City Council press Governor Stassen to order the democratic elections sought by the workers. An attempt was also made to arrange for a delegation from 544-CIO to meet directly with Stassen on the election issue. The governor agreed to such a conference, but, for what proved to be a diabolical reason, he put it off until September 20.

On September 19—the day before our scheduled meeting with Stassen—Blair made his ruling. He certified 544-AFL as the bargaining agent for trucking employees on an industry-wide scale. All CIO petitions for elections were then dismissed on the premise that his order certifying the AFL disposed of the matter.

Both the capitalist dailies and the *Minnesota Teamster* were on the streets with the full text of Blair's ruling hours before 544-CIO got official notice of the decision. The Tobinites, who had thus been granted control over workers they had no right to represent, quickly organized a victory parade of their hangers-on. It was led by an American Legion band.

Blair's decision, as quoted in the *Minneapolis Star Journal* of September 19, 1941, stated: "Upon full investigation and from all the evidence adduced at said hearings and arguments of counsel, and from all the facts and evidence herein, the conciliator hereby finds:

"That the above entitled matter does not present a dispute of the ordinary type between the AFL and CIO but rather presents a dispute between the AFL union of long standing and a comparatively small group of men under a leadership actively affiliated with the Socialist Workers Party, who withdrew from the AFL to avoid being expelled from this organization and who have sought to create a union for their own purposes under a charter from the CIO. . . .

"That the dispute over representation arose on June 9, 1941 by reason of an attempt by certain officers of said union to secede and create a new union under a charter by the CIO.

"That on June 9 there were 5,473 employees in the Minneapolis area, 4,251 were and are paid-up members of General Drivers union local 544, AFL, and have voluntarily paid dues to said union subsequent to said date of June 9, 1941.

"That of 5,473 drivers and helpers in the Minneapolis area, 172 were and are supporters of a group of men who are conducting the Motor Transport and Allied Workers Industrial Union, 544 CIO. . . .

"That to effectuate the purposes of the Minnesota labor relations act and to promote and preserve industrial peace and to safeguard the continued flow of commerce, it is essential that there be one and only one bargaining agent for the general drivers and helpers of the Minneapolis area."

As can be seen, the entire ruling was based on deceitful logic and brazen lies. Red-baiting references to the Socialist Workers Party were used to cover up the complete distortion of facts. Blair dared not admit that "certain officers" of Local 544 were the entire leadership, and that the decision to leave the IBT was taken by almost unanimous vote of some four thousand workers present at the June 9 membership meeting of the local.

No mention was made of the fact that for ninety-one days the transport workers had been striving through 544-CIO to obtain democratic elections, nor was there any effort to justify the refusal to order such elections. Instead, falsified figures were used in an effort to authenticate certification of Tobin's paper union. Blair pretended that 544-CIO's membership consisted only of the 172 workers who had appeared at the hearings he conducted. They had come to testify, however, not to their union membership, but about the methods of intimidation and coercion used by the Tobin machine. Cynically disregarding the facts revealed by those workers, Blair pretended that membership dues had been "voluntarily" paid to the IBT. He accepted as valid the listings in 544-AFL's ledgers, and on that outrageous basis certified it as bargaining agent.

The foregoing omissions, distortions, and outright lies were pointed out by 544-CIO's executive board in the September 25, 1941, issue of the *Industrial Organizer*. Concerning Blair's allegation that recognition of 544-CIO would "defeat the purposes of the Minnesota labor relations act," the board said: "He really means that to recognize the democratic right of the drivers to elections would defeat the aims of Stassen. . . . Blair seeks to set himself up as judge of what is a good union and a bad union. . . . He places the stamp of approval on Tobin's undemocratic regime and gangster policies. . . .

"Democracy is all right to talk about," the board's statement added bitterly, "and to send abroad on the tips of bayonets. But democracy is beyond the reach of the Minneapolis drivers."

Beginning with the issue of the paper in which the above statement appeared, a new slogan was printed at the top of page one. It declared: "Our war for democracy is here, against the bosses, Stassen and Tobin."

A further attempt was now made to have the National Labor

Relations Board override Blair and hold the collective bargaining elections denied by him. We soon found, though, that the NLRB's regional office had orders from Washington to back up the Stassen-Blair line. This Roosevelt agency turned down 544-CIO's appeal for federal action to accord the workers their democratic rights, and it flatly refused to issue complaints against the trucking bosses for signing contracts with the IBT while the issue of union representation was in dispute.

Our next step was to seek a court review of Blair's decision. Since he operated from the state capital in Saint Paul, the matter was taken before a Ramsey County judge, rather than one in Hennepin County where the struggle occurred. After that, as usually happens when workers' rights are involved, the case dragged along in the courts for an extended period of time.

As matters stood at this point, 544-CIO had been effectively walled off in Minneapolis, and there was no realistic prospect of continuing the struggle elsewhere through the United Construction Workers Organizing Committee. Although several IBT locals in the region had sought to join in the revolt against Tobin, they now found themselves in a position similar to ours.

The rebel units in question were situated in Austin, Minnesota; Fargo, North Dakota; and Dubuque, Mason City, Ottumwa, and Waterloo in Iowa. Since these were relatively small towns, the local unions there were rather weak in numbers. For that reason Tobin had been able to move against them without drawing seriously upon the forces concentrated against us in Minneapolis. In each case, moreover, he got help from the local ruling class. This combination of forces enabled the IBT, sooner or later, to force the workers back into line in those towns.

Things were no better concerning the UCWOC's efforts to organize transport workers in Michigan. That campaign had been continued in low key while the fight was raging in Minneapolis, and serious measures to intensify it were not undertaken until early September. By then, of course, Tobin was able to shift many of his thugs to the Michigan front, and the conflict there soon ended in another IBT victory. Once again the futility of Lewis's one-at-a-time strategy had been demonstrated in life; and with that second major defeat, the UCWOC campaign in trucking had virtually spent itself.

Still another adverse development took place in September. The Woll committee arrived in Minneapolis to conduct a loyalty inquisition within the city's AFL movement. Leaders of the Central Labor Union and officers of various local unions were grilled about their past conduct and future intentions concerning Tobin's fight with the "subversives" of Local 544. The committee then left town, after stating that a report of its findings would be made to Green.

Although details of the committee's report were not revealed, its very existence served to intimidate AFL officials in Minneapolis and the surrounding region. They became more craven than ever in their kowtowing to the national union bureaucrats, as was shown by actions taken at the State Federation of Labor's 1941 convention. It pledged support to Tobin against 544-CIO and voted to bar "Trotskyists" from AFL unions in Minnesota.

With blows raining down upon us from most every quarter, the time had come to draw a balance sheet of the changed situation. On the one hand, the Tobin union had been certified as bargaining agent; it had contracts with the employers, and membership in the IBT had become compulsory for trucking employees. On the other hand, 544-CIO had no bargaining rights; it was in no way recognized by the employers, and the courts had deprived it of the right to strike.

On top of that, the union leadership faced trial on trumped-up charges of embezzlement, grand larceny, and seditious conspiracy. The city's AFL movement had been forced into support of Tobin, and the Stalinists were doing their best to estrange the Minnesota section of the CIO from us.

As a result of those combined factors, what had previously been a dynamic organization with great ability to defend the workers' interests was reduced to little more than a union in name only.

Under such circumstances steps had to be taken forthwith to protect the workers, including the best fighters in the union ranks, from pointless risk of further victimization; and that could be done in only one way. Much as it galled them, they had to join Tobin's outfit. Through that move they had the best chance of saving their jobs and of remaining in a position to reopen the conflict against the IBT bureaucracy at the first opportunity. Meanwhile, 544-CIO would simply have to rely upon its few remaining resources, coupled with whatever help could be obtained from the CIO nationally, in an effort to maintain at least nominal existence.

After the leadership reluctantly but unanimously came to the above conclusions, a meeting was called to submit that course for a decision by the union members. I was assigned to make the report. It was an unforgettable experience.

Those in attendance were Local 544's best militants. They had been through seven years of confrontations with the bosses, the capitalist government, and the IBT dictator. Knowledge and experience thus gained had enabled them to carry on the complex 1941 struggle as a disciplined combat formation, one capable of putting up a whale of a fight in the face of overwhelming odds. As seasoned warriors, they were not given to emotional outbursts, and they now demonstrated once again their capacity for self-control under trying circumstances. Yet the very grimness with which these workers discussed the situation into which the union had been thrust illustrated most graphically the depths of their anger and their intense resentment over the injustice that was being done to them.

Agreement was reached at this bitter session on the need for everyone who could, to get back into the IBT. The decision was then carried out in the usual disciplined manner, with gratifying results. Nearly all the militants were able to hold on to their jobs in trucking; a solid bloc of good union fighters penetrated Tobin's outfit, watching hopefully for a chance to take him on again.

Shortly after the union meeting—on October 4, 1941—Grant Dunne killed himself. He was a casualty of two different wars: first a war between imperialist powers and then the war of the bosses against the workers at home.

For the next two days, hundreds upon hundreds of Local 544 members and other trade unionists filed through the mortuary to pay him their last respects. His family then honored me with a request that I deliver the funeral address, and my remarks were published in the October 9 issue of the *Industral Organizer*. Concerning the circumstances of his death, I said:

"Five months after his marriage [to Clara Houck on February 6, 1918] Grant was inducted into the 3rd Pioneer Infantry, and one month later he found himself in the front-line trenches in France. . . . On the very eve of the Armistice he was transporting munitions to the front lines when he was caught with other soldiers in a terrific explosion at an ammunition dump. Grant sustained a severe case of shellshock. He was hospitalized in France and brought back to the United States on a stretcher. On October 12, 1919, Grant was released from Fort Snelling with an honorable discharge. His recovery from his war wounds was slow and he suffered many relapses, especially in the last year of his life. . . .

"In recent years, Grant had seen the world again enveloped in another bloody war caused by the forces of imperialism. He had seen the heavy hands of Roosevelt press on the working class, smashing at every element of militancy in the movement, driving the masses into war. Grant had seen the deep injustices committed against his union by Governor Stassen. He had observed the jackal role played by Tobin, betraying the workers as he always has. . . . He saw the Roosevelt administration lashing out against the union that Grant belonged to and against the party, the Socialist Workers Party, that Grant belonged to. . . .

"As Grant saw the approach of America's entrance into the bloody struggle for markets, colonies and profits, he looked upon his three sons of military age. He thought of the suffering this war might bring to them, as the earlier war had brought to him. . . . These sad burdens aggravated the wounds inflicted upon him in mind and body at the Argonne. All of this was more than he could bear."

Three weeks after the funeral the remaining defendants in the federal case—our numbers now reduced to twenty-eight by a tragic death—went on trial in a Minneapolis courtroom.

Grant Dunne

James P. Cannon   Albert Goldman

Henry Schweinhaut   Matthew M. Joyce

George Novack (left), Warren K. Billings

Roger Baldwin

W. E. B. Du Bois

A. J. Muste

ANATOMY OF A FRAME-UP

12. "Sedition" Indictment

The federal indictment brought against us the previous July contained two counts. The first of these was based on an 1861 statute that had been directed at the armed counterrevolution then being conducted by the Southern slaveholders. This particular measure had never been invoked against the slavocracy. It was now being used for the first time—eighty years later—to frame up socialist and trade union militants! If convicted under that law, we faced penalties of up to six years imprisonment, or a $5,000 fine, or both.

Count one of the indictment charged that "from and before the 16th day of July, 1938," the defendants "did unlawfully, wilfully, knowingly and feloniously conspire . . . to overthrow, put down, and to destroy by force the Government of the United States of America, and to oppose by force the authority thereof. . . .

"The defendants would seek to bring about, whenever the time seemed propitious, an armed revolution. . . .

"Said armed revolution would be brought about and joined in by the workers and laborers and farmers. . . .

"Said workers, laborers and farmers would be . . . persuaded that the Government of the United States was imperialistic, capitalistic and organized and constituted for the purpose of subjecting workers and laborers to various and sundry deprivations and for the purpose of denying to them an alleged right to own, control and manage all property and industry in the United States. . . .

"Members of the Socialist Workers Party would be placed in key positions in all major industries . . . so that said party members could and would induce, persuade and procure the workers and laborers in said industries to join said party, embrace its principles and objectives and obey the commands of its leaders. . . .

"Members of the Socialist Workers Party would be placed in key positions in all trade unions . . . thus enabling the defendants and their co-conspirators to bring about a complete stoppage of work in the major industries . . . and preventing thereby the duly constituted Government of the United States from adequately defending itself against the armed revolution. . . .

"The defendants and their co-conspirators would endeavor by any means at their disposal to procure members of the military and naval forces of the United States to become undisciplined, to complain about food, living conditions, and missions to which they would be assigned, to create dissension, dissatisfaction and insubordination among the armed forces, to impair the loyalty and morale thereof, and finally to seek to gain control of said naval and military forces so that the enlisted personnel thereof would revolt against its officers. . . .

"When the Selective Service Act was passed, the members of said Socialist Workers Party would be urged to willingly accept service . . . and when the appropriate time came to turn their weapons against their officers.

"The defendants . . . would advise, counsel, and encourage the said workers and laborers to arm themselves and to become proficient and trained in the use thereof. . . .

"Workers and laborers would be, and they were, organized into military units which would be armed and drilled and taught how skillfully to use pistols and rifles, which said units would be, and were, called 'Union Defense Guard'; said units would ostensibly be used for protection against violent attempts to destroy trade unions, but were in truth and in fact, designed and intended to be used ultimately to overthrow . . . the duly constituted, Constitutional Government. . . .

"The said defendants and their co-conspirators would, and they did . . . procure certain explosives, firearms, ammunition, weapons and military equipment, for the aforesaid purpose.

"The said defendants and their co-conspirators would, and they did, accept as the ideal formula for the carrying out of their said objectives the Russian Revolution of 1917 . . . and the principles, teachings, counsel and advice of the leaders of that revolution; chiefly V. I. Lenin and Leon Trotsky would be, and they were, looked to, relied on, followed and held out to others as catechisms and textbooks directing the manner and means by which the aforesaid aim of the defendants could, and would be, accomplished; and accordingly, certain of the defendants would, and they did, go . . . to Mexico City, Mexico, there to advise with and to receive the advice, counsel, guidance, and directions of the said Leon Trotsky.

"The said defendants and their co-conspirators would, and they did, endeavor to procure and persuade as many other persons as possible to join with them in their undertaking by printing, publishing, selling, distributing and publicly displaying . . . written and printed matter . . . which advocated, advised and taught the duty, necessity, desirability, and propriety of overthrowing and destroying by force and violence all governments in the world said by the defendants, their mentors and leaders, to be imperialistic and capitalistic, and of the governments so characterized, the Government of the United States of America was said to be the foremost."

Count two of the indictment invoked the Smith Act, an outright thought-control measure adopted in 1940. In this instance, too, we were the first ones brought to trial under that particular law. It carried penalties of up to ten years' imprisonment, a fine of $10,000, or both.

This count alleged that "beginning the 28th day of June, 1940," the defendants "did unlawfully, wilfully, knowingly and feloniously conspire, plan, combine, confederate and agree together and with each other. . . .

"With the intent to interfere with, impair, and influence the loyalty, morale and discipline of the military and naval forces of the United States, [the defendants] would a) Advise, counsel, urge, and cause insubordination, disloyalty, mutiny, and refusal of duty. . . . b) Distribute written and printed matter which advised, counseled, and urged insubordination, disloyalty, mutiny and refusal of duty. . . .

"Knowingly and wilfully would, and they did, advocate, abet, advise and teach the duty, necessity, desirability and propriety of overthrowing and destroying the Government of the United States by force and violence, and

"With the intent to cause the overthrow and destruction of the Government of the United States, would, and they did, print, publish, edit, issue, circulate, sell, distribute and publicly display written and printed matter advocating, advising, and teaching the duty, necessity, desirability and propriety of overthrowing the

Government of the United States by force and violence, and

"Would, and they did, organize and help to organize societies, groups and assemblies of persons to teach, advocate and encourage the overthrow and destruction of the Government of the United States by force and violence, and

"Would be, and did, become members of and affiliated with such societies, groups and assemblies knowing the purpose thereof.

"And the Grand Jurors do present that the said defendants and co-conspirators would, and they did, attempt to carry out and accomplish said conspiracy in the manner set out . . . in the first count of this indictment."

As these vicious charges demonstrated, the federal government was bringing its full weight to bear against us, acting in concert with the IBT bureaucracy. One purpose was to use Minneapolis as the point of departure in a national campaign to wipe out any semblance of trade union democracy, so as to purge organized labor of rebel elements who opposed Roosevelt's war policy. A second aim, plainly enough, was to drive the Socialist Workers Party into illegality and, if possible, to crush it.

Reacting swiftly to this attack, the SWP intensified its public activities nationally. In defiance of the political cops, the party militantly asserted—and continued energetically to exercise—its constitutional right to carry on political and propagandistic work, including opposition to imperialist war.

A dramatic step of this kind was taken in Minneapolis soon after the federal assault started. Following the FBI raids George Novack spoke at a series of public forums held at the SWP headquarters in the city. The topics he discussed were most appropriate to the occasion: "The Revolutionary War of 1776," "The Second American Revolution," and "The Bill of Rights."

During the same period James P. Cannon issued a public declaration, speaking as national secretary of the SWP. As quoted in *The Militant* of July 26, 1941, he said: "Roosevelt's agents were not quite able to erase the tell-tale indications of the real motivation for this persecution. They give their game away in charge No. 4 of the indictment, which accuses us of urging, counseling and persuading workers and farmers 'that the Government of the United States was imperialistic. . . .'

"Roosevelt and his War Party understand very well that an honest workers' party like ours, with firm principles and cadres steeled and tempered in the class struggle, can tomorrow become the accepted spokesman for great masses in the struggle to put an end to the war. The Roosevelt War Party would destroy us before that tomorrow comes. . . .

"We are no pacifists. We shall not turn the other cheek to Roosevelt's attack on our party. On the contrary, we shall see to it that every worker and farmer in this country hears our true views and learns how Roosevelt has engineered this vile frameup against us. This case will be tried by the government in a courtroom in Minneapolis and we shall defend ourselves there. Far more important, however, we shall defend ourselves before our true judges—the workers and farmers of this country. It is their verdict, above all, that concerns us."

As Cannon's remarks implied, there were ample grounds to expect widespread protests against Roosevelt's witch-hunt attack on us. Evidence to that effect had begun to appear right after the FBI raids. The government's reactionary course was denounced in a statement issued on July 28, 1941, by Labor's Non-Partisan League. Speaking as the national political arm of the CIO, the LNPL said:

"Witch-hunting tactics of the Department of Justice under A. Mitchell Palmer in World War I are being revived here as history repeats itself in World War II.

"The Palmer period in the Justice Department has long been recognized by all Americans with any respect for human freedom as one of the blackest in our Government's history, yet one of the key figures of that time is still functioning in a high Justice Department post. He is J. Edgar Hoover, now chief of the FBI.

"It was Hoover who was behind the recent Administration move to jam wire-tapping legislation through Congress, which was defeated only after the CIO became active against it. In the postwar era, Hoover's bureau stooped to searching private Senatorial mail and even tried to frame a U.S. Senator on trumped up charges.

"Today, Justice Department activities again are a menace to fundamental civil liberties and to labor's basic rights. The pattern of activity is the same as in Palmer's day, and J. Edgar Hoover has forgotten none of it.

"In Saint Paul a few days ago a large number of CIO members of Minneapolis were indicted for holding allegedly subversive opinions. The indictment went back to 1938 in strained efforts to find some incident on which to base its action. Not what these

men did, but what they thought, formed the real crime against
them. . . .

"If the Minneapolis teamsters can be jailed for their opinions,
so can anybody. That is why the case is of national importance to
civil liberties."

The American Civil Liberties Union, meantime, had telegraphed a protest to Attorney General Biddle, terming the
implications of the FBI raid "obviously dangerous to the
preservation of democracy." After the indictment was issued, the
ACLU offered its services to the defendants for the announced
purpose of challenging the constitutionality of the Smith Act. A
bit later Vincent Johnson, an attorney representing the ACLU in
Minneapolis, was assigned to cooperate with counsel for the
defense.

Another criticism of the government's action came from I. F.
Stone, a noted journalist, who took up the Minneapolis case in
The Nation of July 26, 1941. Stone wrote concerning the
indictment: "For the first time in peace since the Alien and
Sedition Laws of John Adams a mere expression of opinion is
made a federal crime."

Dissent was likewise voiced by two papers circulated in the
Black communities of the Twin Cities. On August 1, 1941,
companion editorials were printed in the *Minneapolis Spokesman*
and the *Saint Paul Recorder*, asserting: "We are not familiar with
the merits of the case of the government against the Socialist
Workers Party, but we do know that many of its leaders have
repeatedly attacked the enemies of the colored people in this area.

"With the developments in this case and the all-out labor war
between factions occurring so rapidly the general public has not
had an opportunity to get at the real basis for the indictments
voted by the Federal grand jury. . . .

"We cannot, however, deny that members of the S.W.P. and its
leadership or at least many of them named in the indictments
have fought anti-Negro programs and racial bigotry wherever
they found it. That's enough for us to hope the charges upon
which they have been indicted are proven false and that they will
be acquitted."

Although these initial manifestations of support were most
encouraging, a problem still confronted us in promoting the
protest movement to the full. In opposing the Justice Department's action, liberals—such as the ACLU leaders—were expressing progressive sentiments in favor of strict adherence to the Bill

of Rights. But they remained badly confused about the government's real motives in bringing us to trial on witch-hunt charges.

The liberals tended to view the development as rooted in nothing more than a clash between Local 544 and Tobin over matters of internal union politics. Roosevelt, they assumed, had no direct stake in the dispute, and had simply come to Tobin's aid as a political favor to a loyal supporter. In doing that, they felt, the president had made a mistake; he had wrongly involved the government in a matter toward which it should have been neutral. So the liberals hoped to pressure the Justice Department into nullifying the indictment, and they felt confident that their admired Roosevelt would not let the case go to trial.

Such assumptions were, of course, false to the core, and they proved detrimental to the organization of our defense. Predictions that the demagogue in the White House would rectify his "mistake" added to our difficulties in making potential supporters aware that the government would try its best to convict us. Therefore, it was imperative that prompt steps be taken to build an organized defense movement on the widest possible scale.

In that way a systematic propaganda offensive could be conducted to show that the persecution of the Trotskyists was not an aberration, that it was rooted in the Roosevelt administration's determination to gag opponents of its war policy, and that the underlying reason for the indictment was concealed because of widespread antiwar sentiment. To deceive people a fake charge of "conspiracy to overthrow the government" had been substituted. As the renowned lawyer Clarence Darrow once observed, "conspiracy" is an idea invented by a reactionary government to rid itself of its critics.

Systematic efforts had to be conducted through a well-organized defense movement in order to oppose the formidable united front mobilized against us. We were under attack from governmental agencies at the federal, state, and local levels. The Minneapolis employers and the kept press of the capitalist class were up to their ears in the plot. Tobin, his hoodlums, and the top AFL bureaucrats were parties to the assault. And, like curs yapping at our heels, the Stalinists had joined in the campaign to smear us publicly.

With such powerful, determined, and vicious forces arrayed against us, we had to move quickly in launching a broad defense formation. So Felix Morrow, a crack journalist, was rushed to Minneapolis from the party center to help edit the 544-CIO paper, a task with which he was familiar because he had played a similar role after Pat Corcoran was murdered in 1937. That, in turn, freed George Novack, who had been assisting on the union paper, for other activities. Novack was then assigned the central role in building a broad structure which became known as the Civil Rights Defense Committee. He had outstanding talent for such work and was already experienced at it. For an extended period thereafter he served as national executive secretary of the CRDC.

We carefully adhered to a principled approach in launching the defense committee. The SWP sought no artificial partisan advantage from its central role as the victim in the federal case. We insisted, though, on the defendants' right to determine how they would conduct themselves in court, and we resisted attempts to turn the broad committee into an area for conflict over that or any other political issue.

Our purpose was to create a working body with distinct, limited functions. Its proper activities were to publicize the issues in our legal case, mobilize the widest possible support for us on civil liberties grounds, launch a protest campaign against the government's assault on our constitutional rights, and raise funds for defense needs. All who were ready to participate in good faith along those lines were welcomed into the CRDC. Nobody was excluded for factional reasons.

As subsequent developments showed, a united effort of that nature was the best vehicle through which to dramatize the fundamental connection between the actual threat to the rights of the Socialist Workers Party and the implied danger to the rights of all others who were in any way critical of the capitalist order or concerned with protecting constitutional freedoms. A sense of common need was thus generated in the face of a common peril.

Due to realities within the trade unions and within other working-class parties, it was necessary to rely on help from prominent individuals in launching the defense movement. An appeal was made accordingly, and among the first to respond was James T. Farrell, a well-known author. He accepted the chairmanship of the Civil Rights Defense Committee, issuing a statement in that capacity in which he declared:

"This case is the most important involving civil liberties since the trials of the I.W.W. members during the First World War. . . . Unless this attack on our basic rights is checked, it will establish a precedent for subsequent ones. This is precisely the way in which liberty dies. Inch by inch it is eaten away. One precedent after another is established. Repressive and reactionary tendencies are built up until they can, in time, resemble a tidal wave. . . . And we remain free men by defending the liberty of others, as well as of ourselves, whether or not we agree with them."

Two other outstanding individuals came forward to serve as vice-chairmen of the Civil Rights Defense Committee: John Dos Passos, of literary fame, and Carlo Tresca, a prominent labor figure and anarchist leader who edited *Il Martello*, an Italian-language working-class paper.

Step by step, an increasingly broad national committee was formed by the CRDC. It consisted of persons who played leading roles in the trade union and farm movements, educators, radical political leaders, editors, fighters for women's rights, novelists, Black leaders, lawyers, poets, newspaper columnists, and, of special historic import, Warren K. Billings, who had served a long sentence in San Quentin prison along with Tom Mooney as a victim of the San Francisco frame-up during World War I.

A national office was set up by the CRDC in New York under the supervision of Evelyn Reed. Formation of local units was started wherever possible, in cities from coast to coast, and the process was helped along by a national tour by George Novack. As a further aid to the defense campaign, a pamphlet entitled *Witch Hunt in Minnesota* was published by the committee. It set forth the main facts and important issues in the case.

When the trial got under way later on, the myth that Roosevelt would call the whole thing off was definitively exploded, and the nation became witness to an undisguised attack on our ideas by the prosecutors. At that point a new wave of protests appeared. Among them was one from the Workers Defense League, a formation sponsored by the Socialist Party. It said in part: "The Workers Defense League considers the present Federal prosecution of Minneapolis teamsters and others to be unreasonable and unjustified. . . . people's freedom to organize is in serious danger if such actions can be distorted into a conspiracy to overthrow the government."

A statement denouncing the prosecution and supporting the defendants was issued about the same time by the Union for Democratic Action. Its principal officers were Dr. Reinhold Niebuhr, of the Union Theological Seminary, and Freda Kirchwey, editor of *The Nation*. As described in its own words, the

Union was "an organization of American liberals whose definite interventionism is in sharp disagreement with the international and domestic policies advocated by the defendants in the Minneapolis trial." The Union had been formed, the statement declared, "with the purpose of combatting any anti-democratic tendency that may arise in this period of national emergency. The present prosecution of twenty-eight alleged members of the Socialist Workers Party in Minneapolis is undoubtedly evidence of such an anti-democratic tendency. . . ."

Endorsement of our defense campaign was also announced by the General Defense Committee of the Industrial Workers of the World, which said: "The indictments are in reality an attack on the right of working men and women to organize. If the state can indict and convict these men and women and establish such a precedent, labor's rights will be seriously endangered."

By that time the CRDC was distributing a new piece of literature, "Workers on Trial," which gave short biographical sketches of the twenty-eight defendants. This step helped, especially, to win expressions of support and financial contributions for our defense from within the labor movement nationally. As yet, though, such responses of an official nature came mostly from local unions. Backing from within higher labor circles was still confined primarily to union officers speaking as individuals.

Even before the defense campaign reached this level, it is important to note, the Roosevelt administration had already become worried about the scope of the protest movement. So it had undertaken to hoodwink critics of the indictment, using devious methods of the kind reflected in an earlier exchange between the American Civil Liberties Union and Attorney General Biddle.

On August 20, 1941, the ACLU had addressed itself to Biddle in a letter signed by John Haynes Holmes, Arthur Garfield Hays, and Roger Baldwin, all nationally prominent figures. They stated: "The American Civil Liberties Union has examined the character of the evidence on which the indictment rests and has come to these conclusions:

"1. That the charges clearly raise issues of civil liberties in attacking utterances or publications in the absence of any overt acts or even of any 'clear and present dangers' with the sole exception of the charge concerning the organization of the workers defense corps.

"2. That the facts in regard to the workers defense corps show that there was no intent of the Teamsters Union, which was admittedly under the leadership of members of the Socialist Workers Party, to do more than protect union property against threats of vigilante violence. Its activities were entirely public and covered only a few months when apprehension of attack was acute.

"3. That the indictments rest upon two new statutes not previously applied, both of them having been incorporated in the Alien Registration Act of 1940—one of them penalizing advocacy of the overthrow of the government by force, and the other incitement of disaffection in the armed forces. In our judgment both statutes violate the First Amendment of the Constitution; and even if upheld could not be applied to this set of facts under the 'clear and present danger' rule.

"In the light of those considerations it is obviously mandatory on the Civil Liberties Union to engage in the defense with a view to testing in the Supreme Court, if necessary, the constitutionality of the laws and their application to this set of facts."

In his reply of September 4, Biddle told the ACLU: "You state from your examination of the 'character of the evidence on which the indictment rests' that the charges attack utterances or publications, and include only one overt act—the organization of the workers in a defense corps. This overt act, however—arming workers to carry out the purposes to which the utterances are addressed—is clearly sufficient to remove the case from one involving expression of opinion, even if the utterances went no further than that, which they do. You suggest that the facts show the intent was merely to protect union property against threats of violence. But the indictment specifically alleges otherwise, and I am confident that it will be supported in the evidence."

This effort to justify the indictment marked a switch from the line Biddle had taken at the time of the FBI raids upon the SWP. He had been quoted in the *Minneapolis Star Journal* of June 28, 1941, as stating that the principal basis for the accusations against us "is found in the Declaration of Principles adopted by the Socialist Workers Party at its foundation convention, held in January, 1938."

Concerning the government's charges at that time, the *Star Journal* reported that Biddle had stressed a passage in the party's Declaration of Principles, which read: "If, in spite of the efforts of the revolutionists and the militant workers, the United States government enters a new war, the SWP will not, under any circumstances, support the war but will, on the contrary, fight against it."

When a mounting wave of protests followed that flag-waving pitch, the attorney general felt he had blundered in shaping his initial propaganda course. He had underestimated the scope of antiwar sentiment in the country, and he had failed to reckon with the popular belief that those who opposed the war had the democratic right to express their views. So Biddle had to make a turn in his propaganda line—from emphasis on charges of "advocacy" to allegations about an "overt act." To make the switch he falsely represented creation of Local 544's defense guard as "arming workers to carry out the purposes to which the utterances [of the SWP] are addressed."

But the ACLU did not fall for the new ploy. Instead, its opposition to the indictment was stepped up through publication of a pamphlet entitled "Sedition." One passage in that publication asserted:

"The case raises the issue as to whether a union defense corps formed to protect union property against threats of violence can be construed to be part of a conspiracy of a political party to capture the labor movement and use it for the overthrow of the government and the establishment of a workers' government. Every attempt obviously will be made to read that purpose into the one overt act charged. . . .

"The Civil Rights Defense Committee has been created to raise funds for the twenty-eight defendants under indictment. . . . Their appeal for funds has been endorsed by the American Civil Liberties Union, which has participated in the preliminary hearings and will participate in the case at all possible points."

The union defense guard had been organized in 1938 because a fascist-type organization called the Silver Shirts was threatening an armed raid on Local 544's headquarters. Being aware of the lessons taught by previous class struggles, the leadership understood that the union could not rely for protection of its rights upon the capitalist government or its local agencies. So the guard was formed in self-defense, openly and with maximum publicity of the action. In the showdown that followed, its very presence proved sufficent to ward off the threat. Then, after a time, the Silver Shirt movement faded away in Minneapolis, and the guard—which maintained formal existence against future threats of that kind—was used only for things like the monitoring of large social functions.

Despite those facts, charges of the kind now stressed by Biddle were not new. Similar allegations had been made in the fink suit filed against Local 544's executive board back in 1938. The finks' lawyer had accused the union officers of organizing a "standing army," using the "pretext" of being threatened by the Silver Shirts.

After prolonged litigation of the suit in the local courts, a decision was rendered in the fall of 1940 by Judge Paul S. Carroll, who ruled that the union had carried out a legitimate act of self-defense. His findings stated:

"On or about September, 1938, a so-called 'defense guard' was organized. This consisted of certain members of the union being organized into various divisions headed by captains. According to the union's position, these so-called 'defense guards' were organized 'to meet the threat of Silver Shirt leaders and other anti-labor gangsters.' . . . It was not shown that these men were ever armed or did other than general policing at picnics and things of that sort. Upon the record presented to the Court, the so-called 'defense guard' is not shown to have amounted to anything of a serious nature."

Since the FBI had been keeping Local 544 under close surveillance, the Justice Department unquestionably had extensive information about the defense guard from the beginning. It was no doubt equally aware of the Silver Shirt activities. Hence, the political cops knew that the sole purpose of the guard was to defend the union, and that its entire "weaponry" consisted of two .22-caliber pistols and two .22-caliber rifles used for target practice.

That explains why the Roosevelt administration said nothing on the subject until it came to Tobin's aid in 1941—three years after the union guard was formed. The facts were then turned upside down and inside out, so as to bring false charges against us, when the real motive for the federal attack was our opposition to the war. We were accused of forming the guard, not for the union's self-defense, but for ultimate use to overthrow the government. As "evidence" of such intent, according to the *New York Times* of October 9, 1941, Biddle made the grotesque charge that: "Defendants in this case went armed, and signs were shown reading 'Labor should be armed against the coming day.' "

At the same time, hints were leaked to the press that the FBI was scurrying around looking for "further information" about the alleged conspiratorial aspects of the 544 defense guard. The federal cops' quest, as will be seen later, centered on coaching prosecution witnesses supplied by the Committee of 99, so as to "establish the facts" through them.

In the foregoing setting, the Socialist Workers Party convened a plenum-conference in Chicago shortly before the trial began. Formally, it was a meeting of the party's national committee, which was constitutionally empowered to make the necessary decisions between national conventions of the organization. In this instance, though, the gathering was broadened by inviting party activists throughout the country to participate on a consultative basis. That procedure made it possible to hold a widely representative session to consider the problems thrust upon us by the federal attack.

Among the matters taken up by those in attendance was the SWP's Declaration of Principles, adopted in 1938. In that document the party had proclaimed its intention of maintaining affiliation with the Trotskyist world movement. But continued ties with the Fourth International had been made impossible by passage of the Voorhis Act in 1940. So, in December of that year, a special convention of the SWP had voted to disaffiliate from the world body. In keeping with that decision, the Declaration of Principles had been revoked at the same time, and the party's national committee had been instructed to draft revised programmatic expressions in one or another form.

Even though reactionary legislation had forced the SWP to sever its international affiliation, drafts of policy statements prepared thereafter continued to affirm its adherence to the principles of internationalism, its solidarity with the workers of the world, and its defense of the Soviet Union against imperialist attack. In addition, documents prepared in lieu of the rescinded 1938 declaration were brought up to date in the light of new events and of new policy decisions made by the party. Included in the latter category were concurrence with the Fourth International's transitional program for the working class and its allies, advocacy of the formation of a labor party in the United States, projection of a proletarian military policy, and an outline of tasks facing revolutionaries in wartime. Decisions needed to help along this general policy-shaping process were made at the Chicago gathering.

The delegates also pledged the SWP to fight for every bit of democracy attainable under capitalist rule. This was done not only because we appreciated the value of civil liberties in themselves, but also because democratic procedures offered the best opportunities to educate and organize the masses for a transition from capitalism to socialism. For those reasons, the plenum-conference declared, the party would resist every attempt to force it into illegality. Far from going underground due to reactionary pressures, we would struggle with all our energy for our right to maintain public existence.

In addition, a line was laid down for conduct of the defense in court. There would be no watering down of our revolutionary views or evasion of our policies. These would be defended militantly; we would insist upon our freedom under the Bill of Rights to propagate our principles. In a step toward those ends, the witness stand would be used as a tribunal from which to address the working people of the nation.

An understanding was reached, as well, that on-the-spot decisions required during the trial would be made by a majority of those directly involved.

13. Prosecutor's Tricks

Trial of the twenty-eight began on October 27, 1941, before Judge Matthew M. Joyce. We knew from the outset what to expect from this particular judge, since he had also presided over the railroading to prison of WPA strikers in 1939.

U.S. District Attorney Anderson's role as one of the prosecutors was equally predictable. He was an aggressive and unbridled reactionary, whom militants of Local 544's Federal Workers Section had faced before in the WPA trials. Anderson was belligerently ignorant about the fundamentals of working-class politics, and he was certain to focus on appeals to bigotry and prejudice in efforts to turn the jurors against us.

Assistant Attorney General Schweinhaut, the main prosecutor, proved to be a somewhat slicker article. It quickly became clear that Biddle had assigned him the task of giving the government's case a pseudosophisticated political aura for the purpose of confounding those who were protesting against the frame-up. Schweinhaut undertook, accordingly, to twist and distort our views so as to make them appear to have the opposite of their real meaning. As "evidence" for that purpose, he had stacks of books, pamphlets, and newspapers before him at the prosecution table. He also kept FBI agents hanging around in the courtroom and in the adjacent corridor, eavesdropping for snatches of conversation that might be turned to the government's advantage.

The immediate targets of this attack—an exceptionally large group of twenty-eight defendants—were allotted the barest minimum of space in the small courtroom used for the trial. Jammed together like cattle in a slaughterhouse pen, these principled fighters for working-class rights had to listen with burning indignation while the prosecutors described them as sneaky characters engaged in a sinister plot to grab state power by force and violence.

Outside the courtroom, however, the defendants received constant inspiration, which helped them to maintain high morale throughout the trial. Arrangements were made to serve hot meals twice daily for the entire group at the SWP's local headquarters. Cooking duties were performed by comrades not directly involved in the case, and people throughout the state who sympathized with us sent food and financial donations for the commissary. Concrete aid came in another form as well. Among the few spectators able to get into the crowded courtroom were trade unionists who dropped by to show their support of our cause. They would listen to the proceedings for a time, and when a recess was called, one or another of them would press a few dollars into a defendant's hand to help meet trial expenses.

Gathering together for meals twice daily did more than hold down eating costs. These regular sessions had the quality of continuing acts of solidarity, which buoyed our spirits; and at the same time a useful vehicle was provided for the collective shaping of defense policy on a day-to-day basis.

For the latter purpose a steering committee was selected. It consisted of three national officers of the SWP who were among those on trial—James P. Cannon, Albert Goldman, and myself. Our functions were to guide the overall handling of the defense, acting in consultation with the rest of the twenty-eight, and to make quick decisions required while in court. Implementation of our policy course during the actual legal proceedings was then guided by Goldman, who was both a defendant and chief counsel for the defense. He was a skilled trial lawyer with a wide range of experience, which included serving as Trotsky's legal agent from 1937 to the time of his assassination in 1940.

M. J. Myer, an able Chicago lawyer who then shared our political beliefs, acted as Goldman's main assistant. Our legal team was rounded out by Arthur LeSeuer, a Minneapolis attorney with a liberal reputation. In addition, Gilbert Carlson and D. J. Shama of 544-CIO's legal staff helped the defense informally in all possible ways.

One defendant, Nick Wagner, elected to have his own individual counsel—he was represented by Samuel Dolf, a local attorney. There were valid reasons for that exceptional situation.

Wagner, a former organizer for the IBT in Chicago, had been sent to Minneapolis by Tobin as part of the strong-arm force used against the General Drivers back in 1936. After that attack was halted, Wagner was included in the reorganized leadership of newly chartered Local 544. From then on he functioned loyally as a member of the local's executive board; despite his limited political education, Nick identified himself completely with our class-struggle policies at the trade union level, sensing their intrinsic worth. That, in turn, caused the Committee of 99 to finger him to the FBI, and he wound up as one of those indicted for "sedition."

Under the given circumstances, it was advisable for Wagner to have his own lawyer because it helped to demonstrate that he was not an active member of the Socialist Workers Party. So he took that course with our agreement, being careful at the same time to make certain that Dolf did nothing likely to cause the other defendants problems.

Since both national and international interest had been aroused by the indictment, there was extensive press coverage at the start of the trial. Besides the local dailies, newspapers in other cities and the main wire services sent reporters to cover the affair. After the government had finished its presentation, however, the boss press cut down on its attention to the proceedings, and little was reported about our rebuttal of the charges against us.

Fortunately, though, we were not wholly dependent upon the capitalist news media for publicity about our side of the case. *The Militant* was expanded in size in order to provide extensive weekly coverage of the trial for its readers nationally. Local 554-CIO's *Industrial Organizer* played a similar role in getting the facts to workers in the Midwest, a service so widely appreciated that the union paper's circulation grew. In addition, the Civil Rights Defense Committee sent issues of its *Information Bulletin* regularly to labor and liberal organizations throughout the country.

Locally, still another type of communication was developed. Public forums were held at the SWP's headquarters, where political activities continued in the usual manner. These forums, which were well attended, focused on discussion of issues raised in the trial. Considerable literature on such questions was sold to the participants, and sales of this kind were further enhanced when people dropped by the headquarters at other times to ask about publications that had been mentioned in the courtroom.

Several questions of major importance had already been raised in pretrial legal proceedings. The defense had submitted a motion calling for application of the judicial doctrine that the government must show a "clear and present danger" to its continued existence in order to prosecute the defendants on the charges made in the indictment. Joyce flatly denied the motion.

Our lawyers then demanded to know whether we were accused of actually preparing to overthrow the government, or if the charge was one of advocating such action. As matters stood, they argued, the language of the indictment was vague and indefinite. There was a complete lack of any factual evidence as to the nature of the alleged conspiracy and as to the means by which it was to be carried out. A question existed, therefore, whether we were being prosecuted for a criminal offense or persecuted for our ideas.

Anderson said in reply, "The Government will bring out in the trial all the facts which are necessary to prove that a seditious conspiracy existed." And the judge upheld his contention.

At that point the defense called upon the government to provide a bill of particulars regarding the alleged facts of which Anderson spoke, so that a proper opportunity could be afforded us for preparation of a reply to the allegations. As the indictment stood, our legal staff and Dolf joined in arguing, it contained nothing but the conclusions of the prosecutors. There were no details about steps through which the "overthrow of the government" was to be brought about. Moreover, there was no record in the indictment of the roles allegedly played by individual defendants. Blanket charges were made against all persons named; and if the defendants were not apprised individually of the specific accusations against each of them, to put them on trial would be a violation of their constitutional rights.

Schweinhaut handled the rebuttal on this issue. "When a conspiracy is the gist of the crime," he argued, "it is not necessary for the government to allege with great particularity the details of the crime. . . . A bill of particulars would unnecessarily confine the government and limit its testimony." In routine fashion, Joyce ruled in Schweinhaut's favor, and we were unable to obtain advance information about specific charges against us.

At the very least, our lawyers next argued, each defendant should be tried separately, in keeping with the constitutional rights involved. If all the accused were tried together, evidence introduced against one would not necessarily pertain to others. Yet the jury would be unable to relate each piece of evidence solely to the particular defendant involved. A cumulative impression would thus be created in the jurors' minds that every act charged applied to the entire twenty-eight, and they would thereby be denied a fair trial.

Anderson opposed individual trials, stating curtly: "Evidence against one is evidence against all inasmuch as all took part in the conspiracy." As usual, the judge agreed with him, ruling that the defense should not make "too rigid demands" upon the prosecution.

With the legal dice thus loaded against us, the prosecutors proceeded to rig the jury. On the first day of the trial a big panel of prospective jurors—already screened to make sure none were connected with the labor movement—was herded into the courtroom. Our lawyers immediately called for a list of the panel, so that a quick check could be made to peg those most likely to be biased against the defendants. Access to the list was refused, however, and the defense was granted nothing more than the exercise of ten peremptory challenges to eliminate the most unwanted jurors. After those challenges were used, the judge arbitrarily decided who would be chosen to serve.

Of the twelve finally selected, eleven were men and one a woman. Most had middle-class backgrounds. Listed by occupation, the jury consisted of a bank executive, the owner of a grain elevator chain, a lumber company sales manager, the owner of a rural newspaper, a cook for a backwoods jail, a small-town plumber, a hardware clerk, an owner of a general store, a general store clerk, a farmer, a farm laborer, and a garage owner.

Most of the jurors came from rural districts. Although Minneapolis—where the trial took place—was one of the best organized cities in the country, there was not a single trade unionist among them. Nor was there a single Farmer-Laborite; all supported either the Republicans or the Democrats.

Theoretically, these twelve people were to sit in judgment over defendants accused of crimes against the government. Actually, though, they were being called upon to make a sweeping decision—thumbs up or thumbs down, like spectators at a Roman circus—concerning the exercise of working-class rights in capitalist society. Fundamental guarantees set forth in the Bill of Rights were at stake—freedom of thought, freedom of speech, freedom of the press, and freedom of assembly. Hence the jurors bore a grave social responsibility in reaching a verdict, and they deserved honesty from the federal authorities concerning every aspect of the case.

But when Anderson made the opening statement for the government, he sought to conceal—not reveal—the true nature of the trial. Instead of explaining our constitutional right to think for ourselves and to say what we thought, he told the jurors: "The very program of the Socialist Workers Party is a violation of the statutes. . . . It is the position of the government in this case that proof of overt acts is not required and that the conspiracy in itself is unlawful." As those remarks showed, Biddle's earlier attempt to hide the true nature of the indictment with talk about "overt acts" was now thrust aside. The jury was urged to convict us because of our socialist philosophy and principles.

Anderson charged that we espoused the revolutionary doctrines of Marx and of "a more recent writer by the name of Engels." Lenin's teachings were also embraced by us, he added, as were those of Trotsky. Hence, our purpose was to "further the international revolution against organized society." Toward that end we called for defense of the Soviet Union against imperialist attack. In doing so, moreover, we claimed that the U.S. government was imperialistic, which he construed to mean that we were against our own country.

Special emphasis was placed on our relations with Trotsky. Government witnesses would testify, the U.S. district attorney stressed, that some of the defendants went to Mexico City "to get his [Trotsky's] advice and counsel"; and the SWP's program could, therefore, be summed up as "doing in America what was done by Lenin and Trotsky in Russia in October 1917."

To achieve our "subversive" ends, he contended, the SWP carried on organized propaganda of its ideas. Meetings were held to draw in innocents; literature was published for the same purpose; and, of equally sinister import, party members were instructed to be active in the trade unions. By means of the latter policy, he alleged, Local 544 had been brought completely under the party's domination, and an antiwar platform had been promulgated through the local "to hinder and delay the processes" of military conscription.

Anderson denounced the SWP's advocacy of military training under trade union control, and our insistence that it was labor's duty to defend the democratic rights of soldiers and to fight for improved conditions in the armed forces. He charged that our real object was to turn the soldiers against their officers in order to advance "seditious" aims, and that specific evidence of such intentions was revealed in connection with Local 544's defense guard, which had been set up for the "sole purpose of creating an armed force" to be used against the government.

In equally vituperative fashion he assailed us for carrying out class struggle policies in the trade unions. We were accused of fomenting strikes around unreasonable demands for "more and more" from employers and of refusing, no matter what the circumstances, to arbitrate any issue in dispute. Trotskyists, the prosecutor claimed, "always agitate and demand, to cause a condition of unrest in order that there might be a break between the employing class and the employed."

When Anderson had finished his diatribe, we were allowed to make a preliminary statement of our defense against the government's charges. If the jurors were to listen to us with an open mind, we reasoned, they had to be shown that the term *revolution* was a scientific political characterization of fundamental change in the social structure, not a description of wild-eyed bomb throwers. They needed to understand what we really stood for and why. Above all, it was imperative to make them aware of the vital constitutional rights involved in the case. This, of course, was easier said than done; but Goldman, who made our opening presentation, gave it a good try.

"It is a peculiar kind of criminals you have," he told the jury, "who insist upon their right to do what they are doing and to say what they are saying."

The truth was, Goldman emphasized, that this was not an ordinary criminal case. We faced charges under an indictment that had originated in Washington. A political movement had been put on trial because it opposed the war policies of the Roosevelt administration. To conceal that fact, charges of conspiring against the government were falsely introduced, when in reality the whole business was a political prosecution from start to finish.

"The Socialist Workers Party," he said, "is a political movement based on certain ideas which you [the jurors] may not agree with, but it is not a conspiracy. . . . Far from denying the revolutionary nature of our views, we are going to explain those views to you and our right to propagate those views under the Bill of Rights. . . . The party's aim is to win a majority of the people for its ideas through education and propaganda."

Goldman then touched upon specific positions held by the SWP which were to be explained more fully during the defense testimony. These included: why we were internationalists and why that was not a crime; the reasons for our opposition to imperialist war and our right to express these views; the nature of the fascist threat to the working class; why Local 544's defense guard was formed; and the facts about its one and only function, which was to exercise the union's right of self-defense.

Concerning the government's charge that we "fomented strikes," the real situation, he explained, was that a constant struggle went on between workers and capitalists. We didn't need to advocate such a conflict; it was a fact of life. No less false, he added, was the allegation that the defendants imposed their control upon trade unions. They did nothing more than attempt to carry out whatever responsibilities the workers entrusted to them, and in Local 544 under their leadership the best kind of democracy had prevailed.

Turning to our advocacy of a fundamental change in the social order, Goldman pointed out that we preferred a peaceful transition from capitalism to socialism. History had shown, though, that capitalist minorities abroad had resorted to force in an effort to retain power and protect their special privileges. For that historic reason we warned the workers that a similar course would most likely be taken by the capitalists in this country, when a majority decided a change was needed in the social system. It was this prediction of probable resort to force by the present ruling class in the United States—against a future socialist majority—that the prosecution was trying to twist into "proof" that we advocated force and violence against the capitalist government.

After Goldman had completed his statement, detailed presentation of the government's case began. At the outset the prosecutors submitted an inventory of items seized the previous June when the FBI raided the SWP headquarters in Minneapolis and Saint Paul. These items were tabulated in the form of court exhibits to be used as "evidence" against us.

Among the exhibits were a photograph of Leon Trotsky autographed to V. R. Dunne; an armband, a lapel button, and a membership card issued by Local 544's defense guard; and a red banner with white letters reading "Socialist Workers Party." In addition, there were 110 different items of literature. This printed material, which had been taken in varying quantities per item, added up to a total of 2,442 pieces.

Several Marxist classics had been grabbed by the political cops. One of these was the *Communist Manifesto,* written nearly one hundred years earlier by Marx and Engels. Other items in this category were mainly works by Lenin and Trotsky.

Also presented as government exhibits were various pieces of literature published by, or on behalf of, the Socialist Workers Party. Included among them were numerous issues of *The Militant* and the *Socialist Appeal,* copies of the theoretical magazines *New International* and *Fourth International,* leaflets printed for mass distribution, educational brochures, and mimeographed bulletins used for purposes of internal party discussion.

The defense objected to introduction of works by Marx, Engels, Lenin, and Trotsky as "evidence." Fundamental principles embodied in the doctrines of those great teachers were accepted by the SWP, we pointed out, but it did not follow that the party considered every statement by the Marxist masters binding upon its membership. The judge said he would rule on questions of that nature as they arose during the testimony; and in the proceedings that followed he allowed some parts of such material to be used against us, while excluding other parts.

Concerning the prosecution's use of items published by or for the SWP, the defense made no formal objection. We did, however, try to limit the time span involved. The judge was asked to tell the jury that the Smith Act did not become law until June 29, 1940; therefore, items published before that date were not applicable to the defendants. Joyce refused to do so. He ruled that material published before passage of the Smith Act could be used as "indicative of the state of mind" of the defendants.

We also demanded that literary items used against us be introduced in their entirety, instead of tearing quotations out of their proper contexts, as was done in the government's exhibits. That practice, our lawyers argued, was followed for the deliberate purpose of distorting our views in order to falsely picture us as criminals. But the judge ruled in the government's favor on the point.

Objection was similarly made to the use of material written by persons other than the defendants, who in some instances were not even members of the SWP. During the argument over this matter Goldman said: "This is a peculiar kind of a conspiracy, your Honor. It is a conspiracy of ideas. . . ." Where that is the case, he went on, "the government ought to show that the writings and opinions and interpretations of a particular individual are in general agreement with the basic ideas of the party." Judge Joyce, however, didn't consider that necessary.

Another aspect of the government's exhibits was brought out in a clash over excerpts from an editorial entitled "Supreme Court Aftermath," which appeared in the *Socialist Appeal* of March 2, 1939. Goldman contended that the exhibit was clearly inadmissible. "You see, your Honor," he said, "you start with the premise that this is a conspiracy to overthrow the government by force and violence, and then everything that is said and done can be twisted to be part of the conspiracy. . . . I, as an individual, can go out and get a gun to go hunting, but as soon as I am a member of the Socialist Workers Party, if I get a gun, the government says ostensibly I got the gun to go hunting, but in reality I got the gun to overthrow the government by force and violence. We are in a vicious circle there."

In reply the judge cited the last part of the editorial, which read: "The united fighting of labor is so invincible that it can easily teach the courts and their capitalist masters a lesson that the latter will not quickly forget." Concerning that quotation Joyce remarked, ". . . may not this last paragraph, under the charge laid in the indictment with reference to the exercise of force and violence, have relevancy and bearing, even under your conception of the law?"

On occasion the jerking of quotations from their contexts was given an added twist: failure to give the actual source. To cite an instance, one of the government's exhibits was an excerpt from the *Socialist Appeal* of April 4, 1939. When Anderson began reading it to the jury, Goldman interrupted him.

"Pardon me," he said, "I think counsel should inform the jury when he is reading a quotation. . . . This happens to be an editorial by Lenin, in a magazine, I think."

"No, I do not see any quotation," Anderson quickly replied. Then he admitted reluctantly, "but this is an article, however, by Lenin."

"That is right" Goldman added, "written in 1915."

Yet another clash took place over use against us of a quotation from the *Communist Manifesto*. It read: "The communists disdain to conceal their views and aims. They openly declare that their ends can be attained only by the forcible overthrow of all existing social conditions. Let the ruling classes tremble at the communist revolution. The proletarians have nothing to lose but their chains. They have a world to win."

We objected that the government was bringing in a scientific work that had been the basis of movements all over the world for close to a hundred years. In doing so, moreover, the prosecutors had extracted one small excerpt from a pamphlet of close to sixty pages.

Schweinhaut answered that "the second count of the indictment charges a conspiracy to, among other things, advocate, or I mean distribute and disseminate literature which advocates the overthrow of the government by armed force. We say this one does."

Joyce admitted the *Communist Manifesto* into evidence, thereby implying judicial concurrence with the prosecution's contention that its sale and distribution constituted a violation of the Smith Act.

A few more examples will fill out the general picture of the government's use of literary quotations. These will illustrate the method employed to allege that the defendants—regardless of changed times and different historical circumstances—identified completely with every word uttered in the past by leading Marxists.

An excerpt plainly intended to serve the above purpose was taken from a pamphlet entitled *What is Socialism?* written by Goldman himself. The excerpt included these remarks: "Only one type of working class political party has shown itself able to lead the workers in a successful revolution, and that is a party of the type of the Bolshevik party under Lenin. . . . It is because we believe in that theory that we of the Socialist Workers Party are determined to build a revolutionary party of the same type as the Bolshevik party that led the successful revolution in Russia."

Similarly, James P. Cannon was cited as saying in a memorial address for Leon Trotsky: "In his *History of the Russian Revolution,* which he [Trotsky] considered his masterpiece, he gave us a guide for the making of new revolutions, or rather, for extending throughout the world the revolution that began in October, 1917."

Excerpts related to revolutionary trade union policy were used as well. Among the sources drawn upon was an SWP pamphlet entitled *The Founding Conference of the Fourth International,* which reported positions adopted at a world gathering held in 1938. Passages of the following nature were quoted: "The strategical task of the Fourth International lies not in reforming capitalism but in its overthrow. . . . Trade unions are not ends in themselves; but they are means along the road to proletarian revolution. . . . It is imperative everywhere possible, beginning with the youth groups, to organize groups for self-defense; to drill and acquaint them with the use of arms."

A quotation was also read to the jury from an SWP pamphlet containing a document entitled "Manifesto of the Fourth International on the Imperialist War and the Proletarian Revolution." Special emphasis was placed on a sentence therein, which read: "The trade unions can escape burial beneath the ruins of war only if they take the road of socialist revolution."

The prosecution fought especially hard to get into the record excerpts from the Declaration of Principles adopted at the SWP's founding convention in 1938. Goldman objected that the document had been revoked by the party after the passage in 1940 of the Voorhis Act. He noted that the SWP had since approved material containing statements of its views which "differs in no essential point from the old declaration, but it is more carefully worded so some district attorney can't misinterpret it and distort it."

Once again the judge ruled in the government's favor, after which Anderson read parts of the 1938 Declaration of Principles to the jury. What he read consisted of scattered passages of the following nature, which had been culled from a printed document of some twenty-six pages:

"The workers will destroy the whole machinery of the capitalist state in order to render it incapable of counter-revolutionary activity and because it cannot serve as the instrumentality for establishing the new social order. Its place will be taken by a workers' state, based upon the Workers' Councils. . . .

"The Workers' State will not have a professional army, but will depend upon a mass workers' militia, in which distinctions other than those required for technical efficiency will be abolished and democratic control over officers will be exercised by the ranks. . . .

"The most important of the socio-economic measures to be taken by the Workers' State in its initial period is the expropriation and socialization, without compensation, of all monopolies in industry and land; all mines, factories and shipping; all public utilities, railroads, airplane systems and other organized means of communication; all banks, credit agencies, gold stores; and all other supplies and services that the revolutionary government finds it necessary to take over in order to lay the foundations of a socialist society. . . .

"The working class can build a complete socialist society only on the basis of a world division of labor and resources, and world cooperation. The revolutionary party in this country does not aim merely to lead the working class of the United States in revolution, but to unite with the workers of all other countries in the international revolution and the establishment of world socialism. . . .

"The main specific task of the SWP is the mobilization of the American masses for struggle against American capitalism, and for its overthrow. To this end the Party will seek to win the support of the industrial and agricultural workers by its activity within their mass organizations and to establish an alliance between the workers and farmers and other sections of the middle class ready and able to join Labor in a struggle against the big capitalist class. The SWP will support and seek to give leadership to all progressive struggles, whether for immediate or more far-reaching demands, to strikes, organization campaigns, demonstrations, mass actions for relief and jobs and social insurance, mass fights against lynching, evictions, foreclosures, violations of civil rights, and against every type of reaction. While relying primarily on mass actions, propaganda and agitation as the means for furthering its revolutionary aim, the Party will also participate in electoral campaigns, though at all times contending against the fatal illusion that the masses can accomplish their emancipation through the ballot box. . . .

"If, in spite of the efforts of the revolutionists and the militant workers, the U.S. government enters a new war, the SWP will not under any circumstances support that war but will on the contrary fight against it. The SWP will advocate the continuance of the class struggle during the war regardless of the consequences for the outcome of the American military struggle; and will try to prepare the masses to utilize the war crisis for the overthrow of U.S. capitalism and the victory of socialism. . . .

"The policy of the SWP with respect to imperialist war holds good under all conditions. . . .

"It applies also if the United States is in military alliance with the Soviet Union. In the latter case, the SWP would unreservedly support the Soviet Union against imperialism; but would expose the treacherous imperialist aims of the United States in the alliance, would call for the overthrow of U.S. capitalism and its replacement by a revolutionary workers' government which alone could carry forward the war in the interests of labor, of the revolutionary defense of the Soviet Union and of the world socialist revolution."

To round out this general description of the government's exhibits, a seriocomic item should be included. It involved a quotation from a column written for the *Socialist Appeal* of March 9, 1939. The subject was an antifascist demonstration that had recently taken place outside Madison Square Garden in New York City. In the excerpt brought forward at the trial, the columnist had written: "Only the Trotskyists gave leadership to the workers who were ready and willing to fight for their class. Only the Trotskyists were on the line when action was needed. Boy! Were we there! See you in court!"

Despite the strained atmosphere in the Minneapolis courtroom, this literary flamboyance drew general laughter—even from the defendants, who were in an exceptionally good position to grasp the irony of the punch line.

There was nothing funny, however, about the prosecution's intentions in submitting this item as "evidence." In denouncing such practices, Goldman told the jury: "It is one of those columns where somebody tries to be humorous, and I don't think that his humor should be attributed to us, or that we should be held responsible for it."

In sum, the government's devious methods involved everything from dishonest charges in the indictment to the citing of literary quotations out of context in order to misrepresent our views. Bad as those practices were, though, even shadier devices were used to introduce contrived testimony against us.

14. Coached Witnesses

Apart from isolated passages jerked out of revolutionary writings, the government's case rested mainly upon false testimony by Tobinites. They were used to allege that we did and said one thing for public consumption, while we meant and did the opposite in private.

Those who made such charges were members and supporters of the Committee of 99. Some had material interests at stake in attacking us, and others were motivated by personal grudges against defendants. Upon taking the witness stand they performed like trained seals, giving every indication of having been coached by the political cops. Besides that, they were allowed—despite our objections—to sit in court and listen to one another's testimony, a practice which enabled them to use pretty much the same language in answering the prosecutor's questions.

The Tobinites claimed to have held private conversations with various defendants during which, curiously enough, there was never a third party present. Use of that tactic made it their word against ours, so they felt emboldened to lie with reckless abandon. It was in such private talks, the prosecution had them say, that they were initiated into the "real" aim of the Socialist Workers Party, which was to prepare an "armed revolution."

James Bartlett was the government's lead-off witness. His testimony had obviously been well rehearsed, for he exhibited a strangely precise memory. Among other acts of stool-pigeonry, this Tobin agent named most of the defendants as SWP members, described those named as active in the party, and branded each one an advocate of "force and violence." He generalized the latter accusation when Anderson asked what had to have been a prearranged question. As recorded in the official court abstract, that trick was pulled in the following manner:

"Q: Why did you quit, or discontinue as far as you could, your membership in the Socialist Workers Party?

"A: The questions discussed related to the overthrow of the United States form of government, and I did not believe that was right, and I quit."

Anderson also had Bartlett elaborate on various aspects of discussions allegedly heard at SWP meetings or held in private with one or another defendant. A few examples from the official abstract will illustrate the tenor of fabrications presented to the jury.

"Q: And what was then and there said [at a January 1938 meeting of the newly founded SWP] about this new party?

"A: Considerable contrast was made between the Socialist Party and the Socialist Workers Party and it was pointed out during the discussion that the Socialist Party was moving under the illusion that it could bring socialism into effect by use of the ballot box, whereas the Socialist Workers Party entertained no such illusions and maintained that it was necessary for an armed overthrow of the capitalist form of government in order to establish a dictatorship of the proletariat. . . .

"Q: Now what was said there [at later meetings of the SWP in Minneapolis] if you can recall, and state by whom, with respect to use of the unions by the party in seeking control of the government?

"A: I recall one time, V. R. Dunne making a report at a party meeting . . . he pointed out how, under the leadership of the party, developing its program and espousing it in the trade union movement, [the party] was able effectively to take over the city of Minneapolis. He pointed that out as an example of how effectively that could be done on a nation-wide scale if the party had fine leaders with influence and prestige in the important trade unions on a national scale. . . .

"Q: State what further discussion there was at membership meetings, if any, of the use of the unions in connection with the party's taking control of the government.

"A: Well, I cannot recall any specific occasion. There were many specific occasions but most generally at party meetings, the discussions that took place regarding the trade union movement would be with the view that the party must recruit from the trade union movement because the trade union movement was considered the most important.

"Q: For what purpose?

"A: For developing a general strike at' an opportune time, which is generally called a revolutionary situation, so that there could be an effective overthrow of the capitalist government. . . .

"Q: Well, from the discussions at those membership meetings, if this revolutionary situation arose, then what was the program of the party from then on?

"A: According to my understanding, from what I was taught by V. R. Dunne, Carl Skoglund, Oscar Coover and Farrell Dobbs and others, my understanding was that [at] an opportune time, which was called a revolutionary situation, the force of the party would be put into motion in an armed uprising for the purpose of overthrowing the existing government. . . .

"Q: In that discussion was there anything said as to why there should be a class struggle?

"A: It was stated that there could be no class collaboration and still effectively develop a revolutionary movement which would lead to a successful armed revolution. . . ."

As this farce continued, a strained attempt was made to cast Local 544's defense guard in a seditious light. On that subject Anderson led Bartlett into a phony account of a talk with Trotsky when Harry DeBoer and Bartlett had gone to Mexico on a vacation trip. The gist of the tale follows:

"Q: Mr. Bartlett, while you and Harry DeBoer were with Leon Trotsky on this trip, was there anything said about defense guards?

"A: Yes, Leon Trotsky said that he gave the idea to the American party. . . .

"Q: What did he [Trotsky] say about the defense guard movement?

"A: Well, he stated that it should be developed even further on a national scale because it could be used as the nucleus for an armed uprising at the opportune time. . . .

"Q: Well, did he say to whom he had given the idea of this [in the] American party?

"A: Yes, he mentioned Emil Hansen's name.

"Mr. Goldman: Just a minute. I object and move that it be stricken [from the record]. I don't think that the indictment charges Trotsky was a conspirator. . . .

"Mr. Anderson: We charge—include Leon Trotsky as a co-conspirator in this indictment. . . .

"Q: [Anderson] What was said there at that time about Emil Hansen?

"A: [Bartlett] Leon Trotsky stated that when Emil Hansen was about to return to the United States, he had advised him to set up defense guards there, particularly in Minneapolis. . . ."

The *Industrial Organizer* took note editorially of the allegations about private talks in which defendants were supposed to have bared their "real" objectives. It observed: "If everything Bartlett said was true, SWP members did nothing in the past three years but buttonhole Bartlett and tell how very, very revolutionary the Socialist Workers Party was."

Still another ploy was used concerning the *Communist Manifesto*. Bartlett identified for the record a copy of that historic work, stating he had bought it at the SWP headquarters. He claimed to have studied the document carefully and to have discovered that it "advocated force and violence." As will be noted later, the prosecution had a special reason for putting on this particular ham act.

Bartlett's performance was followed by further parading of government witnesses to the stand who either belonged to or supported the Committee of 99. They emulated him in naming defendants as SWP members and linking those named with the alleged conspiracy to overthrow the government. The general nature of their testimony can be summed up through references to specific categories of accusations as those were made by various individuals.

Violet Williams (widow of Tommy Williams) gave the jury this outlandish description of a talk by Ray Dunne: "At one meeting that I attended he said they would put men in key positions in various industries and even stated that the army and navy would have party people in key positions and that when the right time came it wouldn't be any trick at all. He said there wouldn't be any voting; the workers would just take over the government by armed force."

Eugene J. Williams added to those brazen lies. He claimed Ray Dunne told him in private talks: "That the party members, when they were inducted into the army, [were] to form cliques, to kick about anything they could think of to kick about, so it would get into the papers and make the public think they were being treated rotten in the army, words along that line. . . . Dunne stated that at the time of the revolution, the men in the army with their cliques they had formed would take control of everything that they could, the arsenals, and turn the guns on the ones in power."

Roy F. Wieneke undertook to give the jurors the inside dope about Local 544's defense guard, as follows: "In 1939 V. R. Dunne spoke at a membership meeting of the party at which he said that the idea for a union defense guard had come from Trotsky and that masquerading under the object of fighting fascism or the Silver Shirts, it would in reality be the first part of the militia for the Socialist Workers Party. He said that the Socialist Workers Party controlled Local 544 through the leadership there and that would give the party control of the union defense guard."

Elmer Buckingham went a step further in falsifying the concept of workers' self-defense. When the prosecutor asked what Ray Dunne had said at a meeting of Local 544's defense guard, Buckingham answered: "Well, he gave a pretty lengthy speech there. It was in regard to mobilization of all the labor unions in the country and he told us that it wasn't just a local outfit, this here guard that we had here. He says it was happening all over the country, so that when the time of the revolution came, why, labor would take control."

To top it all off, John Novack was called to testify as a government witness. He was a rather pathetic individual, who had somewhat less than the fullest powers of mental perception. Anderson led Novack into an assertion that an SWP member named "Rube," whose last name he didn't know, had told him: "We have guns and ammunition planted in the walls of churches. We have bullets that will go through an inch and a half or two inches of armored plate, which is better than the United States army."

The prosecution surely knew what Novack would say. Yet, outrageous though the above assertion was, he was asked the leading question which evoked it. There could have been only one reason for such a performance. It was a cynical trick designed to shock the jury.

After the prosecution had guided the Committee of 99 witnesses through this sinister burlesque, Goldman subjected them to stiff cross-examination. A number of disclosures resulted concerning the manner in which Tobin's stoolies had worked with the FBI from the time their clique was first organized inside Local 544.

Violet Williams admitted: "The first time I saw an FBI agent at

my house was in the latter part of February 1941. He talked with
Mr. Williams. He was there two or three times after that."

Especially revealing evidence of collusion with the political
cops came out in the questioning of Henry M. Harris. His
testimony for the government had adhered to the pattern
described above. During the cross-examination that followed, an
admission was extracted from Harris that Tommy Williams had
told him to admit Thomas Perrin to one of the clique's meetings.
Goldman then drove the point home, as follows:

"Q: Tommy Williams told you to admit at the meeting in the
Nicollet Hotel, a meeting called of the Committee of 99 for the
truck drivers, to admit Mr. Perrin of the FBI?

"A: Yes.

"Q: And did he point him out to you?

"A: At that time he did not tell me about the FBI, just to admit
a Mr. Perrin."

Harris also verified that he had conveyed an offer of help to
Carl Skoglund in getting his citizenship papers "if he sided with
us." Goldman pressed him for details on this matter.

"Q: Well, how did you happen to make such a proposition to
him?

"A: We had a conversation with the FBI agent.

"Q: And the FBI agent told you that if he [Skoglund] would
side in with you, he would be granted American citizenship?

"A: No. . . . he thought Carl Skoglund might come in with us
if we made such an offer, and I made him such an offer. . . .

"Q: Who was the FBI man who talked with you about this
proposition for Skoglund?

"A: Mr. Perrin."

Another aspect of Tobinite-FBI collaboration was brought out
during cross-examination of Elmer Buckingham. He was among
those who had signed affidavits denouncing leaders of Local 544
as "subversives," which had been submitted to Tobin the
previous April. Goldman demanded to know who had asked
Buckingham for such an affidavit.

"I think it was Mr. Perrin," Buckingham replied.

On redirect examination the prosecution had this witness
change his testimony, undertaking to show that what he had
prepared at Perrin's request had nothing to do with the affidavit
for Tobin. At best, though, this revised story served only to
emphasize the extent to which the government was using an
internal union opposition against the officers of Local 544.

Both Perrin and a second FBI agent, Roy T. Noonan, were called as government witnesses to testify about the raids they had led on the SWP's headquarters the previous June. While cross-examining them, Goldman tried to bring out Tobin's role in instigating federal prosecution of the local 544 leaders. Schweinhaut objected with great vehemence, and the judge ruled that the defendants could ask no questions relating to their conflict with the IBT dictator.

In the course of manufacturing "evidence" for the prosecution, Hoover's agents remembered their frame-up of Teamster leaders in the 1939 Sioux City trial; and, as befits the police mind, they sought to use the victims of that outrage to help put us behind bars. One of those approached was Jack Maloney, who was serving a two-year term in federal prison at Sandstone, Minnesota, as a result of the 1939 frame-up. Years later I asked Jack to describe that episode as best he could remember it. Here is what he wrote:

"One day in the fall of 1941 a guard from the front end came to the machine shop where I was working to escort me to the warden's office. On the way I asked the hack what is this all about and he said you have a visitor. When we got there the warden introduced me to a man who was sitting in his office, stating that the man was an FBI agent, and that he wanted to ask me some questions. Although the agent's name was given to me at the time, I do not recall it. I said to him I have no time for the likes of you.

"The agent said I understand that you may feel bitter towards me, but you should listen to what I have to say. He then outlined to me how the government was proceeding against officials in 544, and Dobbs and some others in New York, for their subversive activities. Because I was a Teamster official and had very close working relationships with Dobbs and leaders of Local 544, he told me, my testimony would be extremely helpful. In return for that, he said, an early parole was assured and he could guarantee a job with the Teamsters when I got out.

"I was outraged. I said to him, you represent the people who harassed me, framed me, and railroaded me into this prison and now you come here and have the guts and poor sense to propose to me that I can get out of this joint by framing some other worker into it. Then I demanded that the warden return me to my cell or work detail. I also told the warden I was aware of my rights and that he should never again subject me to any goddam

interrogation unless my lawyer was present. In leaving I said to
the agent you can go to hell with your offers. I heard no more on
the issue.

"A few days later Shorty Stultz, who was also doing time on
the same rap as me, was called to the warden's office. A bit later
he left the prison in custody of US marshals. Before he was
returned to the prison we learned from the newspapers that he
was a government witness against you and the others on trial in
Minneapolis. Most convicts hate snitches and informers and they
were pretty angry. The warden knew this and Stultz was kept in
the 'rat hole' until he was released on parole a short time later."

"Shorty" Stultz, to whom Maloney referred, was Walter K.
Stultz, who had been president of IBT Local 554 in Omaha,
Nebraska, at the time of his imprisonment after conviction in the
Sioux City case. His testimony against us centered on accusa-
tions that the SWP had tried to take over Omaha Local 554 to use
it against the government.

Those accusations were directed especially against Al Russell,
who had been recording secretary of Local 554 and toward whom
Stultz manifested strong personal animus. With ill-concealed
glee, he identified Russell as an SWP member. Then, using to full
advantage the gimmick of relating a private talk purportedly
held with Russell, Stultz told the jury:

"He said he was not only a socialist and a Socialist Worker, but
was also an ultraleft, and that the only way to get it [power], was
to get it for yourself, grab a rifle and get it—that they would have
to arm and get it."

Two other officers of Local 554—Thomas V. Smith and
Malcolm G. Love—were brought to Minneapolis from Omaha and
put on the stand as government witnesses. Smith testified first.
The prosecution tried to prove through him that we had invaded
the Omaha union with the object of dictating its policies. But
Smith told the jury that those defendants who had been active in
Omaha had come there in response to an official request from the
local for help.

An attempt was also made to show that we had flooded the
union with "subversive" propaganda. Smith said on that point
yes, Russell had once suggested that he read the *Communist
Manifesto*, but he found he couldn't understand it very well. Yes,
when he told Dobbs that he hadn't understood what he read,
Dobbs asked Russell to organize a study class for those interested
in discussing the document. Yes, Russell had organized such a

class and Smith attended it. "We asked him questions and he tried to explain them."

If the prosecutors expected Smith to help them show that our activities in Omaha had been "subversive," the notion was soon exploded. On cross-examination Goldman asked the witness if Dobbs had advocated "force and violence" in private talks or in speeches he had heard. Smith replied:

"I never heard him advocate the overthrow of the government by force and violence during any of those meetings nor in any private conversation I ever had with him did he advocate the overthrow of the government by force and violence."

Under questioning by the prosecutor, Smith testified that he had joined the SWP in the spring of 1940. Goldman asked why he had done so and Smith answered:

"What made me join the Socialist Workers Party? I was an officer of the International Brotherhood of Teamsters in Omaha. I know the conditions we had before this set-up of the Eleven-State Area [IBT over-the-road committee] and conditions in Minneapolis, Saint Paul—at this meeting [in the Twin Cities during January 1938], and seeing the work that Local 544 and their officers were doing, helping out the smaller locals, and their entire board and staff, as I knew them, all of them labor-minded, trying to help the poor, and I found out that they were members of it [the SWP] and I figured that if that was what the Socialist Workers Party was, that put out those kind of people, that that was good enough for me and I joined them."

When Love was called to the stand the prosecutor asked him only a few perfunctory questions, seeking to avoid a repetition of the disaster experienced with Smith. But Goldman refused to cooperate in that attempt. The results are illustrated in the following passage from his cross-examination of Love, beginning with Love's answer to Goldman's question as to why he had joined the SWP:

"A: Why did I join? Well, I will tell you. I joined the party for practically the same reason that Tommy [Smith] gave.

"Q: Did you ever hear Farrell Dobbs make speeches?

"A: I have heard him make a lot of speeches. . . .

"Q: Did he ever say anything about overthrowing the government by force and violence?

"A: No, sir."

Among the government's witnesses were a few who were used for one or another specific purpose. Edward P. Shurick, a radio station manager, identified transcripts of radio talks given by Grace Carlson as a candidate for U.S. senator from Minnesota in the 1940 elections. Excerpts from those talks were then twisted around by the prosecution to claim that she had advocated armed overthrow of the government.

Franklin F. Page, a reporter for the University of Minnesota's student newspaper, testified that he had heard Carlson make a speech advocating "force and violence." On cross-examination Page admitted that the Socialist Club at the university had protested against a distorted story of Carlson's speech which he had written for the student paper.

Eugene F. Gleason, a reporter for the *Cleveland Plain Dealer*, claimed to have heard Carlson advocate use of armed force against the government during a speech she made in that Ohio city.

Elizabeth Humpfner, a Minneapolis nurse, alleged that close association with Rose Seiler had enabled her to perceive that Seiler was no doubt a member of the SWP and agreed with its program.

Charles H. Chalmers, who was in the oil burner business, testified that Ray Dunne—as a guest speaker at a Minneapolis luncheon club—said he had a lot to do with the writing of the Declaration of Principles adopted by the SWP in 1938.

Myrtle Levenius told of buying a copy of the 1938 Declaration of Principles at the SWP headquarters. This had been done not long before the trial, she said, upon instructions from her employer. The employer turned out to be the Associated Industries, successor to the defunct Citizens Alliance which had earned widespread hatred because of its brutal attacks on striking workers.

During this stage of the trial the defense renewed its objections to introduction of the *Communist Manifesto* as government "evidence." The prosecution argued in rebuttal that the document had served as the basis for a study class in Omaha; that Bartlett's testimony had revealed its advocacy of force and violence; and that proof had, therefore, been presented of the defendants' use of the *Communist Manifesto* in violation of the Smith Act. As before, the judge ruled in the government's favor.

This example of the government's methods in prosecuting us was denounced during the trial by Roger Baldwin, director of the American Civil Liberties Union. He did so in a speech at a public meeting held in Minneapolis on November 13, 1941.

"Only one overt act has been charged against the defendants—organization of a defense guard in 1938," Baldwin told the audience, "so the prosecution in the main is based on what they thought. . . . For the first time in our history they are trying men and women for the ideas in the ninety-three-year-old *Communist Manifesto*."

Three days later Robert Minor, acting national secretary of the Communist Party, took an opposite stand. He did so as the principal speaker at a Stalinist-sponsored affair, also held in Minneapolis while we were on trial. Minor was substituting for Earl Browder, the CP's national secretary, who was serving a term in federal prison after having been framed up on passport charges. The frame-up had occurred during the period of the Stalin-Hitler pact. Since then, however, the CP had switched back to support of U.S. imperialism, and it was now fervently backing Roosevelt against opponents of his foreign policy. The president reciprocated by freeing Browder a bit later.

In his Minneapolis speech Minor called for "a national front of all patriotic Americans in support of administration policy," and he denounced the Trotskyists who were on trial in federal court as "fifth columnists" (a term used during the Spanish civil war to describe agents of Franco, the fascist dictator). Referring to the presence of *Militant* distributors outside the meeting hall, Minor urged the audience not to believe "those who have strange sources of money with which to stand on sidewalks and give away papers."

In sharp contrast to the Stalinists' finky role, trade unionists were becoming increasingly critical of the government's tactics in prosecuting the Trotskyists. This trend was reflected in a resolution adopted during the trial by the San Francisco CIO Industrial Union Council. That body declared:

"We condemn the use of government agencies to oppress and harass any labor or political organizations in the pursuit of their legitimate activities, . . . we call upon the Department of Justice to dismiss the indictments against the twenty-eight defendants in the Minnesota case, and . . . we request all affiliated locals to give full moral and financial support to these twenty-eight defendants."

Sharp criticism of the prosecution also came from middle-class circles. A stinging editorial appeared, for instance, in the *Belview Independent*, one of Minnesota's well-known rural weeklies. In its issue of November 7, 1941, this paper asserted:

"Whether we may or may not agree with the Socialist Workers Party's ideals, a great deal more is at stake in this trial than the guilt of the persons charged, and that is whether the people of the United States have the right of freedom of speech, freedom of press and other civil rights. . . .

"Frankly we feel that the entire case is the outcome of the controversy between the AFL and the CIO. Local 544 of the CIO has had the short end of the deal all the way through. In fact, if the letter of the law had been followed, an election would have been called and the members of the union could have voted and made the decision themselves as to which group they wished to have represent them.

"It is hard to believe that their organization would be guilty of fomenting revolution of the bloody type, when a more anti-war organization never existed in the United States. Their reason for opposing the war is not necessarily from the point of view of expense but because they feel that the rank and file of working people of the United States will be spilling their blood for a war that will bring profits only to a few and death and disaster to the working people."

As the views expressed by Baldwin, the San Francisco CIO, and the Minnesota rural weekly signified, there was strong backing for a demand that prosecution of the twenty-eight be dropped; and our defense counsel made a motion to that effect at the trial. Specifically, the judge was asked to instruct the jury to return a verdict of not guilty in the case of each defendant.

Argument for such a directed verdict was presented along the following lines: there was no proof of any conspiracy whatever, unless the very existence of the SWP—a legal party—was held to be a conspiracy; "evidence" submitted against us consisted of speeches and writings, all dealing with an analysis of historical events and with changes anticipated on the basis of scientific prediction; there was no proof of attempts to foment insubordination in the armed forces; all the government could point to was Local 544's defense guard organized for the union's own protection, and the idea that such a small formation could threaten the government was preposterous.

Schweinhaut opposed the defense motion, contending that testimony by government witnesses had proven two things: the hoped-for revolution was expected to come soon, and draftees were urged to create unrest and dissatisfaction in the army. The fact of party membership, he also insisted, showed a clear and absolute intent to overthrow the government by force if the opportunity presented itself. Those things, Schweinhaut argued, clearly demonstrated the conspiracy charged in the indictment.

In his ruling on the defense motion, Judge Joyce ordered that verdicts of not guilty be returned for George Frosig, Walter Hagstrom, Dorothy Schultz, Rose Seiler, and Nick Wagner. He said there was not sufficient evidence that those five defendants had knowledge of the SWP or that they had participated in activities to overthrow the government by force and violence.

Joyce's reasons for freeing the five had an ominous ring. He was telling the jury, in effect, that the SWP—as a party—was being tried on conspiracy charges; and that those who were shown to be active members of the party were automatically to be found guilty, if the jury accepted the government's contention that the SWP itself constituted a conspiracy.

On those premises the judge instructed the remaining twenty-three defendants to proceed with their answer to the government's case against them. In an effort to justify that position, he stated:

"It may seem unreasonable to fear, when the size and power of the United States is considered, that this comparatively small group of individuals could accomplish successfully the objectives charged. But it is well to remember on this point that Hitler went around in a greasy raincoat in his early days and was belittled for his efforts."

Speaking for the five whom Joyce had freed, Dorothy Schultz told the press: "We remain in complete solidarity with the defendants. We must redouble our efforts to save our comrades and friends. The rest of the judge's ruling today means that we must prepare for the worst."

15. "If That Is Treason . . ."

Rebuttal of the government's charges against the remaining twenty-three defendants began on the sixteenth day of the trial. The general line of our testimony had already been worked out through collective discussions, and individual defendants had been selected to take the witness stand for one or another purpose. Broadly stated, our aims were to refute the lie that we were engaged in a criminal conspiracy against the government, to present a comprehensive account of what we really stood for, and to appeal from the courtroom for mass support against the prosecution's attack on our democratic right to propagate revolutionary socialist ideas.

The first witness for the defense was James P. Cannon, who outlined the Marxist fundamentals on which the party based its policies. His testimony was guided during direct examination by Albert Goldman, whose skills as a lawyer were happily supplemented by his knowledge of Marxist politics. Functioning as a team, they turned that stage of the trial into what the *Minneapolis Tribune* described as "a scene like a class room." Cannon's exposition of the SWP's basic views, which he presented in response to questions from Goldman, can be summed up as follows:

The government had turned reality upside down in charging the Socialist Workers Party with a plot to undermine the existing system. A social crisis was developing in the United States not because of any revolutionary conspiracy, but through the operation of two internal laws of capitalism which make inevitable its decline and its replacement by socialism.

One of those laws involves private ownership of the means of production, he explained, and employment of wage labor at less than the value of the products produced by wage laborers. It is obvious that wage workers, who receive for their labor less than the total value of their products, can be customers for only the amount of value they receive in the form of wages. The remaining value created by labor bcomes surplus value, for which the capitalist appropriators must find fields of exploitation at home and abroad. The resulting contradictions of the capitalist system inexorably lead to periodic crises.

The post-1929 economic depression, which resulted from one such crisis of what political science terms overproduction, was an unmistakable sign of the unhealthiness of the social organism called capitalism. It brought upon the working class a scourge of unemployment that operated on a world scale—except in the Soviet Union, where post-capitalist property relations had been established.

Social relations are further aggravated by competition between capitalists, a trend that leads inevitably to the bigger ones freezing out the smaller fry. More and more wealth becomes concentrated in the hands of fewer and fewer monopolists. Meantime, the great mass of people, especially the workers, find themselves confronted with ever-increasing social and economic difficulties; and the number who become pauperized increases.

Fundamental structural factors of the foregoing nature, not socialist propaganda, are the cause of the unending class struggle under capitalism. The greater the bite of the national product taken by the owners, the less goes to the wage workers. This generates a constant conflict of interests between the two major classes, which must culminate eventually in a definitive working-class victory and the establishment of socialism.

Trade unions appeared in this country as the basic organizations through which the workers struggle to defend their interests from day to day. The Socialist Workers Party supports the trade union movement, so as to help the workers resist oppression and strive for improved conditions of life. In doing so we advocate democratic practices through which the unions can be controlled by the rank and file. The party does not seek dictatorial control over those mass organizations, as the government wrongly charges. We strive for leading influence in the trade unions by demonstrating ability to fight for the workers' interests. In that way we seek to gain respect in the ranks, hoping thereby to get a sympathetic hearing for our class-struggle program and socialist ideas.

In talking about perspectives for organized labor we place special emphasis on the need for the working masses to take over the leadership of the country. As the first step toward that end, we urge the workers to make a clean break with the capitalist parties, develop an independent party of their own, and adopt a political program that will genuinely serve the interests of labor and its allies.

The second internal law of capitalism, Cannon continued, involves a conflict between the further development of productive forces and the confinement of those forces within national barriers. In their efforts to solve crises of overproduction, the capitalists look for foreign markets in which to sell their products and in which to invest their excess capital. This trend is inherent in all advanced industrial countries operating on a capitalist basis. They tend to become imperialist powers, which means they seek to exploit other peoples.

But when capitalism enters some new territory, the world sphere open for exploitation begins to narrow down, because the laws of capitalist competition follow like a shadow. The rival imperialists have less and less room for expansion of their spheres of influence, and as a result they come into conflict over redivision of the territorial spoils.

Global clashes of that nature became so intensified early in the twentieth century that they led to the war of 1914-18. The outbreak of bloody struggle on such an immense scale was a signal that the capitalist world system had run up against a profound crisis of historical development. Since then the capitalist nations had continued to be either in a state of war or in the process of preparing for war, and it took only two decades for another world holocaust to begin. As in the case of all imperialist conflicts, World War II was caused by competition between rival gangs of capitalists for markets, sources of raw materials, fields of investment, and spheres of influence. Further conflicts of this kind remain inevitable, moreover, so long as monopolist rule endures.

Roosevelt's claim that he was leading the United States into a war of democracy against fascism was a subterfuge, Cannon warned. The conflict would be imperialist in character. Although fought at the expense of the working class, its purpose would be to advance the world ambitions of this country's capitalists, who stood among the greatest enemies of democracy. Even before the U.S. openly joined in the hostilities, preparations for war were being used as a pretext for cuts in living standards and the curtailing of civil liberties at home; and a victory over Hitler would in no way put an end to the threat of fascism or insure uninterrupted prosperity for the workers. War could be prevented, unemployment abolished, and dangers of repressive rule overcome only by doing away with the capitalist system which breeds war, unemployment, and fascism.

The Socialist Workers Party stands unalterably opposed to imperialist war, he declared from the witness stand. We speak against it, write against it, try to create mass sentiment against it. We support the demand for a referendum vote of the people before the U.S. can make war on any other country. What is more, we shall remain opposed to involvement in an imperialist war even while this country is engaged in such a conflict. We will express that opposition on a political plane, seeking to exercise our constitutional right to call for a different foreign policy.

In opposing imperialist war the SWP rejects any notion of doing so through acts of sabotage or through efforts to foment insubordination in the armed forces. If the party resorted to such conduct, it would discredit itself; it would destroy any possibility of winning a majority to its program, which is the only way in which the social transformation we advocate can be accomplished.

Concerning the armed forces, the party had recently decided to call for military training under trade union control, financed by the government. It had also raised demands that workers conscripted into the military service of imperialism be allowed to elect their own officers, set up grievance committees, and retain their full rights as citizens. SWP members of military age did not seek to avoid the draft by raising conscientious objection. Such a course would isolate them from the working class. For that reason revolutionists submitted to conscription, so as to remain in contact with the worker-draftees and go through the military experience with them.

The imperialist war, for which workers were being conscripted, was in itself an expression of a terrible social crisis, and that crisis would not be solved by war. Mass misery and suffering would grow at a tremendous pace during the conflict. Deep-seated unrest would result, as bitter experiences caused the masses to yearn for a fundamental change in social conditions.

By definition, that is what the term *social revolution* means, Cannon stressed—a basic political and economic transformation of society. An example from U.S. history is the Civil War of 1861-65. That was a social revolution because it destroyed the system of slave labor and property in slaves, replacing it by the complete domination of capitalist enterprise and wage labor.

For a comparable social revolution against capitalism to occur, several preconditions are required. The existing society must have exhausted its possibilities of further development. As a result the ruling class, which can no longer solve the problems it creates, suffers loss of confidence in itself. At the same time the misery and desperation of the masses increases to a point where they come to desire a radical change. Recognition of the need for a social revolution grows, bringing increased acceptance of socialist ideas. Before the desired change can be accomplished, however, there must be a strong workers' party capable of leading the masses in resolute fashion toward a basic solution of the social crisis. To do that the workers' party must be capable of conducting the struggle for socialism in the most economical and effective way.

As matters stood in 1941, the SWP leader noted, serious symptoms of capitalist decay had become increasingly evident in this country. Massive unemployment had existed throughout the 1930s. Such economic restabilization as had been achieved was based for the most part on arms production. Hence, the depression crisis was becoming transformed into a war crisis. This showed that the ruling capitalists were unable to solve their problems; but they didn't know that yet, so they hadn't lost their self-confidence.

The living conditions of the masses had drastically deteriorated during the depression, and, considered in longer-range terms, further impairments of the workers' economic and social welfare were to be expected. Unfortunately, though, the masses were still unfamiliar with socialist ideas, which meant that our party did not have sufficient weight to decisively influence the course of the workers' action in defense of their class interests.

As a minority party, the SWP had to focus on propaganda to popularize its program. That was done by publishing newspapers, magazines, books, and pamphlets and by holding public meetings. At the same time the party sought to play a constructive role within the trade unions and other mass organizations. Efforts were made, as well, to run candidates for public office. The latter activity served as yet another means to make our ideas more widely understood; and, as broadened agreement with our program became expressed through increased support of our candidates at the polls, it would help to test whether the capitalist minority would allow a basic social change to come about through democratic expression of the electorate's will.

The change we visualized would center on establishment of a social order based on common ownership of the means of production, Cannon told the jurors. Industry would be nationalized, wasteful competition eliminated, private ownership of the means of production abolished—along with private profit and the wage system. Use of the term *productive wealth* in that connection does not refer to the personal property of individuals. It means wealth required to produce the necessities of the people—industries, mines, railroads, etc.

Small proprietors, who are not exploiters of labor, will not be interfered with in making such changes. They will be allowed to retain their farms, handicraft shops, and similar small service establishments. A revolutionary government will seek to convince them, by example, of the advantages of socialized enterprises; but until that is accomplished, it will give reasonable consideration to their special needs and problems.

The same considerations wouldn't apply, Cannon added, to industrialists, big landowners, and bankers, who exploit a lot of people. Their holdings will be expropriated and put in the hands of the masses to manage through democratically chosen representatives. Whether or not to compensate those whose holdings are expropriated is not a question of principle. If they are ready to peacefully accept the new order in return for reasonable compensation, that method of effecting the social transformation will be cheaper than a civil war. If they resist majority rule, however, any claim to compensation will automatically be forfeit.

To carry out the necessary social changes, he continued, the instruments of ruling will have to be drastically reorganized. A capitalist government arises from a society based on private ownership of the means of production. As such, it represents in general the interests of the capitalists, excluding from primary consideration the needs of the masses. Therefore, a ruling body of that nature cannot be entrusted with the tasks involved in transforming social relations.

A government of the working class must be set up, with the support of labor's allies. It must frankly represent the economic and social interests of those who toil. That government will have the task of arranging and controlling the social transition from capitalism to socialism. Before that can be accomplished, however, new governmental forms will have to replace the machinery of the present capitalist state, which is designed to serve capitalist interests above all others. The apparatus of rule will have to be reconstructed from top to bottom. Congress could be reorganized, for instance, so as to consist of representatives of the workers and their allies based on occupational units, rather than the tricky method of territorial representation now used by the capitalists.

In Marxist terminology a government genuinely representing the toiling masses is defined as "the dictatorship of the proletariat." But this term should not be confused with the popular impression of dictatorship as the rule of tyrants. Whatever governmental form the capitalists use, they exercise a dictatorship over all social and economic relations, always subordinating mass needs to their own private interests. What Marxists call "the dictatorship of the proletariat" simply reverses that situation, brushing aside the special interests of the capitalists and paying attention, instead, to the needs of those whom the capitalists have long exploited. From the viewpoint of the masses, it will be the most democratic government that has ever existed.

Considered generally, governments are primarily instruments of repression, used by one social class against another. During the first stages of a transition to socialism the revolutionary labor government will continue to fulfill that basic task, except that it will be doing so for progressive purposes. It will serve both to carry out the wishes of the toilers and to prevent the capitalists from obstructing that effort. Then—as the new government of the working masses proceeds to socialize industry, abolish inequalities, raise the income level of the people, and suppress attempts at counterrevolution by the dispossessed exploiters—its importance and weight as a controlling force will gradually diminish.

After a time the social transition will be carried through to the point that exploitation will be completely eliminated and class distinctions abolished, thereby doing away with the conflict of class against class. Need for any official repressive force will thus gradually wither away. The government can then be replaced by administrative councils, whose function will be to plan production, supervise public works, education, health care, etc. As the transition leads to a fully developed socialist society, government over people will be replaced by administration over things. There will no longer be any need for armies, police, jails, and other instruments of repression, so that traditional aspect of government will die out for want of function.

It is this basic perspective concerning the future of humanity, Cannon observed, that makes the Socialist Workers Party internationalist to the core. The modern world has become an economic unit; no individual country is entirely self-sufficient. Hence, present-day problems of the billions of people on earth can be solved only on a world scale. The new social order must be a world order, for that is the only way to achieve the rounded and harmonious development of productive forces that can promote lasting human progress for all.

Since the establishment of socialism is a world task, workers in every country must join together in striving toward that goal. To prevent crippling divisions within the class, all forms of race prejudice must be opposed, as must anti-Semitism. Workers in advanced countries must act as friends of the colonial peoples. Labor must stand for full equality of all nationalities, races, and creeds. Our goal must be total class unity in the struggle against capitalism, and the workers must have international organizations for that purpose.

Given the establishment of a socialist society, he explained, participation in its benefits will be open to all. This may include former individual capitalists, provided they reconcile themselves to the social change and do not take up arms against it. If majority rule is not challenged by force, the legal transition might begin with extensive amendment of the United States Constitution to fit the new regime. Democratic concepts set forth in the Bill of Rights would remain intact, for example, except that they would be further improved and amplified. Existing constitutional guarantees of the right to private property in the means of production, on the other hand, must be completely eliminated.

It is precisely the latter issue, however, that constitutes the nub of the question. Historical precedents show the unwillingness of any privileged, propertied class, no matter how outlived, to leave the scene without trying to impose its will upon the majority by force. As a result every important social transformation has been accompanied by violence. A civil war broke out in this country, for example, because the Southern slaveholders couldn't reconcile themselves to a legal parliamentary victory of Northern capitalism—the election of President Lincoln.

A modern manifestation of this reactionary tendency is found in the rise of fascism elsewhere in the world. When the capitalists are no longer able to maintain a social equilibrium on the basis of democratic parliamentarism, they turn to more open forms of class rule. The ultimate step in that direction is resort to fascism, with the object of breaking up the labor movement by force.

Therefore, significant capitalist support of a fascist movement becomes a terrible warning to the workers. It means that they must take matters into their own hands, or they will suffer the fate that befell the German people under Hitler.

For that reason we advise the workers to prepare themselves so as to prevent the outlived capitalist minority from frustrating the will of the majority. Once faced with a fascist threat, it becomes necessary for labor to organize an effective self-defense. Account must also be taken of the capitalists' aim to use middle-class elements—small farmers, shop owners, professional people—as a recruiting ground for fascist gangs. It is necessary that labor's policies be designed to counter such moves, both to prevent fascist recruitment and because support must be won from significant sections of the middle class before the workers can achieve a social revolution.

To meet any fascist threat that develops, the SWP advocates organization of workers' defense guards to protect union halls, meetings, and picket lines. During 1938 there was, in fact, an upsurge of incipient fascism, which sought to cripple labor by violent methods. In Minneapolis, Local 544 took the lead in forming a union defense guard to meet the fascist hoodlums on their own terms. A bit later, as World War II loomed more closely, new events thrust the would-be Hitlers into the background, and the previous need for workers' defense guards receded. We have, nevertheless, retained the self-defense concept as part of our long-range program, because the fascist threat can be expected to rise again at some future stage of the class struggle.

In describing the clash of class forces during turbulent periods of social change, Cannon outlined the dynamics of the 1917 revolution in Russia. It was the greatest and most progressive event in human history up to that time, he explained, an experience that embodied the doctrines and theories of Marxism with which the Socialist Workers Party identifies itself. In no sense was the Russian revolution an illegal conspiracy of an armed minority, as the prosecution claimed. It came about through collective action by an overwhelming majority of the population.

Councils of workers, peasants, and soldiers—which the Russians called Soviets—were initiated at the outset by the masses themselves. These were so directly representative of the broad population that they constituted the authority recognized by the Russian people, and no policy could be enforced without the support of the Soviets. Hence, when the government set up after the February revolution failed to carry out the mass will, it lost popular sanction. Meanwhile, the Bolsheviks, who were led by Lenin and Trotsky, put forward a policy that accorded with the desires of the workers, peasants, and soldiers, and that enabled the Bolsheviks to gain steadily in influence. By October the Bolsheviks had attained a majority in the Soviets, which made it possible to take control of the government with solid mass support. This revolutionary transformation was accomplished, moreover, without serious violence; nothing more than a little scuffling was involved.

Large-scale violence began only when the forces of reaction launched a counterrevolutionary assault on the democratically elected Soviet government led by the Bolsheviks. A bloody civil war ensued, during which the counterrevolutionaries within Russia were backed by the imperialist powers, including the United States. In the end the Bolsheviks emerged victorious. A workers' state was consolidated on the basis of post-capitalist property forms, that is, nationalization and collective ownership of the means of production.

Shortly thereafter in 1924 Lenin died, and a fight developed between two factions, led by Stalin and Trotsky, over Soviet democracy, the pace of industrialization, and workers' control. The Stalinists had set out to impose bureaucratic rule in all spheres. Their course arose from a drive to reverse the revolutionary internationalist outlook of Lenin's time and to establish an autocratic regime within the Soviet Union, through which to enforce the retrogressive foreign and domestic policies they developed.

As Cannon reached that point in his discourse, Schweinhaut rudely interrupted him. A few months earlier Germany had invaded the Soviet Union, and since then Roosevelt had come to view Stalin as an ally against Hitler. For that reason the White House no longer wanted public criticism of the potential military partner. All governmental agencies had been made aware of the change in line, and the prosecutor acted accordingly in objecting to discussion of the internal Soviet situation at our trial. "What do we care?" he asked rhetorically. Judge Joyce backed up Schweinhaut, ruling that a description of the Stalin regime was "immaterial and unnecessary."

Further testimony about the Russian question was permitted only concerning SWP policy toward the workers' state that had originally emerged under Bolshevik leadership. We support the Soviet Union against imperialism, Cannon told the jury, because it represents a progressive development for the working class. Our opposition to Stalinism doesn't alter our attitude in favor of the Soviet form of industrial production.

This issue, he added, had a direct bearing on the SWP's relationship with Trotsky. We had backed him against Stalin from the beginning. Trotsky's basic analysis of Stalinism had been adopted as part of our own program. In addition, his ideas and interpretations of Marxism in our time were the source from which we got our main concepts about contemporary policies in the international class struggle. We studied those ideas, of course, in terms of developments in the United States and sought to apply them to concrete reality in this country.

Cannon also replied to the government's use of the *Communist Manifesto* against us, which had focused upon a single sentence in that document, reading, "We say openly that [the workers' aims] can be achieved only by the forcible overthrow of all existing social institutions." It should be kept in mind, he explained, that the whole European continent was seething with revolutions and counterrevolutions when the *Manifesto* was written in 1848. No stable parliamentary systems, no democratic processes whatever—through which steps toward a fundamental social change could be initiated—were available anywhere on the continent.

As for our basic attitude toward Marx, he continued, the SWP views him as the most authoritative representative of its ideology. It does not follow, though, that all statements Marx made are accepted as infallible. Marxist theory is neither a revelation nor a dogma. It is a guide to action, which one must know how to apply to one's own time; and the same goes for writings by Engels, Lenin, Trotsky, and other Marxist teachers.

Cross-examination of Cannon was handled by Schweinhaut. What amounted to a sharp debate ensued between the capitalist mouthpiece and the revolutionary leader. Schweinhaut, who was defending a bankrupt social order, used all the legal tricks at his command. But Cannon bested him politically in the confrontation, as a sketch of a few highlights will show.

The prosecutor began by citing testimony that had been given during direct examination, to the effect that expropriation of capitalist property without compensation was not a question of principle. Then he read a sentence from the SWP's 1938 Declaration of Principles, calling for "expropriation and socialization, without compensation." The quotation showed, Schweinhaut insisted, that the SWP did consider it a matter of principle to take such property without compensation. By implication, he was calling the party leader a liar.

That phrase was in the declaration, Cannon replied, but the question of compensation does not involve a principle. We concern ourselves with the welfare of the great mass of the people. The concerns of the capitalist minority are secondary to what we consider the public interest. The capitalists could be pensioned if they agreed not to resist by force the mandate of the majority.

The SWP believes the government is the tool of the capitalists, the prosecutor then argued, so in order to suppress the capitalists the SWP must suppress the government. He meant, of course that the SWP intended to overthrow the government through minority violence.

We would radically change the whole structure of the government, Cannon answered, in accord with the changed will of the majority. Our ideas would gain increased support because of the bankruptcy of the present system and the increasing hardships that result for the masses. The capitalists would try to stop the popularization of ideas inimical to their system and to block organization of an anticapitalist movement. They would turn toward fascist methods. The ruling class would be the ones who substituted violence for a peaceful, democratic solution of the nation's ills.

Schweinhaut demanded to know how the SWP would resist such a capitalist uprising. The same way Lincoln did, Cannon shot back. Lincoln summoned volunteers to suppress the slaveholders' rebellion.

Groping for a new angle on the issue of force and violence, the prosecutor attacked the SWP's position on workers' defense guards. Such formations were intended, he insisted, not primarily for protection of the trade unions, but as an expanding process, as part of the preparation for a struggle to take power.

Defense guards would exist and grow, Cannon rejoined, only insofar as they had an urgent task to perform. If the fascists grew and attacked the unions, the workers had to counter that hostile move by developing and strengthening defense guards. In the course of such a struggle, labor's inherent strength could lead to the defense guards becoming a very effective power.

Since the SWP expected capitalist violence, Schweinhaut added gratuitously at that point, it wanted to start in advance to build up a workers' army.

We couldn't by mere program build up a workers' army, Cannon patiently explained for the benefit of the jury. We couldn't organize workers' defense guards merely because we wanted them. They could appear only when the pressing need for them became apparent to the workers. It was a natural process growing out of the class struggle.

Further on in the questioning, Schweinhaut brought up his pet quotation from the *Communist Manifesto* about "forcible overthrow of all existing social institutions." When the SWP distributed that document, he asked, did it caution against the sentence quoted?

We published it as a historic document, Cannon replied. Our members were expected to govern themselves by the program of the SWP.

The prosecutor next referred to a sentence in a pamphlet entitled *The Founding Conference of the Fourth International,* which read: "The strategical task of the Fourth International lies not in reforming capitalism but in its overthrow." Didn't that mean, he argued, that the SWP did not even intend to attempt anything by legislative reformation? Socialist aims couldn't be attained, Cannon responded, by reformation of capitalism, which is an outlived system.

Taking a different tack in an attempt to picture the SWP as "unpatriotic," Schweinhaut tried some flag-waving. He demanded to know whether the party believed at all in national defense.

We believe in defending the country by our own means, Cannon said, but we don't believe in defending the imperialist government. We are against giving any support to the existing U.S. government or to an imperialist war which it conducts. We will oppose such a war by speaking against it; we will oppose it politically.

Near the end of the cross-examination the chief prosecutor read aloud from *The Militant* of July 12, 1941. He had culled an excerpt which stated: "During the first drivers' strike of May 1934, the employers threw against the embattled transport workers the entire police force of Minneapolis and 5,000 special deputies armed with clubs and guns. In a historic battle . . . the drivers fought the police and deputies to a standstill and chased them off the streets of the city." When he had finished reading, the following exchange took place:

Schweinhaut: "Is that Trotskyism demonstrating itself?"

Cannon: "Well, I can give you my own opinion, that I am mighty proud of the fact that Trotskyism had some part in influencing the workers to protect themselves against that sort of violence."

Schweinhaut: "Well, what kind of violence do you mean?"

Cannon: "This was what the deputies were organized for, to drive the workers off the streets. They got a dose of their own medicine. I think the workers have a right to defend themselves. If that is treason, you can make the most of it."

During this stage of the trial several literary items were introduced as defense exhibits. These included SWP resolutions on the labor party and workers' defense guards; an article by Goldman from *The Militant* of March 29, 1941, explaining why opposition to U.S. participation in World War II did not connote help to Hitler; and passages from Goldman's pamphlet *What is Socialism?* in which he outlined the mass benefits possible through common ownership of the means of production. There were also two resolutions which had been adopted at the SWP's special convention in December 1940: one disaffiliating the party from the Fourth International and the other suspending its 1938 Declaration of Principles.

In addition, efforts were made to introduce into evidence a draft resolution submitted to the SWP's plenum-conference, held shortly before the trial. It contained reformulations of some points in the old Declaration of Principles. The prosecution objected to introduction of this item on the ground that it had been written subsequent to the date of the indictment against us. Judge Joyce ruled that the draft could not be placed in evidence.

Among the witnesses who took the stand in our support were six workers who had belonged to Local 544's defense guard—Richard E. Atherton, Daniel E. Doyle, Harold B. Martin, Kenneth E. McKenzie, Gustave Reierson, and Ole G. Reierson. They testified along the following lines:

It became common knowledge in 1938 that the Silver Shirts were threatening to attack Local 544. The union also learned that Silver Shirt meetings were attended by George K. Belden, head of the Associated Industries. Belden represented a gang of bosses who didn't like the union because it was getting too strong.

To meet that threat Local 544 took the lead in organizing a union defense guard. The newspapers were notified of the action, and the members of the guard were urged to tell everyone they knew what was being done. It was felt that public knowledge of the union's move to defend itself might serve to prevent any threatened attack. Meetings of the guard were held to discuss its defensive functions. Nothing was ever said at those meetings about using the union force against the government.

For a time members of the guard held target practice with .22-caliber guns. Later on, the Silver Shirt threat began to die out and the target practice was discontinued, since there was no longer any need for it. After that, the guard functioned only as monitors at union picnics and as ushers at other large social affairs.

Ray Rainbolt, who had been elected chairman of the workers' defense unit, also testified on the subject. All trade unionists were invited to join the formation, he said, and it had members from several different unions. Decisions concerning the policies of the guard were made by membership vote. Its weapons consisted of two single-shot .22-caliber pistols and two single-shot .22-caliber rifles, which were used for target practice. It continued to function up to the time of a 1940 Christmas party for children of union members. After that the guard went out of existence.

Grace Carlson rebutted testimony by reporters for the *Cleveland Plain Dealer* and the University of Minnesota's student newspaper that she had advocated use of armed force against the government. In doing so she took the opportunity to tell the jury what had actually been discussed on the occasions involved. At the Cleveland meeting her topic was "The Right to Live," and she had centered her remarks on the government's callous policy of spending billions for war while it criminally neglected problems of poverty and disease. Her talk at the University of Minnesota was entitled "The Road to Socialism." She had urged the student audience to study the reactionary nature of the capitalist system, so as to convince themselves of the need to help create a socialist society in this country.

Two University of Minnesota students, John Hart and Earl

Opstad, testified in support of Carlson. In her talk at the university, they said, she pointed out that a majority had to be convinced of the need for a fundamental change before socialism could be established. Speaking in that context, she added that the majority might well have to defend itself militarily because the ruling class would not give up its possessions without a fight.

Roy Orgon, who had been an organizer for the Federal Workers Section of Local 544, told the jury about being assaulted by Tobin's goons the previous June. In outlining his duties as an organizer he also managed to describe how the FWS supported the interests of the unemployed. Then, during the cross-examination that followed, Anderson hypocritically accused the FWS leaders of inciting workers to violence in the 1939 WPA strike. The prosecutor also emphasized that Orgon had been among those convicted of "conspiring against the government" in the federal trial that followed the 1939 walkout.

Earlier in our trial the government's star witness, James Bartlett, had testified that the SWP plotted to "take over" the trade unions by developing "fine leaders with influence and prestige" inside the labor movement. Our dedication to helping the workers use the union power in the service of their class interests was thus debased into its opposite—a cunning scheme to gain influence and prestige for "subversive" purposes. This phony line was torn apart by Ray Dunne, who took the stand to give the jury a true picture of our trade union policy. He refuted, point by point, Bartlett's tale about private talks in which Dunne had allegedly given him the real score about SWP aims.

In addition, the record was set straight concerning a story Bartlett had related in court about an SWP "plot" to oust him from union office. Bartlett had asked help from the Local 544 leaders in getting himself reelected to the presidency of his local, Dunne informed the jury. "I told him that he had become the ordinary, fat little business agent and that the [revolutionary socialist] movement was not interested in supporting that kind of material in the trade union movement."

Yet another attempt was made at this point to tell about Tobin's role in framing us up on "sedition" charges. Schweinhaut leaped from his chair as though he had been given the hotfoot. It was wrong, he objected, to introduce our "feud with the AFL" into the case. The judge again ruled such discussion "immaterial."

While on the stand, Dunne reviewed the background of the

Minneapolis General Drivers Union. He traced its rise as a powerful force within the city's labor movement, described its democratic internal life, and recounted gains the workers had won through the organization.

In addition to helping attain those objectives, he admitted frankly, the SWP was interested in spreading socialist ideas among trade union members. "Our policy was to organize and build strong unions," Dunne said, "so workers could have something to say about their own lives and assist in changing the present order into a socialist society. . . . The Socialist Workers Party supports the organization of a labor party. . . . We want [the workers] to gain experience in their own political organizations, to rely upon their own political parties, as opposed to and separate from the old parties of the capitalist class. We support that idea because we believe that it is a good thing for them to test the methods and experience the methods that have to be used to find their way toward socialism."

Anderson handled the cross-examination. One of his pitches was to accuse the union leadership of precipitating the violence that occurred during the 1934 trucking strikes. But Dunne answered him so effectively that the attempt miscarried.

The prosecutor also made use of a stack of government exhibits containing excerpts from revolutionary literature. These were read, item by item, with emphasis to the jury on "proof" therein that the SWP called for armed struggle to overthrow the government. As each excerpt was taken up in that fashion, Dunne was asked to state whether he agreed or disagreed with what had been written. A battle followed between the unprincipled legal beagle and the principled workers' leader. Dunne refused to be trapped into giving yes-or-no answers to tricky questions. Instead, he sought to put the quotations back into their proper contexts, so that they could be accurately understood by the jury.

I was also called to the stand as a witness for the defense. My testimony centered on a review of the IBT campaign in over-the-road trucking, on our opposition to any form of control over the trade unions other than through a majority vote of the rank and file, and on SWP policy concerning strikes. With reference to the latter subject, I pointed out that a strike is not a game to be played lightmindedly or at will. It involves serious hardships for the workers. Therefore, a strike should be conducted only when necessary to protect the workers' interests, and then the union leadership should do everything possible to help win the fight against the bosses.

Schweinhaut cross-examined me. He insisted that we were quick to call strikes at every opportunity, that we flatly opposed any form of arbitration to settle labor disputes. If that was not the case, he demanded, when did we consider arbitration admissible?

It was wrong for union leaders to rush into arbitration of conflicts with employers, I answered, but under certain conditions action of that kind was sometimes necessary. If a strike was going badly, for instance, and a danger existed that the workers might lose their fight entirely, arbitration would be in order. At times one might also find it advisable to handle secondary issues in that way. As a case in point, the key issue in 1934 was employer recognition of the Minneapolis General Drivers Union. After the bosses gave in on that main demand, we thought it best—in the given circumstances—for the union to accept arbitration of specific wage rates. On the whole, though, such qualifying of the workers' freedom of decision concerning terms of employment was not the best practice, even if it was sometimes necessary.

Another angle was then tried by the prosecutor. He implied that I had lied in my answer to his question, stressing that "you believe there is no such thing as impartial arbitration in disputes between contending forces in the class struggle."

A conflict exists, I explained to the jury, over the division of industrial wealth between wages and profits. There is no such thing as a person whose interests do not trace back, ultimately, to one of those two income sources. Therefore, where issues in the class struggle are concerned, no one can be wholly objective, completely impartial. But in spite of that fact, circumstances sometimes arise in which it becomes necessary for the workers to take their chances on the decision of an arbitrator.

Another clash involved a letter that had supposedly been written to me from Seattle, Washington, on August 11, 1941, and signed by a person I didn't know. It asked me to either come to that city myself or have Ray Dunne make the trip, to help start an SWP branch there. The area showed promise for us, according to this curious request, because Seattle was "adjacent to the military and naval concentration at Fort Lewis and Bremerton, and Sand Point; it is the gateway to Alaska where great military camps are being established."

Schweinhaut now flashed a copy of that letter in the courtroom. What was meant, he asked, by "the reference to the military and naval concentration?"

All I could recall, I replied, was that help had been requested to start a party branch in Seattle. If there was a reference to military establishments, it had made no impression upon me, because I didn't remember such a remark having been made.

The Seattle letter had been written after we were indicted on charges which included alleged efforts to "foment insubordination in the armed forces"; it was phrased in such a way as to fit neatly into that particular charge; the signer was unknown to me; and the prosecutor had a copy of it. Those being the circumstances, the actual source of the letter seemed plain enough—the FBI's bag of dirty tricks.

Schweinhaut concluded his cross-examination after having committed that vile act of forgery; and since I was the last witness for the defense, the time had come for the lawyers to take the center of the stage.

16. A Confused Jury

Counsel for both sides now proceeded to sum up the evidence that had been presented. Here again the government took an edge for itself. Goldman, who made the main presentation for the defense, found himself sandwiched in between the two prosecutors.

Anderson spoke first. He delivered a brutal attack on the defendants, which was intended to evoke antilabor prejudice and other reactionary sentiments among the jurors. We were accused of calling strikes for "unreasonable" demands at a time of "national emergency," and of organizing mass demonstrations for "seditious purposes." Formation of Local 544's Federal Workers Section was branded a plot to take over Minneapolis. "Why," he asked, "did WPA workers need a union? The government takes care of WPA."

The U.S. district attorney emphasized our opposition to imperialist war, our advocacy of military training under trade union control, and the creation of Local 544's defense guard. Those policies, he insisted, were designed to undermine the armed forces of the government and create our own army; they were evidence, in themselves, that we were trying to overthrow the government by force and violence.

Trotsky was named the chief conspirator, the "man who gave the orders" to us. "What business is it of theirs," the prosecutor demanded, "to bring the history of the Russian revolution into the United States? Why don't they go to Russia, if they are so interested in that country?"

Concerning *The Militant,* he said, "It would take a saint to read that literature and not be poisoned by it." As for the Socialist Workers Party, it was "a cancer in the body of the country," and the government wanted "to exterminate this party so that it won't threaten for another century." Never before, he charged, "since Benedict Arnold sold military secrets to the British, has the authority of the government been challenged as it has been by this revolutionary party."

While delivering that vicious tirade against us, Anderson gave Bartlett high praise as a "patriot." He proclaimed his belief in "every word" the Tobinite stool pigeon had uttered from the witness stand.

Having thus wrapped his pet informer in the flag, the prosecutor next made an appeal to religious prejudice. The jurors were urged to have the same kind of simple faith in the government that the disciple Paul had in Christ. "Believe! Believe!" he cried, after stating in a shocked whisper that the defendants held meetings "on the Sabbath." Our conviction was demanded to preserve the sanctity of the family, the home, the church, the schools, and the nation.

Goldman faced the difficult task of following that parade of prejudices with an appeal to reason. "Never before, in the history of a federal court," he noted, "has a jury been confronted with the necessity of listening to the social, political and economic ideas and ideals of defendants, formulated in hundreds of articles and pamphlets, for the purpose of determining whether or not the defendants are guilty as charged in an indictment. . . . I am not here to try to convince you of the correctness of our ideas. . . . I am here, however, primarily to explain those ideas sufficiently well so that the issues in this case will become clear to you."

There were three major charges against us, our chief counsel reminded the jury: conspiring to overthrow the government by force and violence, conspiring to advocate such an overthrow, and conspiring to foment insubordination in the armed forces. The reality was, however, that there had been no conspiracy whatever on our part. We were anxious to proclaim our ideas from the housetops, as was shown by the large amount of SWP literature that had been introduced into evidence.

Against what we had written, the government had counterposed testimony by Tobinites who claimed we said one thing in public but our private intentions were to do something altogether different. After extensive court experience, Goldman observed in this connection, one could perceive something peculiar about their testimony. Trial lawyers had come to recognize that, if all witnesses told more or less the same story, it was a sign they had been coached. This circumstance was not changed by Anderson's protestations about Bartlett's "patriotism" because—as a famous literary figure once said—"patriotism is the last refuge of a scoundrel." It was obvious, therefore, that an accurate judgment could not be formed on the basis of testimony by government witnesses. Decisive weight should be given, instead, to what had been written in official SWP documents.

In that connection, the jurors were cautioned, they should be on guard against the government's crooked tactics in citing excerpts from our documents. His warning against such trickery was presented in a form that had the additional purpose of counteracting Anderson's crude efforts to arouse religious prejudice against us. Goldman referred to an excerpt from the New Testament, Matthew 10:34, where Jesus Christ is quoted as saying: "Think not that I am come to send peace on earth; I came not to send peace, but a sword." Through use of the prosecution's outrageous methods, our chief counsel pointed out, that quotation could be ripped out of context to brand Christ, too, as an "advocate of force and violence."

Goldman, who was a gifted orator, then held the jurors' attention as he gave them a rounded exposition of the party's actual views. His remarks were quite extensive, and only the main points can be summarized in this condensed account.

Our fundamental aim, he said, was to convince a majority of the people that a change to a socialist society was needed. To establish a new social order of that kind, it would be necessary to create a new government of labor and its allies. Use of the term "revolution" in that context did not imply the use or advocacy of violence against the existing government; it simply meant the transfer of economic and political power from the capitalists to the workers.

We did not precipitate the class struggle that existed under capitalism, and jailing us wouldn't end it. A basic conflict went on endlessly between workers seeking higher wages and capitalists anxious to make greater profits. This struggle reflected contradictions in the capitalist system which had become acute, giving rise to unemployment, fascism, and catastrophic wars. We advocated a change from such an outlived system. Since we based our perspectives for that change on winning a majority of the people over to a socialist outlook, it should be apparent that we favored a peaceful transition in the social order, to be brought about on the basis of majority rule.

But we predicted that, even after a majority had come to

support our ideas, the capitalist minority would violently resist a fundamental social change. That prediction, based on historical precedents, in no way implied that we advocated violence; and it was hoped that the jurors would see through the prosecution's dishonest attempt to twist such a prediction into a charge that we advocated overthrow of the government by force.

We didn't deny that we believed in the effectiveness of mass demonstrations. In the history of this country that form of struggle had helped to win significant victories for the masses. It had played a big role, for example, in establishing the right to vote and free education. We continued to advocate—and there would continue to occur—demonstrations and strikes in defense of the rights of the many who are exploited by the capitalists. People would continue to be dragged into court and jailed for such actions, but that wouldn't stop the conflicts.

With reference to imperialist war, the government accused us of two things: that we opposed it, and that we intended to take advantage of a revolutionary situation which we expected the war to create. The truth was that we were against the war because it was a conflict between imperialist nations, fought in the interest of the capitalists only. For that reason we opposed Roosevelt's policy of taking this country into the war. We demanded that the people decide the question of war and peace by referendum vote.

Hitlerism, which represented a fascist regime, had to be destroyed. But that couldn't be done through an imperialist war, which would not be a war to destroy fascism. Wherever capitalists remained in control of a country, including the United States, the danger of fascism would continue to exist. Things would be different, though, if there were a socialist government in this country. It would ask the German people to join with us in creating a cooperative commonwealth throughout the world. Organize your revolt against the Nazis, such a U.S. government would urge the German workers, and establish your own socialist regime. Hitler could not last very long after an appeal of that nature from a socialist United States.

We were accused of conspiring to create insubordination in the armed forces, Goldman continued. The charge appeared to be directed at our call for military training under trade union control, at our proposal that officers be elected by the military ranks, and at our demand that soldiers retain their full democratic rights as citizens. Our advocacy of workers' self-defense was also branded conspiratorial, as was the creation of a guard for that purpose by Local 544. The truth remained, however, as our writings and testimony proved, that our objectives were to defend the rights of citizen-soldiers and to defend workers' organizations against fascist attacks.

The government had spent more time on the trade union question than on any other subject involved in the court proceedings. In fact, this actually had far more to do with the reasons for the trial than the contrived accusations that we had conspired to overthrow the government. But Tobin was involved in the trade union aspects of the case, and the court had ruled that we couldn't discuss his role in the action taken against us. We had thus been prevented from fully explaining our contention that the Tobinites, who had testified that our aim was to use the unions against the government, had given false witness. As the defense testimony had shown, however, the SWP's aim was to have its members active in the trade unions in order to have them do their best to serve the workers' cause and thus to earn a hearing for our socialist ideas.

Concerning the defendants as individuals, Goldman said in his peroration: "All of us represent that type of person who does not think very much about his personal fortunes but thinks of mankind, of society in general. The agony, the death of millions of human beings in senseless wars are not abstractions to us. We feel them keenly and we react to them and we try to create a world where destruction and war and poverty and disease will not be the lot of man. . . . We say that we have reached an epoch where mankind must go forward to socialism or else back to barbarism. . . .

"Permit me to say once more and in conclusion: Our ideas, a product of existing conditions, are indestructible. They will ultimately conquer the minds and hearts of the masses who will struggle for their realization because there is no road to peace and plenty other than the road of socialism."

Schweinhaut spoke next. His remarks, which were relatively brief, focused on two central points. He tried desperately to rehabilitate the character of the government's key witness, Bartlett, whose testimony had been ripped to shreds by Goldman in his speech to the jury. The chief prosecutor asked the jurors to take into account that, although Bartlett "may have made some errors" in his statements, he was not a "deliberate perjurer."

Addressing himself to the issues in the trial, Schweinhaut

stressed the similarity between the Socialist Workers Party and the Bolshevik Party of Lenin and Trotsky. Though small at the time, he emphasized, the SWP could soon become a much stronger force. It might well gain in strength, the prosecutor warned, by "preying upon the distress and despair of people during war and depression," for "hungry men" could be induced to "insurrection."

After the lawyers had finished, the judge did his own summing up of the case. As to the charges against the defendants, Joyce told the jury, it was not necessary for the government to prove the existence of an explicit or formal agreement for an unlawful scheme. Conspirators might come to a tacit understanding to accomplish an unlawful design; they might knowingly work together in some way; and to do so they need not be acquainted with one another. In addition, any act or declaration by one conspirator was to be considered evidence against all those involved.

Joyce then catalogued the government's charges along the following lines: The defendants were officers, leaders, or active members of the Socialist Workers Party. The party declared the government of the United States to be imperialistic and capitalistic. It should be overthrown and replaced by a new government called the dictatorship of the proletariat. The new workers' state would expropriate the capitalists' holdings without compensation and destroy the whole machinery of the capitalist state.

The SWP would oppose any war entered into by the existing U.S. government. It would also oppose national unity and suspension of the class struggle during wartime. People would be incited to open fighting along the lines of the Russian revolution of 1917. SWP leaders had conferred with Trotsky as to the method of carrying out the party's aims. They had sought control of trade unions so as to paralyze industry. Their aim was to develop a general strike, which was called a revolutionary situation, with the object of overthrowing the government; and, therefore, arbitration of disputes between workers and employers was discouraged. Efforts were also made to create dissension within the armed forces and induce the ranks to turn their guns against the officers. A defense guard was organized by Local 544 as a first step in a movement to arm workers nationally. The idea of the guard, which came from Trotsky, was patterned after the method used in Russia. There were some firearms at the union headquarters, Joyce noted at that point for the prosecution's benefit, and target practice was conducted.

Speeches were made by the defendants and literature was distributed advocating the foregoing aims of the SWP, the judge added in listing the government's charges. Reformism was rejected on the grounds that only the overthrow of capitalism could solve the social problems. Class collaboration was opposed as an obstacle to development of a successful armed revolution. It was held that the capitalists would not willingly give up their rule, so they would have to be forcibly removed from power by use of arms.

Joyce next presented a summary of defense testimony. We admitted, he said, that the SWP was founded on Marxian principles. Our aim was to establish a workers' government in place of the existing government, which we termed capitalistic. The change would be based on common ownership of the means of production, elimination of private property in the means of production, and abolition of the wage system and of the division of society into classes. In short, there would be a gradual withering away of the government as a ("so-called," he said) repressive force. It would be replaced by administrative councils. Rule over people would be replaced by government over things.

"Dictatorship of the proletariat," the judge's summation of our views continued, meant a dictatorship only in the sense that it would represent the interests of the workers and would not pretend to represent the interests of the capitalists. The term *revolution* meant only a change in government that would be radical and extreme. No idea of the use of force and violence was intended by that form of expression.

It would be most desirable to have the change made peaceably, and the new regime would be willing to compensate the capitalists provided they voluntarily accepted the new order. But history showed that the capitalist minority would try by violent means to hold onto its privileges, against the will of the majority. Therefore, it was an illusion that an economic change could be effected by persuasion and education, by "legal" and parliamentary methods. (The notion that a social revolution could not be made in a legal manner was Joyce's, not ours. We had defined legality as procedure taken in accord with the democratic principle of majority rule. Accordingly, we had contended that nothing could be more legal than the Russian revolution, which had carried out a majority decision.)

The defendants, said the judge, had testified that the SWP supported trade unions for two reasons: because the party favored anything that benefited the workers; and because unions offered a productive field for the spreading of socialist ideas. They had asserted that, if the U.S. entered the European conflict, such action would be opposed in a political sense; but they would not sabotage the war effort or advocate insubordination in the armed forces.

Joyce concluded his remarks with legal instructions to the jury. The term *revolution*, he stated, did not necessarily imply force or violence. It had to be demonstrated that a conspiracy existed to advocate that a social revolution be brought about by force. Each defendant had to be shown to have acted wilfully, knowingly, and intentionally. Direct evidence was not necessary, however, to prove that intent. Frequently actions spoke more clearly than spoken or written words; therefore, the jurors had to rely in part on circumstantial evidence. They were not present, the judge added, to determine the relative merits of socialism and capitalism, but to determine whether the defendants had conspired against the government.

Then, as reported in the court abstract, the jury retired "under the charge of the officers duly qualified and sworn to keep them to consider their verdict." And if ever a group of people faced a complex task in a befuddled state of mind, this was such an occasion.

The jurors were required to pass judgment on ideas concerning a fundamental change in the nation's social structure, which were held to be "subversive." This task involved an evaluation of over 150 exhibits placed in evidence during the trial, mostly containing passages from revolutionary literature. It was necessary, as well, to assess hours and hours of testimony by government and defense witnesses. The prosecution's allegations concerning "illegal" aims of the SWP, as presented through Tobinite stool pigeons, had to be weighed against our explanation of the party's actual goals. Besides that, an objective appraisal of the issues under consideration had to include recognition of our constitutional right to think for ourselves and to propagate our views in an organized way; also to be kept in mind was the government's duty to abide by all provisions of the Bill of Rights.

Yet those who bore such a heavy responsibility knew little or nothing about the politics of class struggle. Their views on social issues—insofar as any thought had been given to such matters—had been shaped since childhood mainly by subjection to capitalist ideology. Now, probably for the first time in their lives, they had come face to face with avowed revolutionaries, who introduced totally new concepts into their consciousness. That experience had to be a confusing one for them. Doubly so, for it occurred at a time when the White House, with its vast propaganda machinery, was appealing for national unity and class peace.

To further complicate the jurors' problem, the prosecution had deliberately stood the truth on its head throughout the trial. The SWP's views had been distorted in every conceivable manner, so as to make it appear that we meant the opposite of what we said—that we were nothing more than a gang of evil conspirators. No mention was made of our constitutional rights. Instead, the party was described as a "cancer in the body of the country," which it was necessary to "exterminate" in the name of the nation's "sanctity."

As though all that weren't bad enough, the judge had made things even worse. His summation of the evidence was cleverly slanted in favor of the prosecution. He told the jurors to "rely in part on circumstantial evidence" since "actions spoke more clearly than words"—an instruction that could be interpreted as a broad hint to give Tobinite testimony more weight than our explanation of the SWP's aims. Joyce also said, in effect, that political association in support of our aims could be held to be conspiracy if the government's charges that we had "seditious" intent was accepted; and he gave the term "conspiracy" a vague, catchall definition.

Still another indication that the jurors had experienced difficulties in coming to a decision is to be noted in the length of their deliberations. They were out from around noon on November 29 until 8 p.m. on December 1—a total of about fifty-six hours. During that time they reached the following verdict:

All the remaining twenty-three defendants were found not guilty on the first count in the indictment. Five were found not guilty on the second count as well: Miles Dunne, Roy Orgon, Kelly Postal, Ray Rainbolt, and Harold Swanson.

Eighteen were found guilty on count two of the indictment, which involved alleged violation of the Smith Act. Those convicted were James P. Cannon, Grace Carlson, Jake Cooper, Oscar Coover, Harry DeBoer, Farrell Dobbs, V. R. Dunne, Max

Geldman, Albert Goldman, Clarence Hamel, Emil Hansen, Carlos Hudson, Carl Kuehn, Felix Morrow, Edward Palmquist, Alfred Russell, Oscar Schoenfeld, and Carl Skoglund.

A form was provided by the court for the jurors to record their verdict. After it had been filled out, a postscript was added: "The jury recommends leniency."

Once the jurors had been discharged, newspaper reporters questioned them about their deliberations. Stories were then published that a majority had been ready to convict all the defendants on all charges, but a few had wanted to find everybody not guilty on both counts in the indictment. Those opposed to our conviction were thought to include the rural jail cook, the lumber sales manager, and the banker. One of the latter three was quoted as terming the prosecution of twenty-eight defendants at one time remindful of the mass trials held by Hitler and Stalin. A long argument was said to have taken place among the jurors, after which a compromise was reached in the form of the announced verdict.

Whatever validity there may or may not have been to press accounts, one has no way of obtaining an exact and rounded picture of the jury's deliberations. Its outlook and intent, as well as the implications of its findings, can be assessed only on the basis of the verdict that was brought in unanimously.

Under the first count in the indictment we were accused of penetrating the trade unions for ulterior purposes, organizing Local 544's defense guard as the first step toward creation of a rebel army, and actively promoting insubordination in the armed forces of the United States. Tobinite informers were used to testify in support of those allegations. Charges and testimony alike were carefully designed to show that we were engaged in an immediate conspiracy to forcibly overthrow the government. Yet the jury found all of us not guilty on that count, and its verdict had the effect of bearing witness that the prosecution had engaged in a crude police frame-up against us.

Count two of the indictment charged us with conspiracy to advocate both insubordination in the armed forces and violent overthrow of the government. In that connection, as the *Minneapolis Tribune* of November 27, 1941, pointed out, the prosecutors had "sought to show that the instrument through which they [the defendants] sought to accomplish this was the Socialist Workers Party." Judge Joyce had accepted precisely that premise when, after presentation of the prosecution's case, he freed five of the defendants. He ruled at the time that they were not shown to have knowledge of the SWP or to have participated in activities to overthrow the government. Under those circumstances it seems likely that the jury—in completely freeing another five defendants—had simply followed the judge's test: namely, that the party itself was on trial, and that the defendants' guilt or innocence was determined by proof, or lack thereof, that they were active party members.

As for the eighteen who were convicted, the prosecution had failed to produce any evidence against them which the jury found acceptable, other than the ideas expounded by the party. That was shown by the jurors' rejection of Tobinite allegations in support of the first count in the indictment. A question arises, therefore, as to what the jury intended by the guilty verdict on count two. The only testimony about alleged advocacy of insubordination in the armed forces came from Tobinites, whose honesty was obviously doubted. But the jurors couldn't single out that issue in reporting their findings. They were required to return a blanket verdict on the second count, accepting or rejecting all charges involved. Hence, the "insubordination" issue was inseparably linked with the main accusation of advocating overthrow of the government.

It was thus only the charge of "advocating overthrow of the government by force and violence" that the jurors appeared to have accepted as valid. In doing so, however, they were apparently rejecting the ideas presented by the SWP, which were so new and strange to them. If the defendants were thought to be motivated by criminal intent, it is not likely that the guilty verdict would have been accompanied by a recommendation of leniency in imposing penalties upon us.

Taken as a whole, the outcome of the trial was something less than a sweeping victory for the Roosevelt administration. Ten of the twenty-eight in the prisoners' dock were found not guilty on all charges. No one was convicted of any overt act—only for what was thought and said. What is more, the jury's recommendation of leniency—despite the gravity of the issues involved—undermined the moral validity of such convictions as were obtained. These were poor auspices, indeed, for the debut of the Smith Act, which was being used for the first time against critics of the government. Its innate viciousness had been dramatically exposed. As a result recognition grew that our civil liberties were the prosecution's real target—that we were not criminals at all, but victims of a political frame-up. It thus became possible to gain ever wider support of our continuing fight for justice.

Upon receiving the verdict, Judge Joyce announced that sentences—which could be as much as ten years—would be handed down December 8. That left us to sweat it out for a week before learning how long we would be imprisoned. During that period a social was held at the SWP headquarters in the city. It took place on Sunday, December 7.

Many comrades and friends came to the affair to show their solidarity with those who were to be sentenced the next day. It was a congenial gathering. Some played cards, chess, and checkers; others simply held relaxed conversations. A radio provided background music. Then, like a bolt from the blue, the announcer interrupted the musical program to read a news bulletin: The Japanese were bombing Pearl Harbor.

When we appeared in court the next morning, our families and comrades filled the room to overflowing. All were apprehensive. At that very moment Congress was in the process of declaring hostilities against Germany, Italy, and Japan. Roosevelt was urging retaliation for what he termed a day of "infamy" at Pearl Harbor. The capitalist propaganda machine was flooding the country with calls for patriotic support of the war effort, and we had just been convicted of advocating the overthrow of the government by force and violence. It seemed likely that the judge might seize upon the sudden change in political atmosphere to throw the book at us.

Ray Dunne was the first one called before the bench. A hushed silence fell over the room, as all ears strained to hear what the judge was saying. He ordered that Dunne be imprisoned for a term of—sixteen months. As those words were uttered, there was a perceptible easing of tension. Sixteen months is a long time to spend in prison, but ten years would have been far worse.

Eleven other defendants received the same sixteen-month term: Cannon, Carlson, Cooper, Coover, Dobbs, Geldman, Goldman, Hansen, Hudson, Murrow, and Skoglund. Six were ordered to prison for a year and a day: DeBoer, Hamel, Kuehn, Palmquist, Russell, and Schoenfeld.

Our attorneys immediately filed notice of appeal, and the judge ordered a stay of sentence pending the outcome of that action. We were allowed continued freedom on bond while the case was taken to higher courts beginning with the U.S. Circuit Court of Appeals.

There appeared to be several reasons for Joyce's moderation in sentencing us. We had been convicted on thought-control charges only. The jury had recommended leniency in imposing penalties. And during the week that had elapsed since the convictions, there had been an increased public outcry against the government's persecution of the Trotskyists because of our beliefs.

To encourage further protests of this kind, Goldman issued a public statement from the courtroom announcing our determination to continue the fight. "We intend to exhaust every step and every resource for appeal purposes," he said. "Above all, we shall appeal to the American people in an attempt to convince them that the rights of free speech, free press and free assembly are in real danger."

A call for support of those convicted was also issued by the five defendants whom the jury had freed. They stated: "We stand in complete solidarity with our convicted eighteen fellow-defendants, whose only 'crime' is their unswerving devotion to the interests of the working class of people. The convicted defendants and the labor and civil liberties organizations cooperating with them have indicated their determination to appeal the verdict against the eighteen to the higher federal courts. We shall assist them and we urge all workers to back this appeal financially and morally."

The American Civil Liberties Union promptly announced that it would cooperate with the Civil Rights Defense Committee all the way in fighting to overturn the verdict. A statement by ACLU officers declared that, if the convictions stood, the Smith Act "will be a dangerous weapon against civil rights of labor and radicals of all varieties."

An editorial in the December 6, 1941, issue of the *New Leader*, published by the Social Democratic Federation, said: Such an application of the Smith Act and of the 1861 Sedition Act turns them into a threat to civil liberties. . . . all Americans who love liberty—and this does not, apparently, include the Communists—must be vividly aware of what is happening."

A week later the *Call*, which spoke for the Socialist Party, expressed similar views. "As usual in these cases," it asserted, "the prosecution relied on flag waving and on scaring the jury half to death with passages from general Leninist literature torn from their context and dating back for decades. . . . Our condemnation of the fantastic proceedings at Minneapolis is unqualified, and we support to the full the move to appeal the decision."

News of the trial's outcome also brought a flood of protests from trade unions throughout the country. A typical example was a resolution adopted by the New Jersey State Industrial Union Council, CIO. This body pledged support to the eighteen, stating that it "condemns the convictions in the Minneapolis case and protests the use of the FBI to interfere in the democratic procedure of the labor movement."

The *Industrial Worker*, organ of the IWW, said on December 6: "We stick to industrial unionism, while they [the SWP] promote one of the many brands of so-called communist politics. But we see eye to eye with them and with other liberty-loving people on the question of civil rights, the right to have opinions and to express them, whether those opinions please the big shots of finance or not."

Union after union—CIO, AFL, and independent—proceeded thereafter to send donations toward the financing of our appeal to the higher courts.

W. E. B. Du Bois, the noted Black educator, declared his solidarity with the defendants; and Adam Clayton Powell, a Black member of the New York City Council, asserted: "Whenever the civil liberties of any American or any American group are threatened, then the civil liberties of all are in danger, and this is the issue in Minneapolis."

Many prominent liberals denounced the government's persecution of the Socialist Workers Party. Among them was Melvyn Douglas, a well-known Hollywood star, who joined the Civil Rights Defense Committee.

Ironically, right after we were sentenced Roosevelt proclaimed December 15 as "Bill of Rights Day." It was the one-hundred-fiftieth anniversary of the adoption of that document, he noted, and it should be especially honored on that occasion to remind people of the nation's goals in its contemporary "war for democracy."

Commenting on the president's hypocrisy, *The Nation* of December 13, 1941, observed editorially: "The prosecution of . . . Trotskyists for sedition and the conviction of eighteen of them . . . are challenges to every believer in civil liberties. They are an example of the very thing the Bill of Rights sought to make impossible—the imprisonment of men not for what they did but for what they thought and said. . . . We believe that the precedents established by this conviction are dangerous to freedom of thought and expression in America. . . . We believe that all progressives of whatever political orientation must join in the defense of the Minneapolis defendants or permit the establishment of a precedent that may be used some day against any of them."

Roosevelt's fakery about the Bill of Rights was also taken up at a public meeting held by the CRDC in New York on December 15. Around seven hundred attended the affair, including outstanding representatives of civil rights groups and workers' parties. Roger Baldwin, founder of the ACLU, told the gathering: "I am celebrating with you not the glorification of the document, but resistance to a violation of it."

James P. Cannon, one of the Smith Act victims, solidarized himself with Baldwin's cogent remark. "In fighting for the Bill of Rights," he said at the New York meeting, "in its essence, in its application, and not as something to be preserved in a museum, we are conducting a progressive, and at this juncture, a highly revolutionary fight. . . . People with diverse views are rallying around the banner of this splendid committee, the Civil Rights Defense Committee . . . [and this gives] the promise to others, who like us might fall victims, that they will not be friendless in the day of adversity, and in the day of persecution."

Shortly thereafter the CRDC issued a new pamphlet, "The Bill of Rights in Danger," which brought people up to date on the latest developments in the Minneapolis case; and one of the defendants, Ray Dunne, began a national tour to help rally support for our fight to overturn the convictions.

At the same time the Socialist Workers Party took all possible steps to demonstrate its determination to carry on political work in defiance of the government's witch-hunt against us. The party also sought to make clear that it would continue to exercise the democratic right to use all available means to propagate its revolutionary socialist program. Proceeding accordingly, the SWP in Minnesota nominated Grace Carlson, one of those convicted under the Smith Act, as its mayoralty candidate in the Saint Paul city elections, scheduled for 1942. In announcing her candidacy, Carlson asserted defiantly: "I stand for international socialism, for the principles of Marx, Lenin and Trotsky. I believe only a socialist government can bring a lasting peace, and freedom and plenty for all."

Concerning the SWP policy in the aftermath of Pearl Harbor,

an official statement was issued in the name of the party's chief officer, James P. Cannon. It was published in the January 1942 issue of *Fourth International*, the theoretical magazine of the Trotskyist movement at that time.

The party statement declared: "Up to December 8, 1941, when this country officially entered World War II, we considered the war upon the part of all the capitalist powers involved—Germany and France, Italy and Great Britain—as an imperialist war. . . . This characterization of the war was determined for us by the character of the state powers involved in it. They were capitalist powers in the epoch of imperialism; themselves imperialist— oppressing other nations or peoples—or satellites of imperialist powers. The extension of the war to the Pacific and the formal entry of the United States and Japan change nothing in this basic analysis."

Concerning the SWP's attitude toward the Soviet Union and China, on the other hand, the declaration continued:

"We make a fundamental distinction between the Soviet Union and its 'democratic' allies. We defend the Soviet Union. The Soviet Union is a workers' state, although degenerated under the totalitarian-political rule of the Kremlin bureaucracy. Only traitors can deny support to the Soviet workers' state in its war against fascist Germany. To defend the Soviet Union, in spite of Stalin and against Stalin, is to defend the nationalized property established by the October revolution. That is a progressive war.

"The war of China against Japan we likewise characterize as a progressive war. We support China. China is a colonial country, battling for national independence against an imperialist power. A victory for China would be a tremendous blow against all imperialism, inspiring all colonial peoples to throw off the imperialist yoke. The reactionary regime of Chiang Kai-shek, subservient to the 'democracies,' has hampered China's ability to conduct a bold war for independence; but that does not alter for us the essential fact that China is an oppressed nation fighting against an imperialist oppressor. We are proud of the fact that the Fourth Internationalists of China are fighting in the front ranks against Japanese imperialism."

As for the real war against fascism, the SWP said, it could only be waged by a government of the workers and their allies. Only such a government could assure that peace would not be followed by another economic rape of Germany, as was brought about through the Versailles treaty at the end of the first world conflict.

"When the people of Germany can feel assured that military defeat will not be followed by the destruction of Germany's economic power and the imposition of unbearable burdens by the victors, Hitler will be overthrown from within Germany. But such guarantees against a second Versailles cannot be given by Germany's imperialist foes."

The statement issued in Cannon's name also contained a section on our conduct as a revolutionary minority in wartime.

"Our program . . . is today the program of only a small minority. The great majority actively or passively supports the war program of the Roosevelt administration. As a minority we must submit to that majority in action. We do not sabotage the war or obstruct the military forces in any way. The Trotskyists go with their generation into the armed forces. We abide by the decision of the majority. But we retain our opinions and insist on our right to express them.

"Our aim is to convince the majority that our program is the only one which can put an end to war, fascism and economic convulsions. In this process of education the terrible facts speak loudly for our contention. Twice in twenty-five years world wars have wrought destruction. The instigators and leaders of those wars do not offer, and cannot offer, a plausible promise that a third, fourth and fifth world war will not follow if they and their social system remain dominant. Capitalism can offer no prospect but the slaughter of millions and the destruction of civilization. Only socialism can save humanity from this abyss. This is the truth. . . .

"In this dark hour we clearly see the socialist future and prepare the way for it. Against the mad chorus of national hatreds we advance once more the old slogan of socialist internationalism: Workers of the World, Unite!"

As this forthright declaration of the Socialist Workers Party's continuing opposition to imperialist war showed, we made no political concessions to those with different views whose backing was sought in the fight to overturn the convictions under the Smith Act. The campaign through the Civil Rights Defense Committee to win broad support of our appeal to the higher courts was based entirely on the need for united action in order to protect the democratic rights at stake.

About two years elapsed before our case reached the U.S. Supreme Court, and during that period several new developments took place in 544-CIO's struggle against Tobin.

17. Another Kangaroo Trial

Two kinds of "justice" were handed out by the capitalists: frame-ups against workers' leaders who remained loyal to their class, and handsome rewards to some labor officials who had been outstanding in doing the bosses' bidding.

One of those in the latter category was Meyer Lewis, a personal representative of AFL President William Green. Lewis had been rushed to Minneapolis in the summer of 1941 to help Tobin against Local 544-CIO. But after spending only three weeks in the city, he grabbed an opportunity to engage in what promised to be an even more lucrative calling. Lewis went to Stockton, California, where he was given a management job at the open-shop Flotill Cannery. To earn the high salary that went with the post it was necessary only for him to help hold the workers' wages at the lowest possible level. As an experienced labor faker he had the required skills for the task, and the jump in personal income involved squared with what he obviously considered the highest principle in life—his own advancement.

Another recipient of capitalist bounty was Alfred P. Blair, who had been an official of the Brewery Workers Union. In return for his political support to Governor Stassen, Blair was appointed early in 1941 as state labor conciliator. He accepted the post despite strong trade union opposition to the Minnesota "Slave Labor Law," which he was being assigned to enforce. In that official capacity he schemed with Stassen and the employers to strip 544-CIO of its legal rights and to certify Tobin's paper setup as the sole bargaining agent in the Minneapolis trucking industry.

Less than a month after that dirty work was finished, Blair was hired at a fat salary to serve as "labor relations expert" for the Gamble-Robinson Company. This fruit and produce firm had been among the big outfits chiefly responsible for the bloody assaults on picket lines during the 1934 trucking strikes. Since then it had fought the unions at every turn, and it remained a die-hard enemy of organized labor. Blair was equal to the task assigned to him by such a stern master, however, as he showed in December 1941. At that time he rejected the Gamble-Robinson workers' demands for substantial wage increases and forced them out on strike. A contract settlement was then jammed through on cut-rate terms like those in the sweetheart deal made the previous summer between the Tobinites and other trucking firms.

Blair and Meyer Lewis had differentiated themselves from the general run of business unionists only in the sense that they had openly gone over to the bosses' side. The perfidy of Daniel J. Tobin, for example, who ostensibly remained in labor's ranks, knew no bounds after the United States entered the war. To an increasing degree the IBT president functioned as an outright capitalist flunky, and his treachery to the workers can be illustrated by a few quotations from the *International Teamster*.

Writing in the May 1942 issue of the IBT magazine, Tobin forecast "a new era in labor relations when all strikes may be virtually outlawed." Therefore, he advised, every Teamster unit should "employ a first-class statistician in order properly to present its demands before arbitration boards." So far as the IBT was concerned, strike action had already been outlawed by a Tobin decree, and he was merely advocating a contrived substitute for use of the union power. But statistics alone, no matter how elaborate, cannot defend the workers' interests. In fact, the Teamster dictator admitted as much when he complained about "unpatriotic employers" who took advantage of his no-strike policy to "increase their personal profits."

Tobin demanded more from IBT members than abstention from strikes of their own. In the same issue of the *International Teamster* he ordered the truck drivers to act as strikebreakers against other trade unionists. "The general president," he said, "calls the attention of all local unions to his confidential letter of April 3. He again strongly cautions all local unions to continue work and to disregard picket lines. If you are requested by the representative of some other union to refuse to cross picket lines, tell him to take it up with his international union, and that when you get orders from your international union you will act."

Apparently the May directive failed of its purpose to a significant extent, for Tobin next issued a vicious ultimatum. Obey me, he said in effect, or face expulsion from the union, loss of job, and even victimization by the FBI. Such threats were clearly implied when he declared in the IBT magazine of June 1942: "If you can't comply with our international orders, which are founded on necessity, AND ON ORDERS FROM OUR GOVERNMENT, then the best thing to do is to notify the International Union. Then we will protect ourselves. We know how! . . .

"The International Union, in my judgment, will be called upon within the very near future, to forward to the Federal authorities a list of the officers in any district who cause a stoppage of work without having the sanction of the International Union. . . . AND I MIGHT ADD FOR YOUR INFORMATION THAT THE OFFICIALS OF YOUR INTERNATIONAL UNION WILL NOT REFUSE TO COMPLY WITH THE ORDERS OF THE FEDER-AL GOVERNMENT."

To further those repressive aims, the IBT overlord persisted in his efforts to make a horrible example of the Trotskyists. He sought thereby to show that union members who had the impudence to cross him would have fire and brimstone visited upon them without end; and for that purpose he continued to take every conceivable reprisal—no matter how petty, no matter how mean—against the rebels of 544-CIO.

A typically low blow was struck in the aftermath of the sedition convictions in federal court. Local 544-CIO was no longer in a position to maintain a paid organizational staff, so its function-aries applied to the government for unemployment compensation, to which they were entitled. Tobin's lawyers immediately filed a protest with the Minnesota authorities against the payment of any such claims. After that the state unemployment office went through the motions of holding a hearing on the case, and the requested insurance payments were denied. The official ruling was based on a phony argument that the applicants had "separated from AFL-544 by their own voluntary conduct without just or good cause."

The denial of unemployment compensation was part and parcel of an effort to deprive the 544-CIO leaders of economic sustenance in any form. Through an employer-Tobin conspiracy they were blacklisted in the trucking industry, and attempts were also made to prevent them from earning a living in any other way. As a result the victimized union militants were thrust into dire circumstances. Harry DeBoer and Carl Skoglund, for instance, were forced to set up a repair service for household appliances on a shoestring basis, and it barely enabled them to get by. Emil

Hansen and Moe Hork, to cite another example, were finally compelled to leave town for an extended period in order to earn enough to maintain their families.

Reprisals were also taken against anyone in the Minneapolis AFL who was suspected of harboring sympathy toward 544-CIO. One case of that nature involved John Janosco, secretary-treasurer of Upholsterers Local 1895. A complaint was filed against him in the Central Labor Union by 544-AFL on the grounds that he was a "suspected Trotskyite." Tobin himself then pressed specific charges through the International Upholsterers Union. He accused Janosco of "causing to be employed" on the staff of a credit union paper to which Local 1895 subscribed for its members "one Miles Dunne." At Tobin's insistence Janosco was suspended from the union.

For years thereafter the IBT head manifested great anxiety about the possibility of our making a comeback somewhere inside the international. Whenever any sign of opposition to his policies developed within the organization, he was quick to launch into a crusade against the "Trotskyite" danger.

As the attack on Janosco showed, the Teamster bureaucrats constantly hounded the whole AFL movement in Minneapolis. They were backed up, moreover, by the AFL officialdom nationally and by the Roosevelt administration. Under those pressures the Central Labor Union, which had been favorably influenced by the rise of a strong truck drivers union in the city, abandoned such progressive views as it had once held. Its retreat before the wave of reaction began when the clash between 544-CIO and the IBT erupted, and the process of capitulation soon turned into a rout.

Up to June 1941 the AFL unions locally had opposed U.S. entry into the war. By the end of the year, however, that position had been completely reversed. As reported in the *Minneapolis Tribune* of December 13, 1941, the Central Labor Union unanimously adopted a program for "industrial peace" and for "all-out support of the war." That action signaled utter abandonment of resistance to ruling-class moves aimed at piling the burdens of war onto the workers' backs. Instead of fighting against the brutal capitalist policies, most union officials throughout the city helped the White House ride herd on the labor rank and file.

Matters were no better in the Minneapolis Teamsters Joint Council. It had been gutted of leading figures who were worth their salt, even when measured by bureaucratic standards. I. E.

Goldberg, who had been sent to the city as Tobin's mouthpiece, said as much in a report he sent on November 29, 1941, to Joseph A. Padway, general counsel for the IBT. Goldberg complained that "the situation has not produced any outstanding leader with the proper qualifications to carry on in the face of our present problems."

Within 544-AFL the laws of the bureaucratic jungle prevailed. Tobin kept a close eye on the outfit, continuing to maintain an iron dictatorship over it. No democratic rights whatever were accorded to the rank and file. The local officers were given arbitrary control over the workers involved, provided that such control was exercised in slavish conformity with IBT policy. Central to the line thus imposed on the Minneapolis transport workers was support of Roosevelt's war aims abroad and collaboration with the bosses in the industrial sphere at home. That outlook was, of course, readily accepted by Tobin's stooges. They were not the least bit concerned about the violations of class principles thus committed. In their view only one thing was really important—how to become top dog in the local Teamster setup.

Given the prevalence of such personal aspirations within the staff of 544-AFL, it didn't take long for internal dissension to develop. Various cliques arose, each one seeking to knife the others in an issueless power struggle. Early in 1942 this situation led to the dumping of James Bartlett, who had been the government's chief stool pigeon in the sedition trial.

Reportedly, another staff member had been dropped a bit earlier, and he had then used a gun, said to have been obtained from Bartlett, to threaten some of the Tobinite officials. Whatever the actual facts, the 544-AFL executive board seized upon the incident to accomplish a desired end. Bartlett was fired from his union post, after which he turned to the management of some bowling alleys he had acquired while an IBT official.

While all this was going on, workers in the trucking industry had been receiving blow upon blow from the bosses. The sweetheart contracts signed by the Tobinites had been only the first setback. Even the cut-rate terms of employment called for in those shady deals were being violated to an increasing degree, and grievances filed by the workers most often went unsettled. On top of that, job conditions generally were going from bad to worse. In sum, it was being demonstrated that unions can have congenial relations with employers only on the latter's terms, and that the militants who had led the truck drivers since 1934 were in reality guilty of only one thing—they had consistently fought the boss class, acting always in the workers' interests.

Under those circumstances it didn't take long for rebellious moods to spread once more among trucking employees. Resistance stiffened to payment of membership dues to the Tobin outfit. Few workers attended meetings of 544-AFL, and opposition groups within the ranks grew in strength.

In that promising situation 544-CIO sought as best it could to keep in close touch with militant workers who were groping for some way to defend their interests against both the employers and the Tobin gang. But the effort had to be made within the framework of a precarious financial situation. Funds were so hard to come by that it was necessary to suspend publication of the *Industrial Organizer* at the end of 1941. Only two special issues of the paper were published after that—one in February 1942 and the other during May of that year. Even paying the rent on a modest headquarters had become a problem. On the whole, the union's situation was such that activity could be carried on only by volunteer organizers, who had very limited means at their disposal.

Handicapped though it was, 544-CIO nevertheless managed to take maximum advantage of an opportunity that developed at Waterman-Waterbury, a furnace manufacturing company. Employees in the shipping division there belonged to 544-AFL, and a company union had been formed in the production end. Each of those setups had contracts with the firm, which were not due to expire until February 1, 1942.

A recruitment drive had already been started at Waterman-Waterbury at about the time Blair had certified the Tobinites as official representatives of trucking employees on an industry-wide scale. The drive was conducted in cooperation with CIO Machinists Local 1140, and the workers involved jumped at the chance to have the CIO represent them. Those engaged in production were taken into Local 1140; the drivers, helpers, and shipping room employees into 544-CIO. A demand was then made upon the state labor conciliator to certify the two CIO locals as bargaining agents for their members, but the conciliator ordered the workers to abide by the boss-dictated contracts that had not yet expired.

Anticipating a crooked ruling from the Stassen administration, CIO Locals 544 and 1140 had also filed petitions with the

National Labor Relations Board, demanding an employee election at the company. This dispute involved production workers over whom the IBT had no normal claim, and for that reason it would have been quite sticky for the NLRB to back up a Stassen-dictated ruling in favor of 544-AFL. So the Roosevelt agency decided to order an election, scheduling it for January 30, 1942.

At that point the Tobinites began to go berserk. First they tried to have 544-CIO barred from the ballot, claiming that Blair's earlier decision made their setup the "exclusive representative" of Minneapolis trucking employees. But the attempt failed. Then they had IBT Warehouse Local 359 put on the ballot—alongside 544-AFL—as a means of opposing both the CIO unions. During the electioneering that followed, the company joined with Tobin's goons in threatening reprisals if the workers didn't "vote right."

Despite such acts of intimidation, CIO Locals 544 and 1140 won the contest by large majorities. The two CIO unions thus became the duly certified bargaining agents at Waterman-Waterbury, and the management had no choice but to recognize that fact.

The significance of the vote was not in the number of workers involved, which was relatively small. What really counted was that, for the first time since June 9, 1941, a group of trucking employees had been allowed the democratic right to name the union of their choice—and they had chosen 544-CIO. Their decision was a clear indication what the outcome would be if industry-wide balloting was held in motor transport, and for that reason the boss press buried skimpy reports of the election results among the ads on inside pages. Despite that dodge the news got around fast by way of the grapevine. Word was spread at the same time that further elections would be sought at other companies, and militants throughout the trucking sphere manifested eagerness to help get such moves going.

Tobin, who was far from a fool, quickly grasped the implications of our victory at Waterman-Waterbury. So he pressed forthwith to have the authorities carry through yet another legal frame-up against us.

Means for the desired action were already at hand. Months earlier the Hennepin County grand jury had indicted four leaders of 544-CIO—Miles Dunne, Moe Hork, Kelly Postal, and Nick Wagner—on several counts of "embezzlement" and "grand larceny." Their trials had since been postponed repeatedly; in ordering one of the postponements District Judge Frank E. Reed had observed sardonically, "By the early part of December there may be no defendants in this case."

He was referring, of course, to the federal "sedition" trial; but the defendants in that frame-up had not gone directly from the courtroom to prison, as Reed's crack hinted might be expected to happen. Five officers of 544-CIO, who were among those tried, had been found not guilty. Although some of the other union leaders had been convicted, they remained free on bond pending an appeal to higher courts. In only one instance had there been a withdrawal from the scene. After Nick Wagner was freed by Judge Joyce, his lawyer had arranged for the embezzlement-larceny charges against him to be dropped on the condition that he would return to Chicago.

Except for Wagner, all the leaders of 544-CIO remained active (Hansen and Hork not yet having left to find work elsewhere), and under their guidance the union was showing renewed signs of vitality. That alarmed the bosses, as well as Tobin. They joined with him in bringing pressure for quick action on the Hennepin County indictments, and Kelly Postal, secretary-treasurer of the organization, was made the primary target.

Postal had been indicted on six different counts. One of these involved a check for $1,000 that had been made out on January 22, 1940, in the middle of the fink suit against officers of Local 544. It was a cashier's check, drawn as a precaution against the finks seeking to tie up the union treasury. The check was finally cashed on June 11, 1941, after the union membership—upon voting to leave the AFL and join the CIO—had instructed the officers to take all necessary steps to defend the local's property from its enemies. Before cashing the check for that purpose, Postal had been advised by counsel that in previous instances of this kind the courts had uniformly held that a seceding local union was entitled to retain its property.

But the grand jury had ignored such legal precedents. Every indictment voted against officers of 544-CIO rested on the false premise that all the local's funds and other holdings belonged to Tobin. In this particular case, therefore, it was alleged that Postal had "embezzled" $1,000 out of the IBT president's treasury.

A jury trial on that charge began February 2, 1942, before Judge Levi H. Hall in district court. Gilbert Carlson and D. J. Shama served as counsel for the defense. The prosecution, under the direction of County Attorney Ed Goff, tried to lay the groundwork for a "conspiracy" angle that could be applied on a sweeping basis to other officers and to active members of 544-CIO.

In that attempt Goff relied almost exclusively on testimony by Tobinites, whose fantasies had already been rejected by the jury in the sedition trial. Seven of these dubious characters took the stand. Four of them had also been witnesses for the prosecution in federal court. Two of the others were of the same stripe, having been members of the Committee of 99. The seventh was T. T. Neal, Tobin's receiver in charge of 544-AFL. They told a rehearsed story which had been concocted in an effort to back up the charge in the indictment.

After hearing both the prosecution and defense testimony, Judge Hall ruled as follows: "By a resolution of the majority of the Local 544 membership, he [Postal] was directed to turn over all the monies of the union to the Union Defense Committee. That this resolution, directing him to turn over the monies was open and avowed, cannot be disputed, as it was heard, according to State witnesses, through the loud-speaker system, even by those assembled outside the building. The membership of the union must have believed they had a right to transfer these monies by resolution, as they attempted to do. Postal, the defendant, was the agent and steward of the membership and turned over their money at their direction."

The judge then instructed the jury to bring in a verdict acquitting Postal of the charge under which he had been tried.

Hall's ruling struck at the heart of the embezzlement-larceny frame-up charges. He upheld the local union's right to keep possession of its funds in transferring affiliation from one parent body to another, and the defense's contention that the action taken was decided upon through a democratic vote of the membership. As for Tobin's claims, the ruling accorded him no rights whatever in the matter.

It thus appeared that the whole plot to use the money issue against the rebel union leaders was about to come apart at the seams, and that caused the IBT mob to lash out in desperation. After the Postal verdict, one of them was reported to have threatened: "We're going to stop those people soon." How they went about that was described in a public statement issued by Miles Dunne:

"At ten minutes to noon on Friday, February 20th, three men, each holding a revolver in his hand, entered the headquarters of Local 544-CIO at 827 Twelfth Avenue South. In the headquarters were Kelly Postal, Ray Rainbolt and Harry DeBoer. . . . The trio of gunmen were unknown to the 544-CIO organizers. They were dressed in plain dark overcoats. The largest of the three carried, in addition to a gun, a wrapped baseball bat.

"The gunmen ordered the 544-CIO leaders to 'Stick 'em up.' When Rainbolt laughed, the largest said, 'This is no laughing matter.' The gunmen searched the 544-CIO men, found no weapons, and ordered them to face the wall with their hands up.

"They asked the names of their victims. When DeBoer told his name, the largest gunman lifted the ballbat and hit DeBoer over the head, back and legs until the latter crumpled in a corner. Mr. DeBoer has been representing Local 544-CIO in current negotiations with the Waterman-Waterbury company, where 544-CIO recently won a National Labor Relations Board election from the AFL.

"The gunmen ordered Rainbolt and Postal to stay quiet with their hands up, and left. They had been in the headquarters about three minutes.

"Local 544-CIO reported this attack to the Minneapolis chief of detectives and to County Attorney Ed Goff.

"Local 544-CIO charges that Daniel J. Tobin, president of the AFL Teamsters International, is responsible for this armed attack on Local 544-CIO leaders. Should any Local 544-CIO leader be attacked or murdered, we shall hold Tobin personally responsible.

"Such tactics as those resorted to today are consistent with the unprincipled and violent struggle that Tobin has been waging in Minneapolis since June, 1941, against the drivers and warehousemen of this city. Local 544-CIO is calling the attention of the national labor movement to the attack on its leaders by Tobin gunmen."

Dunne's statement was reported in the *Minneapolis Tribune* of February 22, 1942, including the passages blaming Tobin for the assault. That got a response from the IBT hooligans, who tried to pretend an imaginary attack had been cooked up as a "typical Dunne stunt." Then, seeking to make the victims appear the criminals, they hypocritically protested in the *Minnesota Teamster*: "A city ordinance provides punishment for those giving false information to police or to a newspaper. Justice demands the offenders be prosecuted."

Neither the police nor the county attorney showed any interest in apprehending the three gunslingers. Through its own investigation, however, 544-CIO obtained the license number of the out-of-state automobile they had used. That information was given to the authorities, but, as could be expected, nothing was ever done about it.

If the reactionary plotters thought the assault would scare off the 544-CIO leaders, they were due for another disappointment. The CIO local went right ahead with negotiations at Waterman-Waterbury, and shortly afterward it secured a one-year contract with the company. Wage hikes ranging from ten to fourteen cents an hour were won for the various job categories involved. These stood in marked contrast to the six-cent increase accepted earlier by 544-AFL for workers at other companies. Besides that, provisions were included for job protection and for enforcement of the agreement—two vital issues on which the AFL had defaulted badly.

News of the Waterman-Waterbury contract gave added impetus to the urge among Minneapolis trucking employees to get out of the AFL and into the CIO. It also threw a scare into the employer-Tobinite conspirators, who hurriedly launched a two-pronged counterattack against us. One of their moves involved Blair's action the previous September certifying 544-AFL as industry-wide bargaining agent.

Blair's decision had been challenged by 544-CIO through a petition for a judicial review in the Ramsey County courts. Tobin's lawyers then leaped in to vigorously oppose such a review. In doing so they used every conceivable argument, including a claim that certification of the IBT had brought "peace, calm and repose" to the industry. District Judge Carleton F. McNally seemed to feel, however, that the court should make some pretense of fairness. He decided to review the matter, and that was being done in a rather leisurely manner when Waterman-Waterbury signed with the CIO.

McNally then speeded things up, apparently under pressure from the bosses. Before long he upheld the Blair decision, which had denied the motor transport workers the democratic right to choose their bargaining agent. His ruling meant that employee elections in trucking would still be blocked in Minneapolis, as a safeguard against the resurgence of 544-CIO.

By that time the second phase of the counterattack was well under way. It had opened in the form of a campaign by the Tobinites to have Kelly Postal retried on the remaining indictments against him. The first trial on the $1,000 count, they contended, had been poorly handled by the county attorney. According to the *Minnesota Teamster* of February 12, 1942, the "bumbling prosecution" failed to refute defense testimony that a majority of the Local 544 membership went into the CIO. "Records" introduced at the earlier Blair hearings should have been used to show that "all members were in 544-AFL." Besides that, the IBT could supply "evidence showing the operations of the bolters."

Concerning the indictments against Miles Dunne and Moe Hork, even the Tobin gang appeared to feel that they could not be prosecuted successfully. Neither of them had been in direct charge of union funds, as had Kelly Postal, who was secretary-treasurer of the local. So, as things turned out, the charges against Dunne and Hork were quietly dropped, and this aspect of the conspiracy to strangle 544-CIO was focused entirely on the secretary-treasurer of the organization.

County Attorney Goff soon announced that Postal would be tried again. This time the charge was first degree grand larceny, involving a sum of $5,000 which had allegedly been embezzled from Tobin. The money in question had been turned over to Filling Station Attendants Local 977, AFL, in the form of a loan from Local 544. Since the two unions had close ties, the loan had been arranged—with the approval of Local 544's membership—as a means of safeguarding the local's funds as it transferred from the AFL to the CIO.

For the second trial, the *Minnesota Teamster* jubilantly reported, "extensive preparations" were being made by the county attorney. Strong "evidence" would be presented, and it would be stressed that Postal "took the money after he was out of the union [IBT] and in the CIO."

A snag was encountered, however, when no local judge could be found who would take the case. An out-of-towner was then brought in from another judicial district, and the defense attorneys, Carlson and Shama, filed an affidavit of prejudice against him. Quite a legal hassle followed. In the end the trial was handled by Arthur W. Selover, one of the most reactionary judges in the Hennepin County district. On top of that, the jury was packed with middle-class individuals who knew little or nothing about the labor movement.

William Compton, an assistant county attorney, served as prosecutor. In his opening speech Compton used the IBT line that "only a conspiratorial minority" within Local 544 had gone over to the CIO "for their own ulterior reasons." After that he paraded Tobinites to the witness stand. They spun tales about a "Trotskyite conspiracy," but not even those fabricators dared pretend that Postal had taken union funds for his own use. Their object was to brand all officers and active members of 544-CIO as "thieves," claiming there had been a "conspiracy" of the CIO to "steal Teamster funds." Judge Selover accepted this crooked testimony into the record, repeatedly overruling objections from defense counsel.

When the defense began its presentation the judge reversed his tactics, upholding the prosecution in blocking testimony which would have given the jurors the real score about the local's break with Tobin. But the prosecutor-judge combine was unable to keep Ray Rainbolt off the witness stand. Speaking authoritatively as recording secretary of Local 544 and as head of the Union Defense Committee that had been formed in connection with the local's switch to the CIO, Rainbolt refuted the charges against Postal. In doing so he gave testimony accounting for every penny of Local 544's funds that had been turned over to the Union Defense Committee by decision of the membership. When he had finished, defense counsel pointed out that neither larceny nor embezzlement had been committed. In transferring its affiliation to a different parent body the local had simply taken steps to safeguard its funds, and that had been done in an entirely legal manner.

On balance, there were no real differences between the two cases against Postal. The charges, the prosecution's alleged evidence, and the rebuttal by the defense were essentially the same in each instance. This time, however, the line taken by the judge was different. Hall had upheld Local 544's right to keep possession of its funds when it broke with the IBT. Selover did just the opposite.

He cited a clause in Tobin's constitution providing that a Teamster local could not be dissolved so long as seven members dissented. The jury was then instructed: "If you find that seven or more members dissented to secession from AFL-544 to the CIO when the vote was taken last June 9, then such vote was ineffectual and the union remained in existence and has a right to possession of all monies including the $5,000 involved in this case."

Selover's charge to the jury did everything but directly order a guilty verdict against Postal. He ruled, in effect, that Tobin's "laws" stood higher than the rights of the union membership; that Local 544 had acted "illegally" in carrying out a decision arrived at through application of the democratic principle of majority rule; and that refusal to submit to a veto by a handful of the IBT dictator's stooges was a "crime."

After getting those instructions the jurors tried to consider their verdict. Hours later they reappeared before the judge and told him they were deadlocked. At that point Selover made his directive more explicit. If Local 544 had violated the IBT constitution, he said, Postal must be convicted. Under that pressure the jury finally came in, on April 24, 1942, with a verdict of guilty.

Judge Selover then sentenced Kelly Postal to a term of up to five years in state prison. Defense counsel moved at once to appeal the conviction to the Minnesota Supreme Court, and a stay of sentence was granted pending the outcome of that action.

Yet another monstrous injustice had been committed by the frame-up artists. Kelly was a veteran of World War I who had seen a lot of action in the frontline trenches. He was also a combat veteran of thirty years' standing in the trade union movement, and throughout those years he had selflessly fought in the interests of his worker comrades. Now this principled man of unimpeachable integrity faced the prospect of sitting in a prison cell where he would bear the stigma of an "embezzler."

Although 544-CIO was eager to save Postal from that fate, it was no longer in a position to raise the large sum needed to finance his appeal to a higher court. Rank-and-file trade unionists, who deeply resented the frame-up, sent in voluntary contributions for the purpose. But these were not sufficient to meet the costs involved, and significant aid could no longer be expected from CIO officials nationally.

When this country had entered the war in December 1941, John L. Lewis had headed a parade of top union officers to the White House, where they had given Roosevelt a no-strike pledge. They had acted, of course, without troubling to consult the rank and file in advance. The labor bureaucrats had simply decided on their own to help the government regiment the workers in the wartime service of imperialism, whether the workers liked it or not. As a corollary, it had been necessary for the bureaucrats to make peace among themselves, at least temporarily; and that had led Lewis to end his feud with the AFL building trades hacks by dissolving the United Construction Workers Organizing Committee, with which Local 544 had become affiliated when it left the IBT.

Dissolution of the UCWOC left 544-CIO entirely on its own. Even before that, the local had been reduced to a remnant of its former self, due to the combined assault by Tobin, the employers, and the government. Another shred had now been torn from that remnant by John L. Lewis, and virtually nothing was left of it. After months and months of hard fighting, we had finally suffered total defeat.

There was no longer any realistic basis on which to continue the trade union struggle, though a way still had to be found to defend Kelly Postal. So 544-CIO asked for help from the Civil Rights Defense Committee, which responded immediately. George Novack, executive secretary of the CRDC, quickly set a campaign into motion to win support for Postal within the labor movement nationally. His action was backed up by James T. Farrell, CRDC chairman, who wrote a brochure describing the outrage committed against the 544-CIO leader. Sufficient funds were raised in that way to finance Postal's appeal in the courts, and numerous trade unions adopted resolutions protesting the frame-up.

On June 18, 1943, the Minnesota Supreme Court upheld the conviction. In doing so the higher judicial body used a fake argument as an excuse for the raw decision. The verdict showed, it contended, that the jury had found there was "bad faith on the part of the defendant."

Three days later Kelly Postal was thrown into the state penitentiary at Stillwater, Minnesota. And as the cell door clanged shut behind him, the CRDC intensified its campaign on his behalf, demanding that he be granted an executive pardon.

To help the campaign along, Postal sent the following message to the CRDC as he entered prison: "I believe that the principle of trade union democracy, which was the chief issue in this case, made it worthwhile to make the appeal [to the Minnesota Supreme Court]. Even though we have lost the battle, we have not lost the war. Trade union friends all over the country have been aroused at what they know is a violation of trade union democracy. I am confident that they will support your committee as it continues the fight for this principle."

His prediction of significant popular support in the fight for a pardon proved accurate. Many thousands of signatures were collected through circulation of petitions in shops and factories, at truck terminals, in union halls, and at union meetings. The famous class-war prisoner Warren K. Billings spoke out in support of Postal, as did A. J. Muste, secretary of the Fellowship of Reconciliation. Backing came from within the Minnesota section of the National Association for the Advancement of Colored People. Both the American Civil Liberties Union and the Workers Defense League joined in the fight for a pardon.

A clear indication of the scope of the pardon movement can be perceived in a Tobinite smear attack on the CRDC campaign, which appeared in the *Minnesota Teamster* of September 9, 1943. It read: "A warning to unions in Minnesota against a fund solicitation scheme among labor unions on the advertised pretense of getting the release from prison of a man who stole union funds, was given this week by Minnesota labor leaders. . . . The pretense for begging money from unions is to try and gain the release from Stillwater prison of Kelly Postal, who was sentenced up to five years for first degree larceny."

Events were to show, however, that slimy tricks of that kind failed of their purpose. There were too many in the ranks of labor who, unlike the Tobin gang, had some principles. Support of the pardon demand mounted steadily. It became so strong, in fact, that the Minnesota authorities decided they had better do something about turning off the heat.

On the morning of May 29, 1944, Postal got a surprise order to accompany a prison guard to the warden's office. There he found the state parole board waiting for him. His release from prison was being considered, the board informed him, if he would stay out of Minnesota. As Kelly reported later, one of the board members said: "Tobin and the Minnesota AFL officials are opposed to your release, but we don't want another Mooney-Billings case on our hands." He was then returned to his cell to think the matter over.

No question of principle was involved in Kelly's accepting parole rather than continuing the fight for a pardon, and in his case there was compelling personal need to get out of prison as quickly as possible. His wife was terminally ill with cancer. When he was sent to the penitentiary she had gone to Oregon to live with one of their daughters, so she could have the necessary care. Kelly wanted desperately to be with his sick wife, and for that reason he decided to accept parole on the conditions laid down by the board.

Late in the afternoon of the same day Postal was taken back to the warden's office. Upon being informed of his decision, the board granted him a parole on the spot. That very evening—after having served around eleven months of his prison term—Kelly was put aboard a train bound for Canby, Oregon. There he was placed under supervision of the Oregon authorities, who insisted that he go to work immediately at whatever employment he could find. That turned out to be one of the toughest jobs in a saw mill.

By then the eighteen found guilty in the federal sedition trial had also been put behind prison bars.

18. Pardon Campaign for the Eighteen

Ever since the convictions under the Smith Act, support of our appeal to the higher courts had been mounting steadily. The extent to which backing came from trade union quarters was especially significant. During 1942 around one hundred fifty central labor bodies and local unions, speaking for over one million workers, passed resolutions protesting the violation of our constitutional rights; and a steady stream of financial contributions to the Civil Rights Defense Committee flowed in from those sources.

Aid from other spheres developed to a similar degree. Among those who spoke out in our defense were Black leaders, academic figures, and editors and writers for liberal publications. Various radical groups also solidarized themselves with the eighteen in the fight against the Smith Act frame-up. But the Communist Party was not among them; it continued to applaud Roosevelt's witch-hunt attack on us.

So brazen was the CP's betrayal of democratic principles that its conduct was pointedly denounced by Roger Baldwin, director of the American Civil Liberties Union. Baldwin had long been a member of the International Labor Defense, a one-time progressive organization which had degenerated badly after falling under Stalinist control. At this point, however, he suddenly resigned from the ILD. His action was reported by the *Daily Worker* of June 9, 1942, in a way that reflected the CP's pride in its "patriotism."

This gutter sheet, published by flunkies of the Moscow bureaucracy, said: "Mr. Baldwin gave as his reason for resigning the fact that the ILD supports the government in its prosecution on sedition charges of the Minneapolis Trotskyists whom he and his organization are defending."

Baldwin's dramatic repudiation of the Stalinist finks was all the more remarkable in view of the war hysteria being manufactured at the time. The White House used that propaganda device to appeal for "patriotic" acceptance of every step taken in connection with the "war against fascism." Those steps naturally included the move to jail the eighteen, and heavy governmental pressure was brought to bear in an effort to block expansion of the movement in our defense. Not only that. The Roosevelt administration looked for additional means of stifling the Socialist Workers Party's continued denunciation of the imperialist warmongers.

A move having the earmarks of a new plot against us was made in the fall of 1942. Two FBI agents appeared one day at the SWP's national office in New York. They introduced themselves as operatives for the Justice Department's "sabotage division" and asked to see the principal officer of the party. Since they had come in broad daylight on this occasion, asking for official consultation, it seemed advisable to talk with them. We had no intention, though, of subjecting one individual to possible entrapment by two frame-up specialists, so both Jim Cannon and I sat in on the conversation.

We were told that the FBI was investigating a railway wreck which had occurred about a year and a half earlier. The agents said the train following or preceding the one involved in the accident had carried officials of the Soviet Union, and therefore they were checking out the possibility that the wreck had resulted from a miscarried act of sabotage by enemies of the Stalin regime. Then they proceeded to put on a soft-cop, hard-cop act.

One of the FBI men assured us that we were not considered definite suspects. They were merely looking into every angle and had come to us in the process because the party was known to be opposed to the Stalinists. "To show good faith," he added, they had first approached the SWP leadership, but they wanted a list of party members in order to question others on the subject.

We pointed out that the party was politically opposed to sabotage as a tactic in the fight for social change and that our position on the question had often been expressed publicly. The government knew all about our views, moreover, so the visit we were receiving signified to us that another crude frame-up was in the making. It was the height of insolence to ask our cooperation in such an attempt, and under no circumstances, we declared, would they be given membership lists.

"If you don't cooperate," the hard cop then threatened, "we can make real trouble for you."

"That is quite obvious," we replied, "since your outfit is already railroading eighteen of our people in a Smith Act frame-up. But you don't frighten us. Go ahead and make your trouble."

Right after the FBI visit, Cannon issued a statement reporting what had happened, and it was prominently displayed in *The Militant* of November 21, 1942. Nothing further was heard on that particular subject, but we soon learned that still another step had already been taken in the campaign to harass the SWP and disrupt its political work.

Toward the end of November complaints began to pile up about *Militant* subscribers not receiving the paper. The fault appeared to lie somewhere in the postal service, and Albert Goldman, our general counsel, went to Washington to find out what was going on. There he learned that, beginning with the issue of November 7, 1942, mailing of the paper had been deliberately held up. The postal authorities refused to give him an official explanation of their action. They did admit "off the record," however, that future numbers of the Trotskyist weekly would also be held up, pending examination by the Justice Department to determine if they were "non-mailable"; and notice was soon received that three consecutive issues, dated November 7, 14, and 21 were "being disposed of"—that is, destroyed.

Destruction of the November 21 issue was especially diabolical. For one thing it carried Cannon's statement about the FBI's "sabotage" caper. That issue also reported the arbitrary conduct of the postal officials. Therefore, on top of everything else, news of the paper's suppression was being suppressed, for the capitalist media made no mention of the attack upon our weekly.

Word of this government move against us was gotten around, nevertheless, and a protest was immediately sent to Washington by the ACLU. Labor and liberal journals soon began to follow suit, as did several radical publications. Not so the Stalinists. They were quick to approve suppression of *The Militant* and to advocate similar action against all public organs critical of the Roosevelt administration.

In one sense the CP hacks got their way The government did more than continue its censorship of *The Militant*, allowing some issues to be mailed after long delays and destroying others. In December the practice was extended to our monthly theoretical magazine, *Fourth International*.

Then Postmaster General Frank C. Walker issued a notice for us to appear at a Washington hearing on January 21, 1943. We would be called upon at that time, he said, to "show cause" why the second class mailing rights of *The Militant* should not be revoked. Fundamentally, the threat constituted another violation of our democratic rights, and, if carried through, that governmental crime against us would become further compounded by material factors involved. Loss of second class rights could be almost tantamount to exclusion from the mails because of the higher rates charged for other forms of postal service. At the very least, such a punitive measure was bound to create a serious obstacle to distribution of our press.

We were also confronted with twenty-seven excerpts from *The Militant*, which the Justice Department had labeled "objectionable." These fell into the following broad categories: attacks on the imperialist aims and the war profiteering of big business; criticism of Roosevelt's foreign and domestic policies; and characterization of the war as imperialist.

The hearing was conducted by three of Walker's official flunkies. Goldman represented *The Militant*, and Osmond K. Fraenkel appeared for the American Civil Liberties Union. Both Goldman and Fraenkel presented extensive arguments in support of the paper's legal right to express the ideas which had been set forth. What was more, Goldman added, the facts on which the views presented were based could be shown to be completely accurate.

William C. O'Brien, counsel for the Post Office, handled the rebuttal of arguments in our defense. He summed up the essence of the Roosevelt administration's methods when he said flatly: "We are not concerned here with questions of truth and falsity. It does not make any difference if everything *The Militant* said is true." Justification for rescinding the paper's mailing rights, he contended, lay in the "effect" its ideas might have.

Both Goldman and Fraenkel leaped on that crude assertion of dictatorial authority. "Once you establish the precedent that the decisive factor is possible effect," Goldman objected, "then the danger is great that all the jails in the country will be filled."

Fraenkel declared: "This effort to revoke the mailing rights of *The Militant* constitutes the gravest threat to freedom of the press that has thus far arisen in the war."

During the Washington hearing, it came out that Attorney General Biddle had urged Postmaster General Walker to initiate the proceedings against our weekly paper. "Since December 7, 1941, this publication has openly discouraged participation in the war by the masses of the people," Biddle had written to Walker on December 28, 1942. Its views, he said, appeared to be "calculated to engender opposition to the war effort as well as to interfere with the morale of the armed forces." Therefore, the attorney general concluded, "I suggest that you may wish to consider the issuance of an order to show cause why *The Militant* should not be denied the second class mailing privilege."

This was the same Biddle as the one who had carried out Roosevelt's order to prosecute us for sedition. He was represented at the postal hearing by the same Henry A. Schweinhaut who had served as chief prosecutor in the Minneapolis federal trial. Schweinhaut appeared to be working full time at hounding the Trotskyists, and Roosevelt later rewarded him for those services with an appointment to a federal judgeship.

A few weeks after the hearing, on March 3, 1943, Walker revoked *The Militant's* second class mailing rights. After that the paper had to be sent as third or fourth class matter, which was much slower in delivery and a good deal more costly than second class. The monthly magazine, *Fourth International*, was not directly involved in the matter of second class mailing rights, but it was also subjected for an extended period to censorship and delay in delivery.

Walker's action against *The Militant* brought intensified support of our protest campaign. But the Roosevelt bureaucracy stubbornly persisted in interfering with our use even of third and fourth class mail service. The April 24, 1943, issue of the paper, which contained a May Day manifesto, was declared "nonmailable"; and those numbers which did go through were held up as long as two weeks for censorship by the Justice Department.

At that stage the *New York Times* joined in the criticism of the government's interference with our press. On April 28, 1943, this influential capitalist newspaper said editorially: "It is difficult to sympathize with *The Militant* editors, who admittedly do not approve of the present war. . . . But encroachments of freedom of the press always begin with publications we can do without. . . . any newspaper could be coerced, and published opinion would be at the mercy of the Attorney General and the Postmaster General."

Similar criticisms followed in *Colliers* magazine, a national weekly of large circulation; also in the *Chicago Daily News*, the *Philadelphia Record*, and the *Chicago Tribune*, all prominent capitalist dailies.

After that, the Justice Department's censorship of the Trotsky-ist press was eased considerably, as was the delay in its delivery through the mails. Close to another year elapsed, though, before those difficulties were fully overcome. *The Militant's* second class mailing rights were not restored until March 18, 1944.

While the prolonged battle over the censorship issue was going on, we had been receiving further blows from other governmental quarters. On September 20, 1943, the U.S. Court of Appeals for the Eighth Circuit issued a weasel-worded decision upholding the conviction of the eighteen under the Smith Act. Our attorneys thereupon petitioned the U.S. Supreme Court to reverse the lower court's ruling. Such action was called for, they argued, because the Smith Act was unconstitutional and it had been used against us in an unconstitutional manner.

Our petition cited the first of the original ten amendments to the U.S. Constitution, which are known as the Bill of Rights. The First Amendment explicitly states: "Congress shall make no law . . . abridging the freedom of speech, or of the press." That provision, we contended, was violated by the Smith Act, which abrogated our right to freely express our views.

But the U.S. Supreme Court refused even to review the case of the eighteen, and its antidemocratic stance exposed a myth about the judicial process. According to capitalist propaganda the highest court acts objectively and consistently to interpret constitutional principles in the light of changing times and conditions. In reality, this is not the case, as its attitude toward us demonstrated.

Basically, the judicial process is designed to serve ruling-class needs. The only constant involved is the upholding of constitu-tional guarantees extended to capitalists—the right to private property in the means of production, and comparable matters. On paper, the Bill of Rights is just as explicit as the constitutional protection of capitalist property. But the high court's history shows that supposedly inviolable guarantees to the exploited masses have been undermined and whittled down through a variety of legal devices, each one designed to meet specific capitalist needs at a given juncture. Workers' rights have been infringed upon through court action, then partly restored, only to be violated anew; and this consistent pattern of inconsistency has been attuned to the ebb and flow of the class struggle. Taken as a whole, judicial interpretation of the Constitution has reflected two opposite trends: increasingly specific protection of capitalist interests, and ever-deeper erosion of the workers' democratic rights.

The class approach used by the judiciary can be seen in its overall handling of the Smith Act. When our case reached the Supreme Court in 1943, the country was deeply involved in a world imperialist conflict. The masses generally were under the illusion that it was conducted as a progressive struggle against fascism, and there was wide disagreement with our reasons for opposition to U.S. participation in the war. In those circumstances a large section of the population tended to acquiesce in the use of the Smith Act against us, the first time it was invoked.

At the same time, though, many others became concerned about the witch-hunting aspects involved in the conviction of the eighteen. Most people in that category supported the war, but they didn't want precedents set in the name of the "war effort" that would serve to weaken their own democratic rights. So they responded to our appeal for protests against the sedition frame-up.

The Supreme Court—which, as Finley Peter Dunne's "Mr. Dooley" said, "follows the election returns"—was thus confronted with a dilemma. It wanted to sanction our imprisonment, but not at the risk of stirring up a political hornets' nest by formally declaring the Smith Act constitutional. In that contradictory situation, the top judges decided, their best course was to do nothing. They simply allowed the decision of the lower court to stand, thereby causing us to be jailed in accordance with ruling-class needs of the moment; and through that procedure the way was still left open for them to make one or another pragmatic ruling on the thought-control law itself later on, as might be required under changed political circumstances after the war.

It took only a few years for such an occasion to arise. In 1949 the government tried the Stalinists on sedition charges, a move that demonstrated the evil consequences of the CP's unprincipled conduct in supporting the earlier imprisonment of the eighteen. During that year several leaders of the Communist Party were convicted on counts under the Smith Act. They appealed the convictions to the U.S. Supreme Court, and in opposing them the Justice Department cited the outcome of the Minneapolis case as legal justification for the move against the CP.

The federal assault on the Stalinists took place in a political climate marked by a "cold war" against the Soviet Union and other workers' states and by witch-hunt attacks in this country on those who opposed the imperialist line. The political atmosphere worsened when the Korean War broke out and a wave of ultrarightism, led by Senator Joseph R. McCarthy, began to dominate the U.S. scene. Under such conditions the sheer weight of reaction seriously obstructed the development of a movement in defense of the victimized Communist Party leaders. Actions on their behalf had been made twice difficult, moreover, because of the extent to which the CP's finky conduct during World War II had alienated labor and liberal circles. Consequently, not many were ready to emulate the Socialist Workers Party in defending the CP's constitutional rights as a matter of democratic principle.

When the appeal from the 1949 convictions reached the Supreme Court during the Korean War, the court took full advantage of the isolation the Stalinists had earned for themselves. Their case was used as a convenient vehicle for a decision upholding the constitutionality of the Smith Act. The court ruled that the law in question was directed at "advocacy" of violent action against the government, not at mere "discussion" of ideas; that the Communist Party was a "highly organized" formation engaged in a "conspiracy" to seize power; and that use of the law against that party was necessary because of the "inflammable nature of world conditions."

Later on, though, the foregoing interpretation of the thought-control law was sharply modified. This took place between 1957 and 1961, as still other convictions under the Smith Act reached the high court. All the defendants in these later instances were alleged to be members of the CP. Yet the court now found it impolitic to automatically reconfirm the ruling it had made in the first case involving Stalinists.

The political climate was changing. The Korean War had ended and McCarthyism had fallen into disrepute. Mass actions were developing in the Black struggle for full equality. A student radicalization was beginning that would later serve to trigger massive protests against the U.S. intervention in Vietnam. New signs of dissidence were cropping up in the trade unions. In sum, a spirit of nonconformity was arising, with a marked tendency to evolve toward widespread opposition to ruling-class repression.

Faced with those developments, the Supreme Court judges decided to shift gears on the Smith Act issue. The primary object was to forestall a massive campaign for outright revocation of the vicious thought-control measure, and steps were taken accordingly to soften it by means of a rewriting through judicial interpretation. The revised rulings made between 1957 and 1961 can be summed up along the following lines:

Advocacy of forcible measures against the government could not be prohibited so long as there was no effort to instigate action toward that end. Where plans to use force and violence for the overturn of capitalist rule were alleged, the organization in question had to be of sufficient size and cohesiveness to pose a substantial danger of achieving its goal. That organization had to be presently inciting its members to action aimed at overthrow of the government at the first propitious moment. Only those active members of the accused organization having guilty knowledge and intent could be convicted. Mere membership was not in itself sufficient grounds for conviction.

On the basis of the above reinterpretation of the Smith Act, convictions of alleged CP members were in some instances reversed by the Supreme Court. The freeing of those victims tended to discourage further prosecutions under the given law for the nonce, and that served, in turn, to alleviate pressures for its repeal.

This thought-control device has thereby been kept alive. So it continues to present a statutory medium through which people can be prosecuted, in violation of the Bill of Rights, on charges of "advocacy" aimed at "eventual" overthrow of the government by force and violence; and to serve that purpose the law can be given all the necessary teeth by judicial fiat, whenever the capitalist overlords so desire.

As the class struggle grows sharper in the future, the ruling class can be expected to call for new legal devices on the part of the judiciary like those manifested between 1943 and 1961. It can also be anticipated that the Supreme Court will comply with such political demands. Its erratic handling of the Smith Act for witch-hunting purposes leaves little doubt on that score. If, for instance, the legal interpretation developed by 1961 had been applied in the case of the eighteen, a decision would have been in order to set us free. But at the time, when we asked the top federal judges to protect our constitutional rights, their reply was curt and cowardly: "Petition denied."

An order was then issued requiring us to present ourselves for incarceration about a month later, on December 31, 1943, and we responded to the court's antidemocratic ruling with a public statement which declared:

"History proves that prisons and force have never destroyed

progressive ideas. We go to jail confident that our socialist ideas will ultimately be adopted by the masses who have suffered under a dying capitalism. We shall come out of prison ready to continue the struggle on behalf of the working masses."

On December 31 all but three of the eighteen assembled at the SWP headquarters in Minneapolis. From there we proceeded in a column of twos, accompanied by newspaper reporters and photographers, through busy downtown streets to the Federal Court House. After being taken into custody by U.S. marshals, our march was continued to the county jail, where we spent New Year's Eve.

The next day, January 1, 1944, Grace Carlson was removed to the federal women's prison at Alderson, West Virginia, and fourteen of us were transported to the U.S. penitentiary at Sandstone, Minnesota. The fourteen included Cannon, Cooper, Coover, DeBoer, Dobbs, Ray Dunne, Geldman, Goldman, Hamel, Hansen, Hudson, Morrow, Palmquist, and Skoglund.

For personal reasons Kuehn, Russell, and Schoenfeld surrendered themselves in a separate group to U.S. marshals in New York. They were then locked up in the federal prison at Danbury, Connecticut.

Life behind bars was especially rough for Grace Carlson. Like Kelly Postal, she had to sit alone in a prison cell, totally isolated from her party. The rest of us were relatively better off in the sense that we at least remained in close association with some of our comrades.

SENTENCE NOTICE TO INMATE

DOBBS, Farrell   No. 2005-SS

White   Age 36   Res. New York City, N.Y.

16 Mos. Conspiring to overthrow govt. by
        force, & subversive activities.
No Fine
Sentence Begins: Dec. 31, 1943
Received: Jan. 1, 1944
El. for Parole: June 9, 1944
Cond. Rel. Date: Jan. 24, 1945
Exp. of Sentence: Apr. 30, 1945

(Corrected 1-1-45)   T. P. Hedges,
                               Record Clerk

Farrell Dobbs's sentence notice card

Not long after we were incarcerated, Judge Joyce added a macabre touch to the whole affair. He ordered destruction of the written matter used as "evidence" against us in the 1941 trial. He was merely following court routine, yet it seemed a symbolic climax to the "sedition" frame-up—the burning of our literature.

Meanwhile, the prison authorities had let us know what time factors would be involved in regaining our freedom. This information was provided on small cards headed "SENTENCE NOTICE TO INMATE."

As will be noted, a date was included on which one would be eligible for parole. But in the case of the eighteen we had no intention of seeking release from prison on that basis. Unlike Kelly Postal's situation, none of us were confronted with personal difficulties which made it urgent to get out as quickly as possible. Therefore, we were in a position to carry on a fight for presidential pardons, a tactic which was preferable in this instance. It served both to emphasize that our rights had been violated and to put mass pressure directly on Roosevelt, who was the master architect of the "sedition" frame-up.

For those reasons a pardon campaign had been launched right after the Supreme Court rejected our appeal. It was conducted by the Civil Rights Defense Committee, which by this time was well geared for such action. New literature was published in order to bring people abreast of the latest developments in the case, and George Novack toured the country extensively to further stimulate campaign efforts. A petition drive was started with the aim of getting support from thousands of individuals in the fight for unconditional presidential pardon of the eighteen. Declarations in our favor were sought at the same time from well-known figures in various circles, from the labor and liberal press, and from mass organizations.

Warren K. Billings helped out with a statement asserting: "The best fighters for the working class have been subjected to frameups by the capitalist class and its agents. This is certainly true of the eighteen in the Minneapolis case. . . . This is an attack upon the entire labor movement and it must be met with the united action of all labor."

Shortly after we were imprisoned the CRDC campaign was inadvertently given a boost by the witch-hunters themselves. In February 1944 Albert Goldman was disbarred from the practice of law on the grounds of his conviction under the Smith Act. Outcries of protest quickly followed in liberal circles, as did increased backing of the pardon demand. Growing numbers of liberal editors, prominent intellectuals, and academic figures began to speak out on our behalf.

A number of Black leaders were equally responsive to the appeal for continued support of the eighteen. The NAACP and the March on Washington movement called upon Roosevelt to right the wrongs that had been committed against us. Comparable sentiments were expressed in other spheres as well. Organizations ranging from formations of working farmers to student groups spoke out in our favor. There was also a steady increase in the volume of individual signatures on pardon petitions.

Special attention was paid to CRDC activities within the labor movement. At the outset declarations of support were sought from trade union officials who were relatively progressive or at least subject to pressure from progressive forces within their organizations. An outstanding response of the kind we sought came from Gabriel De Angelis, financial secretary of Local 365, UAW-CIO, in Long Island City, N.Y. De Angelis took up the case of the eighteen in a talk over radio station WEVD in New York City. As quoted in *The Militant* of June 10, 1944, he said:

"This prosecution is the most sweeping government attack upon democratic and labor rights in many years. . . . In refusing to hear this case, the Supreme Court has set an extremely dangerous precedent which can now be used against other trade unionists and minority groups. That is why my union . . . [is] giving full moral and financial support to this case."

Similar backing of the pardon demand came from state CIO councils in Michigan and New Jersey. The action taken by those influential bodies served, in turn, to stimulate responses from other trade union sectors, and the campaign to bring pressure upon Roosevelt from within the labor movement gained steadily in momentum.

These successes enabled the CRDC to raise funds needed for the defense effort. There were legal expenses to be met. Expenditures were required for printing, postage, etc., in connection with the pardon drive. Financial aid had to be extended to families of the eighteen, and ten dollars a month—the maximum allowed by the authorities—was sent to each of the prisoners. The latter sum enabled us to get a few "luxuries" from the prison commissary, such as sharp razor blades and soap that didn't take your skin off. In addition, the CRDC managed to provide books we wanted to study during our enforced idleness from political activity.

As demands that Roosevelt grant us presidential pardons mounted within the labor movement, Tobin sought desperately to stem the tide. In some cases the IBT head wrote directly to union officials who were supporting our cause. He urged them to reverse their positions, arguing that their policy was self-defeating because the Trotskyists were "endeavoring to destroy the American labor movement by boring from within." Those steps were accompanied by a running attack on the CRDC campaign in the Teamster magazine. In the May 1944 issue, for instance, pardons for the eighteen were opposed on the basis that "some of those men . . . were afterwards found guilty of embezzlement of the funds of the organization in Minneapolis."

Tobin's filth was matched by the Stalinists, who vied with him in slandering the pardon movement. CRDC supporters were denounced in the *Daily Worker* as "tools" being used by "Hitler agents." The CP hacks also emulated the IBT dictator in directly attacking influential labor figures who backed the demand that Roosevelt free us from prison. As a result it didn't take long for the two of them to develop a tacit united front, as was demonstrated at the 1944 state conventions of the AFL and the CIO in Minnesota.

The Tobin-dominated AFL gathering went on record "condemning the attempts of the eighteen convicted seditionists to use the good name of the unions. . . . in petitions calling for their release from prison." A duplicate stand was taken at the Stalinist-controlled CIO session. It voted to condemn "the disruptive and seditious activities of this group" and to oppose "any aid or comfort to those serving terms in the federal penitentiary."

As the unprincipled actions of those two conventions showed, reaction had gained full sway over the Minnesota labor movement, and in that climate the Stalinist–right-wing bloc committed still another outrage. The Farmer-Labor Party was liquidated into the Democratic Party.

During its early years the FLP had functioned as an independent political setup, opposing both the Democrats and the Republicans within Minnesota on the basis of a reformist program. The movement was then under nominal control of organized labor, and it enjoyed the support of almost every trade union in the state. Beginning in 1936, however, the reformist organization underwent a change.

At that time the Communist Party, which was making a "peoples' front" turn, sent its forces into the FLP. There the

Stalinists entered into what became an on-again, off-again alliance with the opportunists of the right wing. Between them, these elements gradually succeeded in turning the Minnesota formation into a tool of Roosevelt's national political machine, especially on the issue of preparation for U.S. entry into the war. Within the state this trend was accompanied by cynical election deals with local Democratic politicians and by moves to strip organized labor of any voice in shaping party positions.

A trade union revolt against the FLP machine resulted. By 1939 the Minneapolis AFL had struck out on its own in local politics. The Central Labor Union ran its own candidate for mayor that year and again in the spring of 1941. Both campaigns were conducted on the basis of platforms drafted by organized labor, which included planks opposing U.S. involvement in imperialist war. This emerging political formation had firm roots in the working class, was subject to trade union control, and had the potential to develop into an independent labor party on a city and state scale. All this changed, though, after the attack on Local 544 came out into the open in mid-1941.

During the showdown that followed, the Minneapolis Central Labor Union capitulated to Tobin in the trade union fight and to Roosevelt on the war issue. A 180-degree turn in political line naturally resulted. The progressive local trend toward formation of an independent labor party was aborted by the AFL bureaucrats, who began to prepare the unions for adaptation to the Democratic Party.

When the 1943 Minneapolis elections were held, the AFL central body endorsed Hubert H. Humphrey as its candidate for mayor. He was an unknown figure, from outside labor's ranks, who was seeking public office for the first time. Previously a candidate had been required to run on a labor platform to receive such backing. But Humphrey got union support despite a demagogic declaration in which he said, "I have not made any commitments to organized labor or to organized capital."

Shortly after the city elections the Central Labor Union sponsored a banquet at which politicos of various stripes were invited to speak. They joined in calling for "unity of all liberals" behind candidates for Congress who would be favorable to Roosevelt. One speaker was Humphrey, who coyly remarked that "after all the talk about unity there must be some place to come home to." Humphrey then introduced the leader of the Democratic Party in Minnesota as the next speaker.

A few months later, in April 1944, the union bureaucrats joined with the political careerists and Stalinists to destroy what little remained of the once-vigorous Farmer-Labor movement in the state. The FLP was absorbed by the Democratic Party at an amalgamation convention. After twenty-six years of independent existence as a force in Minnesota politics, the reformist organization had gone over entirely to the capitalist two-party system. To camouflage that surrender the changed setup was given the hybrid name "Democratic Farmer-Labor Party."

The criminality of this deed, from a working-class viewpoint, was further compounded by the circumstance that dissolution of the FLP took place at a time when sentiment for independent labor political action was rapidly increasing nationally. Much had happened since the top union officials made their no-strike pledge in December 1941. Roosevelt had responded to their servile act with a phony declaration that "equality of sacrifice" would be demanded from capital and labor. He had also purported to impose a freeze on both wages and prices, but, as is always the case under the present system, there was nothing equitable about the practices that followed.

The wage freeze was rigidly enforced on the basis of an arbitrary ruling called the "Little Steel formula." Jobs were also frozen in many instances by administrative decree, and speedups were intensified on production lines throughout industry. The so-called policing of prices, however, was a farce. The cost of commodities went up and up, causing the workers losses in purchasing power and consequent lowering of their living standards. For the capitalists, on the other hand, "equality of sacrifice" turned out to mean skyrocketing profits.

In the face of those flagrant injustices, pressure for defensive measures began to mount within the trade unions. Dissatisfaction among the coal miners, for example, became so intense that in 1943 John L. Lewis felt compelled to abandon his earlier no-strike pledge and lead a fight for wage increases. A series of walkouts followed, through which the miners broke the "Little Steel formula" and won significant pay hikes. Their victory precipitated widespread demands upon the labor bureaucrats to rescind all no-strike pledges. When those demands were ignored, the workers began to take matters into their own hands. "Wildcat" strikes, conducted in defiance of top union officials, broke out in auto, rubber, and other industries.

The new trend in political attitudes was dramatically manifested at a mid-1943 convention of Labor's Non-Partisan League in

Detroit. The delegates present represented about two hundred thousand members of affiliated CIO unions in Wayne County. They called for "immediate establishment of an independent party of labor and working farmers" in Michigan.

Further expressions of sentiment for independent labor political action were voiced soon thereafter among unions in New Jersey, New York, and Pennsylvania; by the summer of 1944 a quite extensive campaign for the formation of a national labor party had developed.

This upsurge of labor militancy, which stemmed from Roosevelt's discriminatory policies on the home front, helped greatly in winning support for the CRDC campaign. It thus became possible during August of that year to submit the formal demand for pardon of the eighteen in a most impressive manner; the necessary preparations for that step had already been completed.

Earlier George Novack had visited us in the various prisons where we were held. At that time appropriate formulations were worked out concerning questions on the pardon application form about our future intentions, if the president freed us. Among other things, we were supposed to promise never again to commit the "crime" for which we had been jailed. Nothing of the kind was done, of course. Our answers to all questions were phrased so as to reaffirm the revolutionary socialist principles for which we had been framed.

On August 3, 1944, Novack made a trip to Washington where he handed our applications to the Presidential Pardon Authority. He brought along a formidable array of material expressing mass support of the pardon demand. There were resolutions from over three hundred trade union, Black, and labor fraternal organizations; petitions signed by some twelve thousand individuals; hundreds of letters from prominent figures in labor, Black, liberal, civil liberties, and fraternal circles; scores of editorials and articles from the labor, liberal, and working-class political press condemning the sedition convictions.

Those demanding unconditional pardon of the eighteen included four international unions: Textile Workers, CIO; Retail, Wholesale, and Department Store Employees, CIO; United Transport Service Employees, CIO; and International Ladies Garment Workers, AFL. There were also several top union officials who joined in the demand: R. J. Thomas, president of the UAW-CIO; John Green, president of the CIO Marine and Shipbuilding Workers; Irving Abramson, president of the New

Jersey CIO Council; and John Gibson, president of the Michigan CIO Council. In addition hundreds of local unions had adopted resolutions in our support. All told, backing was received from labor organizations representing more than three million members.

Within the Black movement, declarations in favor of presidential pardons came from the NAACP, the March on Washington organization, the Negro Labor Committee, the Future Outlook League, and the Mass Movement League. A number of Black leaders, educators, and members of the clergy spoke out on our behalf as individuals. Similar backing was voiced by the two largest labor fraternal organizations: The Workmen's Circle and the Workmen's Benefit Fund.

But this massive support of the pardon demand was contemptuously brushed aside by Roosevelt. He did so, moreover, without even troubling to examine personally any of the declarations on our behalf. The whole thing was handled by his underlings, who sought to justify the president's imperious attitude by citing administrative technicalities.

On October 6, 1944, U.S. Pardon Attorney Daniel M. Lyons notified us that our applications had been denied. The request had not been submitted to Roosevelt, he wrote, since "the President's rule provides that in the absence of a favorable recommendation from the United States Attorney or the trial Judge, an application for executive clemency shall not ordinarily be presented to him. Our study of the application fails to disclose a justification for submitting these cases as an exception to the rule. . . . [because] the Attorney General feels. . . . he could not properly present this case to the President with a recommendation favorable to the exercise of clemency."

News of this raw decision precipitated a new flood of protests addressed to the White House. Before all of the eighteen had served their time a total of some six hundred labor and progressive organizations, speaking for about six million members, had registered disapproval of the president's high-handed conduct.

The six who received sentences of a year and a day were granted conditional release from prison on October 20, 1944. The term *conditional* meant they were being accorded time off the full sentence for good behavior, but if the authorities considered them guilty of misconduct during that interval, they could be rejailed until the entire sentence had been served.

Public affairs were arranged in Minneapolis and New York to welcome home the six. Roger Baldwin of the ACLU spoke at the New York gathering. "This has been the worst case in years," he said, "and the best defense I have seen in a long time."

A few weeks later, on January 24, 1945, the remaining twelve of the eighteen were allowed to return home on conditional release. As had been the situation of those freed earlier, we had to report regularly to a probation officer during the "good time" period. In our case, which involved sentences of sixteen months, this went on until the full term expired on April 30, 1945.

Once again, though, Carl Skoglund remained the object of federal punitive measures. On July 3, 1942, the Immigration and Naturalization Service had hauled him before M. M. Joyce, the judge who had presided over the earlier sedition trial. Joyce had denied Carl's application for citizenship and ordered him deported to Sweden. But communication with that country was severed under the wartime conditions then prevailing, so the order could not be carried out.

When the war came to an end, however, the deportation attack was renewed, and the CRDC organized yet another campaign in Skoglund's defense. For some years it remained possible to keep him at liberty on bond. Then, during the McCarthy period, the situation changed.

Carl was suddenly seized and imprisoned on Ellis Island, after which steps were taken to deport him, with less than twenty-four hours' advance notice. His lawyers quickly got a court writ blocking the move, but the immigration authorities tried to ignore it. He was spirited aboard a ship leaving for Sweden and held there until about ten minutes before sailing time. Only at that point, after the defense committee had taken swift protest action through Socialist Party leader Norman Thomas, was he brought back for continued internment ashore in compliance with the judge's order.

Somewhat later Skoglund's release was obtained on bond, but his freedom of movement was greatly restricted. He had to report at frequent intervals to the Immigration Service, where petty bureaucrats subjected him to indignities. Things remained pretty much that way, with the threat of deportation constantly hanging over him, until the day of his death.

While the eighteen of us were in prison we had ample time to second-guess ourselves on the handling of the fight that had broken out in 1941. Could a way have been found to postpone the showdown with Tobin, we wondered, until objective conditions took a turn for the better? Our conclusion was that it could not have been accomplished in a principled manner.

At the core of the dispute lay the war issue, which overshadowed all other questions. Tobin was determined to gag Local 544's opposition to U.S. entry into the imperialist conflict then raging. If we had allowed him to do so, hoping thereby to duck a fight for the time being, it would have appeared that we tacitly approved Roosevelt's foreign policy. On that crucial issue, therefore, our role would have become that of trade union misleaders and would have been no better than that of the unprincipled labor bureaucracy.

Once we had compromised with the IBT head on such a vital matter, moreover, further demands upon us would have followed. Among those would have been compliance with his wartime no-strike pledge, which enabled the employers to take back many concessions the workers had won through struggle. We would also have been called upon to act as strikebreakers against other trade unions. Efforts to maintain peaceful relations with Tobin would thus have thrust us, one step after another, away from our class-struggle course and toward adaptation to class-collaborationist policies.

Such a shift in line would have led, in turn, to disorientation of the Socialist Workers Party's cadres in the Teamsters. It would have become necessary for them to act more and more in violation of the revolutionary concepts they had come to embrace. Their conduct would have grown less and less distinguishable from that of trade unionists who had succumbed to the wartime pressures generated by the capitalist class. Under those circumstances some of them might even have ceased after a time to think and conduct themselves like revolutionary socialists; they might conceivably have degenerated into business agents of the ordinary type found in the labor movement.

As matters actually stood, however, none of that had happened. Our line had been to continue Local 544's public opposition to imperialist war, refusing to accept any kind of "patriotic" moratorium concerning action in defense of working-class interests; to press for maintenance of labor's independence in relation to the capitalist state; and to fight for rank-and-file control over the trade unions, in keeping with basic democratic principles.

In carrying out those policies, the SWP cadres gave a magnificent account of themselves. They demonstrated that the difference between a nonpolitical trade unionist and a politically educated revolutionary militant is a qualitative one. Although up against insuperable odds, they fought like tigers to the bitter end, always seeing beyond the personal and organizational difficulties of the moment to the new horizons attainable through a socialist transformation of society. Tobin got not one single renegade from among those basic cadres; and when the twenty-eight went on trial for sedition in federal court, the prosecution could find no defendant who was ready to turn state's evidence in an effort to get off scot-free. A compelling demonstration was given under intense fire that the Socialist Workers Party is a party genuinely devoted to revolutionary socialist principles, a party dedicated to truthful service of the working class.

Although we lost the immediate battle, our exemplary fight in Minneapolis contributed to the fundamental education of workers. Before it was over we had forced the demagogue Roosevelt to openly display his antilabor visage, thus exposing the capitalist government's true role in the class struggle. Similarly, the clash with Tobin laid bare the treacherous role of union bureaucrats in general, since he was a typical example of the breed.

A knowledge of those developments should prove instructive to contemporary members of the labor movement. If studied as a whole, the events in Minneapolis can help workers prepare effectively—in terms of both trade union and independent political actions—for coming struggles against the bosses, their lackeys in public office, and their servitors within the ranks of labor.

Looking back on the vicious reprisals taken against us by the forces of reaction, I concur with the view Carl Skoglund once voiced on that subject. "These were the penalties the bosses visited upon militants in the vanguard of the workers' struggle," he said. "But our ideas always will prove more powerful than their economic sanctions, the courts and the prisons.

"We are still on the receiving end. But our principles—carried forward by another mighty movement of the masses—are bound to triumph, as the truth always does.

"I am as sure of that as I am of daylight after the passing of night."

Kelly Postal   Grace Carlson (left), Dorothy Schultz

Eleven of the Minneapolis defendants at a dinner celebrating their release from prison. Clockwise: Clarence Hamel (turning toward camera), Harry DeBoer, Farrell Dobbs, James P. Cannon, Emil Hansen, Oscar Coover, Sr., Carl Skoglund, Carlos Hudson, Jake Cooper, V. R. Dunne, Max Geldman.

Afterword

In its transitional program for socialist revolution the Fourth International asserts: "All talk to the effect that historical conditions have not yet 'ripened' for socialism is the product of ignorance or conscious deception. The objective prerequisites for proletarian revolution have not only 'ripened'; they have begun to get somewhat rotten. Without a socialist revolution, in the next historical period at that, a catastrophe threatens the whole culture of mankind. It is now the turn of the proletariat, i.e., chiefly its revolutionary vanguard. The historical crisis of mankind is reduced to the crisis of the revolutionary leadership."

Verification of the latter statement will be found in the history of the Minneapolis Teamsters. The leadership problem confronting labor today is pinpointed by the contrast between the opening and closing phases of the General Drivers Union's story.

In 1934, at the outset of the period covered in my four-volume account of developments within the International Brotherhood of Teamsters, workers throughout the country were becoming radicalized under the adverse pressures of a severe capitalist crisis. Combative moods were growing in intensity among them, and they were ready for organized action on a massive scale in defense of their class interests. The way was thus open to build strong trade unions. These could serve both as direct instruments of struggle within industry and as a base from which to launch independent labor political action on a national scale in a fight for supreme power.

In Minneapolis an unusual situation existed at the time of the upsurge in labor militancy. Locally, there was an exceptional relationship of forces between the main radical tendencies. Among the Trotskyists expelled from the Communist Party in 1928 had been the most capable trade unionists in its Minneapolis branch. When the potential for mass action developed later on, those seasoned fighters took the initiative in helping the workers conduct effective strikes in support of their demands upon the bosses; and in doing so they were able to beat the Stalinist hacks in a direct contest for leadership of the city's key labor contingent, the trucking employees.

We had a similar advantage over the social democrats. Many had previously left that tendency in Minnesota to help form the Communist Party in 1919. Since then the social democrats had remained quite weak in the state, especially in Minneapolis; and as the Teamster struggles unfolded, most of the militants among them were won over to the Trotskyist party.

With the Trotskyists thus constituting the dominant force in the radical movement locally, it was possible for us to play a decisive role in the broad ranks of labor. We mobilized the trucking workers of the city for action on the basis of our class-struggle line. Both the local AFL officialdom and the IBT bureaucracy were outflanked through development of the combat momentum needed for the union ranks to brush aside all internal obstacles standing in their way. The trucking employers were defeated in battle, and a strong Teamster organization was consolidated in Minneapolis. After that our class-struggle course was extended into the surrounding area by means of a campaign to unionize over-the-road drivers. On the electoral plane, when the Stalinists and right-wingers made a shambles of the Farmer-Labor Party in Minnesota we pushed for reorganization of independent mass political action, by steps that could lead to the development of a labor party based on and controlled by the trade unions.

Those accomplishments were made possible through the interplay of two basic factors. One of these was the skillful and considerate leadership of the workers by revolutionary socialists. The other was our championing of trade union democracy. Full membership participation was encouraged in the organization's internal affairs. Freedom to express all points of view was upheld, as was the workers' right to set policy by majority vote.

As successes in the fight against the employers were achieved through this combination of able leadership and internal union democracy, the workers acquired increasing awareness of their great strength in class unity. They also began to get a better notion of what was needed to defend their interests. But variations existed in their grasp of class relations under capitalism and of the bosses' inherent antagonism to organized labor. Perceptions of that basic issue ranged from only elementary trade union consciousness in most instances, across intermediate stages of class-struggle understanding reached by more limited numbers, to attainment of a revolutionary socialist outlook by a few. This unevenness in levels of development presented no serious obstacle to progress, however, so long as labor generally remained in a state of upsurge. Workers who had become more advanced could take advantage of the existing struggle momentum to activate their lagging comrades. Step by well-timed step, in accord with the pace of events, effective forces could thereby be mobilized for action in the trade union and political spheres.

The concrete manner in which the situation was handled at each stage of developments within the Teamster movement has been detailed in my four volumes. These were written to provide something more than a description of the events that transpired. I have attempted to place the reader in the position of the revolutionists who guided the union ranks—retrospectively looking over their shoulders, so to speak—as they assessed each successive problem and decided how to deal with it. My purpose was to help find clues to ways and means of transforming labor's potential class power into a dynamically active force in the continuing struggle against the capitalist exploiters.

The reader should keep in mind, of course, that both the precise strategy and specific tactics set forth in the books on the Teamsters were attuned to a concrete situation at a given time and place. For that reason the methods then employed cannot be applied mechanically under new and different conditions. But an imaginative interpretation of the fundamental concepts we translated into action during the 1934-41 period should be helpful to militants in grappling with today's problem of labor leadership.

In addition, material dealing with the roots of present leadership defaults in the trade unions will be found in the series on the Teamsters. The main threads of the analysis presented there can be summarized briefly as follows:

Nationally, the relationship of forces on the left was unfavorable to the Trotskyists during the 1930s. We were a small propaganda group. Our activities had to center on assembling the initial cadres for the reconstruction of a revolutionary socialist party in the aftermath of the Stalinization of the Communist Party. The advantageous position of the Minneapolis comrades was, therefore, unique. Elsewhere in the country our movement did not have the required strength and opportunity to play a leading role in labor struggles to the extent that we found possible in the Teamsters.

Nationally, both the Stalinists and social democrats had us outnumbered; and those tendencies—each representing a particular form of reformism—acted more or less in concert with the business unionists who constituted the labor officialdom. As a consequence, the workers of the nation lacked leadership of the kind needed to help them safeguard and promote their class interests.

The misleaders were able to prevent the labor upsurge from going beyond the unionization of the unorganized mass production workers into the CIO, although much more was possible at the height of its energies. They managed to tie the new industrial union movement to the Democratic Party, beginning with the 1936 national elections, thereby keeping the workers mired in capitalist politics. By mid-1937, class-collaborationist norms were reestablished to a large extent in setting trade union policy. Reliance on help from the Roosevelt administration was substituted for use of the union's full power, and a staggering setback resulted for the CIO with the defeat of the Little Steel strike.

Because of those leadership defaults the combat momentum of the insurgent masses was crippled and eventually broken. Even though strikes continued to occur episodically, the tide of battle had turned. A change in mood came over the union ranks. Militants found it more and more difficult to draw reluctant elements into action. Cautious attitudes became more pronounced, and a more conservative climate developed. To an increasing extent the best fighters found themselves swimming against the stream, except during those interludes when new struggles flared up briefly.

In that changed situation the bureaucrats took one step after another toward restriction of the democratic and fighting spirit in which the CIO was born. Consolidation of their control over the organization proceeded at the same time that dictatorial rule was being reimposed within the AFL. Bit by bit, such rank-and-file democracy as had been established during the upsurge was undermined. The unions were gradually brought under the domination of an officialdom ready to act in "partnership" with the employing class.

Roosevelt took advantage of the opportunity provided by these developments to implement the imperialists' key objective at the time. He lined up the labor bureaucracy in support of preparations for war, and, as a necessary corollary, he launched a witch-hunt against militants who resisted his foreign policy. This was made all the easier for him by labor's previous failure to take the independent political road, which left the capitalists in unchallenged control of the government. He had a free hand to use a wide range of repressive devices, including assignment of the FBI to a primary role as political police.

Such were the circumstances in 1941 under which General Drivers Local 544 clashed with IBT President Tobin over the war issue. By then adverse developments nationally had thrust us into a position where we had few reliable allies and many enemies. Under FBI guidance, opportunists within the local union had organized a clique which acted in collusion with Tobin and with various governmental agencies in attacking the democratically elected leadership. Tobinite goons, aided by hacks from the national AFL, joined in the assault. Those reactionary forces were backed up by the city administration, the county courts, and the state government. On top of that, Roosevelt moved against us on three more fronts: through the National Labor Relations Board, the Immigration and Naturalization Service, and the Department of Justice.

Faced with so formidable a combination of foes, an isolated local union had no way of successfully defending itself. We were reduced to fighting a rearguard action, doing so as skillfully as possible in an effort to minimize the losses suffered in our defeat.

Local 544's victimization was the prelude to a larger tragedy. From then on the workers collectively have paid a heavy price for the class-collaborationist policies imposed upon the trade unions by the bureaucracy's betrayal. Included in the cost were U.S. entry into World War II and subsequent wars in Korea and Vietnam. So long as monopoly capitalism exists, the danger of further imperialist attacks on other countries will continue, along with the threat of nuclear holocaust.

Here at home, meanwhile, the boss class has imposed harsh restraints upon the trade unions through antilabor laws, court injunctions, outrageous fines, and frame-ups of militants. Inflation and unemployment have reduced living standards, eroded job security, and thrust many into poverty. Oppressed nationalities, especially, have suffered from deprivation of their economic, social, and democratic rights. Women continue to face discrimination on every level. The masses generally have experienced attacks on their civil liberties as efforts to organize in defense of their interests have been disrupted by the FBI, CIA, and other agencies of the political cops. In addition, capitalist greed has led to dismantling and decay of social services, rape of the environment, and other crimes against the people.

One of the major factors preventing effective struggle against economic and social deterioration has been accelerated degeneration of the labor officialdom since World War II. Right after the war, from 1945 to 1947, bureaucratic control over the trade unions was temporarily shaken by a massive resurgence of working-class militancy. But once again the misleaders of labor succeeded in preventing the formation of an independent labor party and thus kept the workers tied to capitalist politics. Since that time they have moved, one step after another, toward intensified subservience to the ruling class.

So far as officials in the upper strata of the union bureaucracy are concerned personally, capitalism works fine. Huge salaries, expense accounts, and other emoluments enable them to maintain high living standards. Job security—for themselves—is implicit in their control over the workers' mass organizations, as is assurance of lavish pensions when they retire. For those reasons the union bureaucrats, like the bosses, consider anyone who wants to change the existing system an "irresponsible radical."

But there is one catch in this otherwise ideal situation for the labor skates. An illusion must be maintained that they are effectively representing the workers in collective bargaining. Without that false face their basic role as de facto agents of the bosses would be exposed, and a majority in the union ranks would begin looking for a way to do a housecleaning job on them. To avoid that danger they must get occasional concessions for the membership from the employers. On balance, these must be sufficient to convince a considerable section of the workers that the class-collaborationist line followed by the bureaucrats is acceptable. In that way, so long as the economy is on the upgrade, a relatively stable component within the union membership can be maintained for use in suppressing internal revolts.

If the bureaucracy mobilized the ranks for struggle to win the needed concessions from the bosses, however, a climate would be created in which its control over the unions would be jeopardized. So another course has been taken. The top labor officials have supported the ruling class on most social and political policy questions, hoping to get in return at least minimal employer responses to the workers' economic demands.

These officials have gone a long way toward converting the trade unions into auxiliary instruments of repression acting in collusion with the capitalist authorities. Among the consequences has been the clamping of collective bargaining into an iron vise. One jaw consists of restrictions imposed upon organized labor by the bosses' government. The other takes the form of bureaucratic controls within the unions themselves. Through this combination of repressive forces the workers have been subjected to steadily intensifying exploitation at the hands of the capitalists.

An equally reprehensible situation exists concerning struggles by doubly oppressed layers of society, such as oppressed nationalities and women. Those movements are largely ignored, or at best given little more than lip service, by the trade union bureaucracy. If, however, the ruling class shows open hostility toward a particular oppositional tendency—as it did in the case of Malcolm X, for example—the labor fakers are quick to oppose that tendency as well.

In the sphere of capitalist foreign policy, especially, the top union officials play the role of lickspittles. That has been illustrated most fully in the criminal support given by George Meany and his cohorts to the brutal assault on the Vietnamese by the U.S. imperialists and in their reactionary opposition to the American antiwar movement.

Up to now the labor bureaucrats have gotten away with this treachery. But new trends are developing that will undermine their control over the workers' movement. U.S. imperialism is falling into increasing difficulties at the center of the developing world capitalist crisis. Under these circumstances the labor bureaucracy's class-collaborationist practices will have less and less success in obtaining collective-bargaining concessions from the employers. And, at the same time, the ruling class will move in devious ways—as in New York City's contrived financial crisis—to protect capitalist profits by driving down the workers' living standards.

As these trends persist and worsen, the workers are bound to become more combative, more disenchanted with official union policy, more rebellious. The top bureaucrats, whose domination over the unions will thus become threatened, are certain to react viciously. They will intensify the present use of red-baiting and violence against internal oppositions; and, parallel with such actions, their self-serving alliance with the employers and the capitalist government will be further tightened.

As that contradictory situation unfolds, opposition to the present official union policies can be organized on an expanding scale. Large numbers of workers can be brought, in stages, toward adoption of a class-struggle program required to defend their interests—if the left-wing forces in their midst proceed with the necessary patience and astuteness.

It would be unwise, for instance, to begin with efforts to vote incumbent officials out of office so that correct policies might be instituted forthwith by a new leadership. The bureaucrats could normally counter such a move rather easily at the present juncture. They would need only to direct an appeal to the more backward sections of the union membership, claiming no more was involved than the "outs" trying to dump the "ins." Since arguments in favor of new policies would seem rather remote to many workers upon first hearing them, the reactionaries could easily fog the issues. There would be no real prospect of immediately ousting the incumbents, and a false impression could be created that they are immune to removal through an election contest.

If the rebel forces proceed, instead, by pressing at the outset for official adoption, or at least tolerance, of policies that will enable the workers to fight off the capitalist assault on their living standards, better results can be obtained. As things get worse under the present officers, broadening layers of the membership will become more open-minded toward new ideas and methods of action. Awareness will grow that organized labor is on the wrong track programmatically. Pressures will mount for a major shift in line. When the incumbents fail to respond adequately, more and more workers will come to recognize that the leadership personnel must be changed, and they will be ready to act accordingly.

Moves toward reconstruction of the leadership in the foregoing manner will very likely become possible mainly at the local union level during the first phase of developments. But action at that level will in itself serve to put heavy pressure on the lower echelons of the general bureaucratic structure. Instead of the bureaucracy splitting the workers to maintain its sway, the workers will be able to split the bureaucracy in their fight for rank-and-file control over the unions.

Efforts toward that end can be set into motion along the lines followed in bringing William S. Brown, Patrick J. Corcoran, John T. O'Brien, and other union officials over to the workers' side in the fight during the 1930s to build a more effective Teamster organization. (See *Teamster Rebellion*, chapter 4, and *Teamster Power*, chapters 13 and 17.) A recent positive example was the 1977 Steelworkers Fight Back campaign of Ed Sadlowski, who is a district director, and other staff members and local officials of the United Steelworkers against the encrusted, class-collaborationist I. W. Abel bureaucracy.

The relevant elements of the class-struggle program needed by the trade unions should be introduced realistically on a transitional basis. In that way the unfolding labor radicalization can be guided from its present stage toward higher forms of development along the following lines:

Proposals for immediate action should center on problems involving the workers' urgent material needs and the defense of their democratic rights. It is also important that the fight around those issues be attuned to the existing levels of consciousness in the union membership. Then, as significant forces are set into motion through that approach, several things take place. Rank-and-file militancy rises. Increasingly sharp clashes with the bosses result, during which the workers begin to shed class-collaborationist illusions and acquire class-struggle concepts. Lessons thus learned during industrial conflicts can prepare the union ranks for an advance toward action on a political plane. In short, a foundation is laid from which to initiate transformation of the trade unions themselves into instruments capable of developing far-reaching revolutionary perspectives.

As the transitional process from where they are to where they should be continues, the workers' attention can be focused on broad questions which go far beyond day-to-day issues on the job. They will learn in that way to generalize their thinking in class terms, and the development of a conscious anticapitalist outlook will follow.

If, during the course of their experiences in struggle, the labor militants are helped to analyze the causes of the social and economic ills facing them; if they are aided in perceiving the essence of an outlived capitalism—they will learn that the existing problems are not incidental and episodic at all, but the consequence of a deep structural crisis of the system. They will then see why governmental control must be taken away from the capitalists by labor and its allies.

Basic to such a rise in the workers' class consciousness is understanding that a fundamental change must take place in the role of the trade unions, which constitute the existing form of mass organization among the workers in this country. These broad instruments of struggle must be turned away from reliance upon so-called friends among the capitalist politicians. They must break off the self-defeating collaboration with the bosses' government, that has been imposed by bureaucratic misleaders. The unions must be transformed into mechanisms for independent and militant action by the workers all along the line. Restrictions on the right to strike must be vigorously opposed and freedom to exercise that right firmly asserted. Internal union democracy must be established so that all questions can be decided on the basis of majority rule. Then, and only then, will organized labor manage to bring its full weight to bear in confrontations with the employers at the industrial level.

Whenever conflicts of significant magnitude erupt within industry today, the government intervenes on the employers' side; and this interference is bound to intensify as capitalist decay gets worse. From this it follows that trade union action alone will prove less and less capable of resolving the workers' problems, even on a limited basis. Objectively, industrial conflicts will assume more and more a political character, and even the most powerfully organized workers will be faced with an increasingly urgent need to act on the new and higher plane of politics.

Therefore, efforts to build an effective left wing in the trade unions will run into insurmountable obstacles unless the workers move toward resolving the problem of political action. A vigorous campaign must be conducted to break the labor movement from subordination to capitalist politics and to launch an independent labor political organization. This campaign will have to focus initially on educational propaganda for a change in labor's political course, but it should not be conducted in an abstract, routine manner. Ample opportunity will be found to concretize the propaganda by drawing the lessons of setbacks caused by the misuse of labor's inherent political strength. This can lay the basis for an advance, as soon as it becomes realistic, to an agitational campaign designed to convince the ranks of the urgency of forming a labor party.

In the process of creating their own mass party, based upon and controlled by the trade unions, the organized workers can draw unorganized, unemployed, and undocumented sections of their class into a broad political alliance. Labor will then be in a position to act both in a more unified manner and through advanced forms of struggle.

The workers will learn to generalize their needs, as a class, and to address their demands on a political basis to the capitalists, as a class. Political confrontation of that kind—for example, the nationalization of a given industry under workers' control—will raise labor action as a whole to a higher plane and at the same time impart new vigor to the continuing trade union struggles. Increased militancy within industry will serve, in turn, to reinforce activity in the political sphere. In that way interacting processes will develop through which the workers will attain greater class consciousness, more complete solidarity, and, hence, mounting ability to outfight the bosses.

Before unity of the exploited masses can be attained, however, still another of organized labor's existing policies must be thoroughly reversed. The labor movement must champion and give unqualified support to the demands of the Blacks, Chicanos, Puerto Ricans, Indians, and other oppressed national minorities, and of women and youth.

As Leon Trotsky insisted in discussions during the 1930s, the American workers must learn to act politically and to think socially if they are to attain the class consciousness and solidarity needed to defeat the exploiters. This is the opposite of the narrow class-collaborationist course pursued by the labor bureaucracy and the privileged layers they reflect. Thus, as a matter of principle, the trade union movement must use its power to actively fight for such progressive demands as affirmative action programs against racial and sexual discrimination on the job, in the union, in hiring, housing, health care, and education; the right to abortion and childcare; busing and bilingual, bicultural education; the right to a free college education for all youth.

If unconditional backing of that kind is given, the labor movement will be helping itself in a double sense. The strengthening of anticapitalist struggles on other fronts will make it harder for the employing class to concentrate its fire on the trade unions. The greater the scope of mass confrontations with the bosses' government, the more effectively will labor be able to involve its natural allies in the development of independent political action on a massive scale. This was true in the 1930s and it is even truer today, when women, oppressed nationalities, and workers under twenty have become the majority of the American work force and a substantial component of the union movement.

In addition, the experience of the Vietnam War holds an important lesson for the trade union movement. The labor bureaucrats sided with the imperialist aggressors in that conflict, against the welfare of people in the U.S. and in violation of the rights of another nation. But many in this country, who had the insight and courage to uphold the democratic principle of self-determination for colonial peoples, opposed the assault on the Vietnamese. Taking to the streets in vast protest demonstrations, they organized one of the most powerful mass movements in U.S. history. This domestic resistance made it politically untenable for the U.S. capitalists to proceed at all hazards with their attempt to conquer the people of Vietnam, who defended themselves heroically and effectively. In the end the imperialists were frustrated and defeated. The intended victims established the right to manage their country's affairs as they may choose. Here at home, all who are fighting for their own democratic rights, for changes in social and economic policies, acquired new struggle momentum from the setback dealt to the U.S. imperialists abroad.

Organized labor can profit by following the example set by the antiwar movement. If trade unionists aid the victims of U.S. imperialism in other countries—and at the same time back all progressive causes within the United States—they will earn extensive support for their own struggles. An anticapitalist united front can thus be built, both nationally and internationally, and, as it grows in strength, the relationship of class forces will be changed to the decisive advantage of the workers and their allies.

During the advance toward attainment of those goals yet another vital problem must be kept in mind. History shows that, as mass resistance to the capitalist exploiters grows, they will supplement the government's repressive role with extralegal forms of attack on those in rebellion. Some aspects of that trend have already become a familiar part of industrial and social struggles in this country: use of hired thugs and vigilantes against strikers, for instance, and of Ku Klux Klan-type terrorism against oppressed nationalities. Those are only fore-runners of even harsher measures to come as the social crisis gets more acute. The most diabolical of the extralegal onslaughts will take the form of a fascist movement—heavily financed by monopoly capital—which will try to smash the trade unions and other protective organizations of the oppressed masses.

In looking for means of defense against such assaults, it would be fatal to rely on the bosses' government, no matter how liberal its face. Capitalist politicians in public office are themselves tools of the ruling class, which instigates the legal and extralegal violence used to keep the masses in line. Therefore, these Democrats and Republicans will do nothing effective that cuts across the needs of their masters, which means they can be expected to shield and abet the repressive forces—surreptitiously, if not openly.

If those who become targets of capitalist violence are to protect themselves, they must prepare for self-defense, as required at each new stage of the class struggle. It is the duty of the trade unions, especially, to show initiative in this respect, and all potential victims of extralegal attacks should be drawn into a united defense movement on the broadest possible scale.

At every juncture in the unfolding social conflicts, the workers and their allies need guidance from a revolutionary socialist party. That is the reason for the existence of the Socialist Workers Party. Its scientific analysis of the class struggle provides in fullest measure the political consciousness and program that the anticapitalist movement must have. There-fore, it is uniquely qualified to shape the basic proposals, broad strategy, and tactical steps required for the most effective mass action.

In the course of events, increasing numbers of militants who come to recognize those facts will be ready to join in building such a party on an expanding scale, as they did in Minneapolis during the 1930s. As members of the revolutionary party, they will learn fundamentals involved in the fight against capitalist exploitation as well as lessons of past class struggles on a world-historical scale. Through that education they will become better equipped to apply valid principles in today's conflicts. Their capacity will become enhanced to exert helpful influence within the broad mass movement in ways that will add to its efficiency in action, to its prospects for ultimate victory.

Such growth in the numerical strength and influential role of the revolutionary socialist party is, in the last analysis, decisive for the acquisition of supreme power in the United States by the workers and their allies; for only that kind of politically advanced formation, geared for combat in a scientific way, can lead the masses successfully in defeating the capitalists and their repressive apparatus.

It will then be possible to assume governmental power through assertion of majority rule, after which economic and social relations can be reorganized on a rational basis. An enlightened society can be constructed along socialist lines, in which there will be peace, freedom, equality, and security for all.

As the Teamster story demonstrates, the principal lesson for labor militants to derive from the Minneapolis experience is not that, under an adverse relationship of forces, the workers can be overcome; but that, with proper leadership, they can overcome.

Index